CAN EAST ASIA COMPETE?

Innovation for Global Markets

SHAHID YUSUF
AND
SIMON J. EVENETT

THE WORLD BANK
Washington, D.C.

A copublication of
the World Bank and
Oxford University Press

1818 H Street, NW
Washington, DC 20433

Telephone 202-473-1000
Internet www.worldbank.org
E-mail feedback@worldbank.org

First printing September 2002
1 2 3 4 05 04 03 02

A copublication of the World Bank and Oxford University Press.
Oxford University Press
198 Madison Avenue
New York, NY 10016

ISBN 0-8213-4998-8

Cover design by Naylor Design Inc., Washington, DC

Library of Congress Cataloging-in-Publication Data
Yusuf, Shahid, 1949-
Can East Asia compete? : innovation for global markets / Shahid Yusuf and Simon J. Evenett.
p. cm.
Includes bibliographical references and index.
ISBN 0-8213-4998-8
1. Technological innovations—Economic aspects—East Asia. 2. East Asia—Economic policy. 3. East Asia—Economic conditions. 4. Finance—East Asia. 5. Competition, International. I. Evenett, Simon J. II. Title.

HC460.5.Z9 T422 2002
338′.064′095—dc21 2002028868

CONTENTS

Box

Figures

Tables

FOREWORD

The recent history of economic development argues against complacency—rapid and stable growth is something of a high-wire act that is not easily sustained. Yet a group of East Asian economies did manage to defy expectations for nearly three decades. The 1997–98 economic crisis interrupted this remarkable sprint, and even though some of the countries appear to have gotten their second wind, their average growth rates are slower. All economies in the region are in the grip of uncertainty and are casting around for a mix of policies and a political economy that will restore their earlier and effortlessly magical performance.

As is becoming increasingly apparent, an investment-led, state-directed approach that derives much of the demand pull from exports of manufacturers may not yield the impetus it did in the past. The middle- and upper-income economies of East Asia in particular are past the stage when such a recipe would be sufficient to generate annual gross domestic product growth of 7 percent or more. For most of them the answer to their economic ambitions is likely to lie in more complex and variegated approaches that blend significant institutional deepening with efforts to combine resource mobilization and much greater levels of innovativeness and productivity. How they might achieve this is the subject of this study, which is part of a project on East Asia's future development prospects conducted jointly by the World Bank and the government of Japan. By drawing upon some of the latest research findings, the authors show how the East Asian model responsible for the "miracle" of past decades can be modified and augmented so as to return those East Asian economies that persevere with reforms to a high growth trajectory.

Against the backdrop provided by the 1997–98 crisis and the tentative recovery of East Asian economies thereafter, this study presents the context in which new policies will be deployed, and by analyzing the options the authors indicate how a combination of institutions and polices would buttress the innovativeness that will be the basis of East Asia's competitiveness.

The great merit of this book, and one that should recommend it to a broad audience, is that it lucidly summarizes the issues currently being debated and suggests how the discourse can be moved to the next stage and provide East Asian policymakers with the guidance they are urgently seeking.

Nicholas Stern
Chief Economist and
Senior Vice President
Development Economics
The World Bank

Jemal-ud-din Kassum
Vice President
East Asia and Pacific
The World Bank

PREFACE

In late 1999 the government of Japan suggested that the World Bank examine the future directions of economic change in East Asia, with the emphasis on how the approaches to development followed in the region might evolve in the early 21st century. The Bank was highly receptive to the idea of analyzing the longer-term implications of the 1997–98 crisis and assembled a team that worked closely with senior Japanese policymakers and scholars. This team defined a broad-ranging study to ascertain the directions of change and to suggest policies for East Asian economies that would sustain their past growth momentum within a changing and more competitive globalizing environment.

This volume is the first of a series of publications that we expect to emerge from the study, and as such seeks to map the terrain that forthcoming books and papers will scrutinize much more closely. East Asia's industrial competitiveness was the stuff of legend in the 1980s and 1990s. Can the region sustain this competitiveness in manufactures and extend it to new products and services? This is the central question this book addresses. Experience suggests that most East Asian economies can rise to the challenge, but success is by no means a foregone conclusion. The 1997–98 crisis revealed a number of obstacles that countries will have to surmount. Moreover, their future performance is likely to be inextricably bound with their capacity to implement institutional changes and to build innovation capability, which is increasingly the arbiter of competitive strength. How East Asian economies, especially those in the middle- and upper-income groups, might fully realize their potential to innovate will require policy, organizational, and institutional initiatives at many levels. By drawing on a wide spectrum of research, this book delineates the key issues and suggests how East Asian economies might grasp the policy nettles that lie ahead. We hope that for the general reader interested in development, this book will provide an accessible window on future possibilities and a sense of the complexity of the development effort that encourages deeper reading. We also hope that the specialist will find this a handy and stimulating progress report of events along a broad front together with a look beyond the frontier that contributes to the debate on development.

The Development Economic Research Group at the World Bank provided us with the ideal environment for conducting the research for this volume, and we are deeply grateful to Paul Collier, the director of the group, for his support, for providing us with a spacious intellectual environment, and for encouraging us to exploit the opportunities offered to the full.

Equally vital was the financial backing of the government of Japan through its Policy and Human Resources Development Fund and the access we enjoyed to senior public officials, who gave generously of their time and provided valuable feedback on earlier drafts of this book. We are deeply indebted to Haruhiko Kuroda, Masahiro Kawai, Kiyoshi Kodera, Rintaro Tamaki, Junichi Maruyama, and Takatoshi Ito. The study has been greatly enriched through our many detailed conversations with Eisuke Sakakibara, who has taken a deep interest in the research since its inception.

Members of the international steering committee of the study reviewed the initial draft of this work. Our special thanks go to Masahiko Aoki, Jemal-ud-din Kassum, Homi Kharas, Eisuke Sakakibara, Il Sakong, Sven Sandstrom, Tharman Shanmugaratnam, Nicholas Stern, Joseph Stiglitz, and Xiaochuan Zhou for their advice and for sharing with us their deep knowledge of the East Asian region. The staff of the World Bank's Tokyo office organized the seminars at which drafts of the study were discussed, and we very much appreciate the assistance provided by Shuzo Nakamura, Mika Iwasaki, Tomoko Hirai, and Hitomi Sasaki.

Our research efforts were greatly enhanced by Soumya Chattopadhyay, Farhan Hameed, and Marc Shotten. We thank them for adding value in many ways. Mir Anjum Altaf, Kaoru Nabeshima, Shekhar Shah, and three anonymous referees gave us detailed comments on later drafts and contributed to the quality of the final product. Rebecca Sugui expertly facilitated the production of the manuscript. The leap from finished manuscript to published book was efficiently orchestrated on the tightest of schedules by our editors, Nicola Marrian and Janet H. Sasser of the World Bank Office of the Publisher. They good-humoredly introduced much-needed discipline and made sure that what started as a glint in our eyes achieved publication.

September 7, 2002

ABBREVIATIONS AND ACRONYMS

AFTA	ASEAN Free Trade Area
AMC	Asset management corporation
APEC	Asia-Pacific Economic Cooperation
ASEAN	Association of Southeast Asian Nations
B2B	Business-to-business
CDMA	Code division multiple access
DSL	Digital subscriber line
EU	European Union
FDI	Foreign direct investment
G	Generation
GDP	Gross domestic product
HDD	Hard disk drive
HTML	Hypertext markup language
ICT	Information and communication technologies
IPR	Intellectual property regime
ISP	Internet service provider
MNC	Multinational corporation
NPL	Nonperforming loan
OECD	Organisation for Economic Co-operation and Development
R&D	Research and development
TFP	Total factor productivity
TVE	Township and village enterprise (China)
WAP	Wireless Application Protocol
WTO	World Trade Organization
XML	Extensible markup language

CHAPTER 1

EAST ASIA ENTERS ROUND TWO

In 2000 the East Asian economies collectively grew by nearly 6 percent, compared with just 1.6 percent in 1998. This performance would seem to provide convincing evidence of the speed and strength of the region's recovery from the 1997–98 crisis. It confounded some predictions that the severe financial shock was likely to result in a gradual U-shaped revival of business activity, as occurred in Latin America in the 1980s. This growth also appeared to reaffirm beliefs in the robustness of the region's key economies and confirmed the findings of research on 160 crisis episodes, which suggested that countries are likely to return to their precrisis growth rates within two to three years (Park and Lee 2001). By 2001, however, growth rates again faltered as the economic slowdown in the United States and Europe spread to East Asia. Even though growth revived in 2002, the questions remain as to whether East Asian economies have adequately remedied the systemic weaknesses that precipitated the crisis, can sustain their competitiveness, and are likely to return to their earlier growth trajectory.

A NEW DYNAMIC: WHY AND HOW

Despite Japan's Herculean fiscal efforts to offset weak consumer spending and revive its economy from a decade-long stagnation, its economic outlook remains uncertain.[1] Thus the region's largest economy is providing less stimulus to the rest of East Asia through import demand, foreign direct investment (FDI), and bank credit than in the recent past. Moreover, even if Japan could resolve the problems caused by banks' nonperforming assets and improve the investment climate, the economy is unlikely to expand by much more than 1.5 to 2.5 percent over the coming decades.

The Japanese approach to organizing and managing the economy lost much of its luster during the 1990s. This and the problems the crisis revealed in other economies has undermined faith in the East Asian model, which emphasized growth through resource mobilization and government-coordination of heavy investment in export-oriented industries.

The recent history of East Asia suggests that growth should accelerate as the tempo of economic activity in the countries of the Organisation for Economic Co-operation and Development (OECD) picks up. However, whether East Asia can maintain rapid growth over the medium and long term will depend on how the acquired strengths of individual countries react to institutional reforms and efforts to develop knowledge-based sectors. These would sustain a dynamic conducive to long-run competitiveness and growth, and would encourage leading, as well as some lagging, sectors to push toward the frontier of technological possibilities. Much depends, though, on how these measures link with policies to enhance the economies' openness to trade, factor flows, and ideas that contributed much to periods of rapid growth in the second half of the 20th century (Maddison 2001).

Innovating to Grow

The economies of East Asia can be divided into two groups. In the lower- and lower-middle-income category are countries such as Cambodia, Indonesia, the Lao People's Democratic Republic, and Vietnam, whose comparative advantage is in the resource-based and low-tech manufacturing industries. The middle- and higher-income economies range from the Philippines and Thailand at one end of the spectrum to Hong Kong (China), Japan, and Singapore at the other. While some of these middle- and higher-income economies still have substantial low-tech industries in the tradable sectors, they are under increasing pressure to move into middle- and high-tech activities. China straddles these two groups and is emerging as a formidable competitor for economies in both categories as it acquires high-tech capabilities, while at the same time consolidating its position in low-tech products, forcing the low-income countries to match or exceed China's industrial productivity in order to remain competitive in world markets. In the longer term China's domestic market is likely to offer significant opportunities to its neighbors. Over the near term this market will remain modest for the kinds of products most East Asian economies export, although demand for resource-intensive products from Southeast Asia will increase. China is also a market that is difficult to penetrate for a variety of reasons that have less to do with tariff barriers than with constraints imposed by severe competition from local producers, marketing arrangements, logistics, and local regulations.

The closer integration of East Asian economies with others in the region and with the global economy—an integration that is likely to increase if trade and capital account liberalization continue—opens the door to fresh opportunities for growth. By the same token East Asian economies, especially the smaller and more open ones, will also be exposed to sharper competition and the risk of shocks. As we see it, the middle-income economies have little to gain by turning back the clock in an attempt to find security in delaying or reversing economic integration. Such a step would almost certainly slow development, and while it might have short-run political support from some groups, this would be unlikely to endure as the costs became more apparent. The drawback of temporarily halting reform and liberalization is that precious momentum is lost, and countries that do so risk being left behind if capital and technology go to their competitors.

The middle- and upper-income economies of East Asia are past the stage where increasing resource mobilization and investment is a recipe to embrace for the next decade and beyond. In practice such a strategy, which resembles the one still being followed, could entail a substantial waste of resources. Levels of investment are already high in much of East Asia, and ratcheting up accumulation, even where this is possible, will yield meager, if any, returns. However, given the wide gaps in industrial efficiency and the possibilities for catching up, if not leapfrogging, technology provides the surest avenue to growth. Except for the low-income economies, innovation will be the engine of growth for much of East Asia now that the initial resource-intensive phase of industrialization is ending. Innovation in a broad range of areas, from products to services and business organization, will be the principal source of increases in productivity and in export competitiveness.

In this study we argue that innovation in three intersecting areas will raise the likelihood that East Asia's middle- and higher-income economies will resume sustainable growth. The first part of our argument is that an environment that stimulates innovation derives from spending on research and development (R&D) by public and private entities in a competitive milieu that, in turn, maximizes the incentives to innovate and commercialize findings by existing firms as well as by new entrants. Networking among firms can promote innovation and efficient resource use and is both more likely to occur and more fruitful when many producers agglomerate in urban clusters. The most effective clusters are ones where a few core activities, such as electronics, biotechnology, apparel, and software, are powerfully reinforced by suppliers of inputs and business services, such as financiers, lawyers, marketing specialists, and accountants. Moreover, successful clusters rely on policies supporting openness, which encourage many-stranded links with other clusters worldwide. In other words, product and process innovation is a function not just of investment in R&D, but also of the clustering of networked firms in an open and competitive policy environment.

The second and related set of arguments presented in this study focuses on the financial sector and business services. This is because a significant share of future growth will derive from the expansion of services, both traditional ones as well as newly created services; gains in the efficiency levels of the services sector, because these currently lag far behind those of the industrial countries; and closer interaction between services and manufacturing. A strong services sector facilitates industrial development, and some of the commercially most successful innovation occurs when consulting, information management, and marketing services, for example, are combined with manufacturing in the biotechnology sector, automotive, engineering, and apparel industries as well as many others. Efficiency gains and innovation depend on competitive pressures and openness, but through much of East Asia, the dynamism of services is predicated on implementing policy reforms that stimulate competition, revisiting the role of regulation, and building a larger skill base.

A third area closely interconnected with the other two is information and communication technologies (ICT). This is important in three respects. First, ICT is a field where a huge amount of innovation is occurring and is likely to continue. In the 1990s growth in the higher-income countries was increasingly influenced by ICT-related investment and the productivity gains triggered by advances in ICT. A second reason why ICT is so intrinsic to the innovation process is that by greatly facilitating communication, collaboration, and competition, it has enhanced the productivity of research globally, while at the same time multiplying the pathways for the diffusion of technology. A third reason for seeing ICT as integral to innovation-led growth derives from the fusing of ICT with key business services. Whether considering finance, marketing, or logistics, the future efficiency and competitiveness of these subsectors depends largely on leveraging ICT. The cost, convenience, and accessibility of telecommunications services will in large part determine the extent to which ICT contributes to innovation. Hence an analysis of these aspects of ICT and the regulation of both telecommunications and the Internet becomes a central part of the ICT story in the context of growth.

An innovative economy draws much of its energy from openness and competition. In the East Asian context these are synonymous with trade and capital flows. For close to three decades trade and capital flows, together with resource mobilization, have served as the drivers of growth in the region. Now, as development shifts to a higher plane, growth fed more by innovation will continue to derive its strength from closer regional and global integration by way of increased trade, FDI, and knowledge flows. Research suggests that such integration of the middle- and high-income economies can not only provide the spur of wider markets, greater competition, and faster dissemination of technology, but that through policy coordination it can also enhance macroeconomic stability, further strengthening the incentives for accumulating knowledge with a long-run payoff.

Growth through innovation thus depends on the investment in R&D and the environment in which findings are put to effective use; a strong and efficient business services sector; the promotion of ICT as an end in itself and as a means of bolstering both manufacturing and other business services; and the coordination of these with steps to increase the regional integration of East Asia and its ties to world markets.

Technological Capability

The contribution of technological capability to competitiveness and to growth is inducing both governments and firms to build the R&D capital essential for developing and assimilating technology. R&D capital entails investment in skills, research facilities, technology acquisition, and institutions to promote the deepening of knowledge and to protect intellectual property rights. R&D outlays, which capture some of the accumulation of R&D capital, are rising, reflecting governments' actions to raise spending both directly by using public funds and indirectly by offering inducements to private entities. This increase also demonstrates firms' greater readiness to secure or enhance their own market positions by embarking on research, whether in-house or through contracts with institutes and universities.

In terms of research spending, the middle- and high-income East Asian economies have drawn abreast of OECD front-runners. Japan and the Republic of Korea, for example, both spend close to 3 percent of their gross domestic product (GDP) on R&D, with business spending providing most of the impetus (table 1.1). China has been raising its outlay on R&D since the early 1990s, reaching 0.65 percent of GDP in 1997, and Malaysia has also increased its spending.[2] Thus technological advances are unlikely to be hampered by the overall volume of resources available for this purpose. For the middle- and lower-income countries the constraints will arise from their limited capacity to use available funds productively if research talent is scarce, institutional supports and incentives are weak, and firms are not geared toward commercializing their research findings effectively. Hence the significance of other factors described in the following paragraphs.

Joint Research

Research partnerships have grown as firms in the OECD countries, as well as in East Asia, have multiplied their links with each other and more fully developed and leveraged the potential of universities and research institutes to produce marketable innovations. This is reflected in part by the rise of cross-border ownership of patents and cross-country strategic technology alliances (figures 1.1 and 1.2). Innovative activity is further promoted by an upsurge in entrepreneurship,

Table 1.1 Research and Development Expenditures, Selected Economies, 1997

Economy	Percentage of GDP
Sweden	3.85
Japan	2.92
Korea, Rep. of	2.89
Finland	2.78
Switzerland[a]	2.74
United States	2.60
Germany	2.31
Israel	2.30
France	2.23
Netherlands[a]	2.09
Denmark	2.03
Taiwan (China)	1.92
United Kingdom	1.87
Australia[a]	1.68
Norway	1.68
Canada	1.60
Singapore	1.52
Italy	1.08
Russian Federation	0.95
China	0.65

a. 1996.

Source: National Science Foundation (2000).

and with it the entry of firms that are important vehicles for introducing new goods and services, production techniques, and mechanisms for building more commercially productive relationships with vendors and customers. However, by intensifying competition, a heightening of innovation can also accelerate the exit of firms whose business models fail the market test. The surge of new entrants in Korea is reflected in the number of workers employed by new firms—approximately 9 percent. The numbers are also rising in Japan and Singapore (Entrepreneurial Fresh Air 2001). In China the collective and private sectors, which account for three-quarters of industrial output, are expanding rapidly. These signs of initiative reinforce accumulated manufacturing capabilities.

Industrial Clusters

Although the direction of causality between clustering and industrial growth is debated, clustering is associated with specific localization

Figure 1.1 Number of Patents with a Foreign Coinventor, by Sector, OECD Countries, 1980–84 and 1992–96

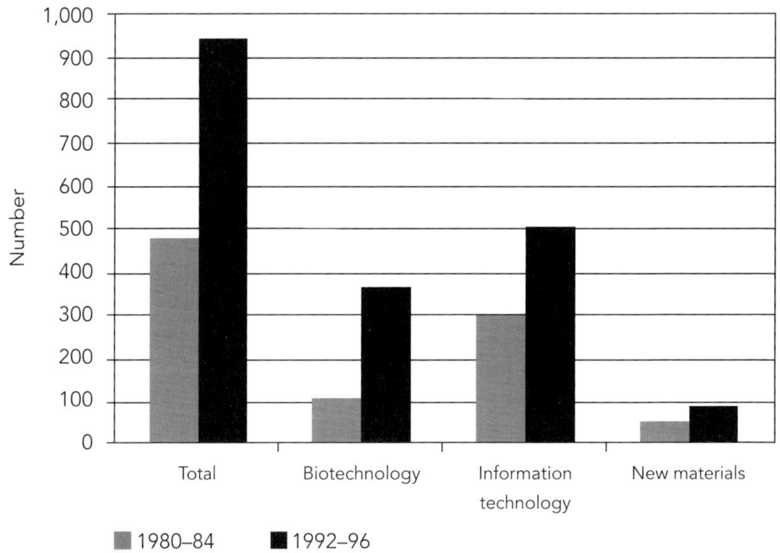

Note: OECD = Organisation for Economic Co-operation and Development.
Source: OECD (2000).

economies resulting from the contiguous presence of many firms drawn from a single industry. Clustering spurs innovation and allows firms to benefit from generalized urbanization economies associated with the availability of diverse skills and infrastructure, from the cross-fertilization of ideas and learning, and from face-to-face contacts (OECD 2001a). Numerous clusters already flourish in East Asia and produce everything from buttons to electronics and cane furniture and are a source of continuous, incremental innovation; however, few high-tech clusters exist outside Japan. A prominent example of a highly networked and innovative cluster is Hsinchu Park, outside Taipei in Taiwan (China), and similar clusters are developing in China in Beijing and Shanghai or are being seeded in the Multimedia Development Corridor near Kuala Lumpur in Malaysia. An understanding of the spatial dimensions of development, the potential for creativity and learning in cities (Glaeser 1997; Hall 2000), and the factors nurturing urban clusters will be central to development in the 21st century.

Impact of Large Urban Clusters

Cities can strongly influence production and productivity by serving as centers for the clustering of industries and services serving domestic and global markets. They are also crucibles for stimulating consumption, developing tastes, spreading new consumer habits, and engendering different lifestyles. As East Asian economies are rapidly discovering, high savings and investment can launch a country's industrialization, and for a time exports can be an important source of demand. Ultimately, however, domestic consumer spending, especially by urban consumers, is vital to sustain stable growth. Moreover, sophisticated and cosmopolitan urban consumers can push local producers into refining their offerings and also provide the market for testing and launching new products. As populations age, the mix of products people demand will change, and services that provide medical care and living assistance, for example, will absorb increasing shares of spending in cities. These trends foreshadow the emergence

Figure 1.2 Share of Patents with a Foreign Coinventor, Major OECD Economies, 1985–87 and 1993–95

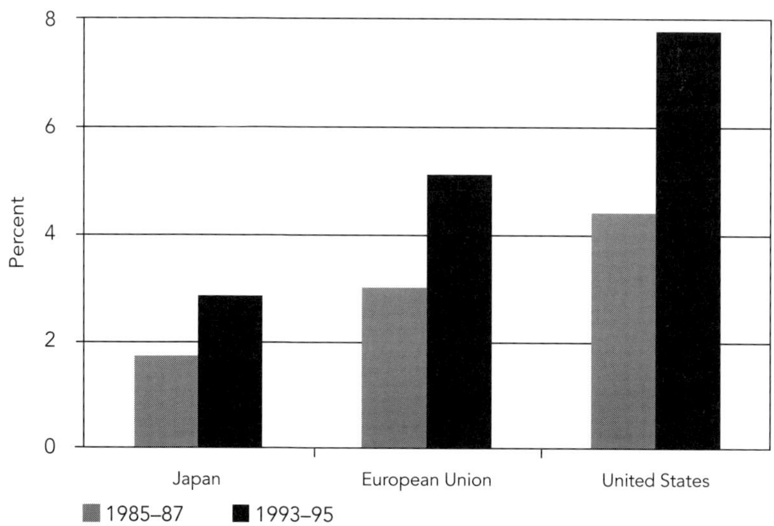

Note: OECD = Organisation for Economic Co-operation and Development.
Source: OECD (2000).

of economies dominated by services, among which high value added businesses in areas such as entertainment, media, education, and medical care will be the major determinants of growth and employment, as they already are in the United States and Europe.

Opportunities for Service Sectors

Recent studies by Baily and Zitzewitz (1998) and McKinsey and Company (2001) have underscored the inefficiency of the services sectors of middle- and high-income East Asian economies. In Japan and Korea productivity in such services as construction and retailing is between 40 to 60 percent of the U.S. level. Closing this gap is one of the surest ways to accelerate growth. This lends urgency to the steps being taken by, for example, Japan, Korea, and Malaysia, to consolidate their banking sectors, clean up their loan portfolios, recapitalize their banks, improve their accounting practices, and strengthen their legal frameworks for enforcing commercial and financial rules. Deregulating other services and opening sectors to foreign competition are badly needed. The case for deregulation of the services sector is reinforced by the greater role that producer services will play in firm competitiveness, first, by bringing into existence market-monitoring institutions, such as rating agencies and accounting and legal services that reliably scrutinize company performance with respect to clearly defined indicators; and second, by facilitating entry through venture capital funds.

ICT and Technological Change

The growth in and diffusion of ICT permits the rapid and efficient transfer and use of vast quantities of information, impinging on a range of factors significant for future growth. As computerization and connectivity expand in East Asia, the role of ICT will widen even more, especially for purposes of e-commerce. In 2000 Korea had the highest proportion of people with mobile phones of any country worldwide (54 percent), while China had the largest absolute number of people using cell phones—85 million (table 1.2). Moreover, as of 2001 individuals whose first language was not English accounted for more than half of all Internet users, with the majority of these being in East Asia.

Table 1.2 Cell Phone Subscriptions, Selected East Asian Countries, 1996–2000 (millions)

Country	1996	1997	1998	1999	2000
China	6.85	13.23	23.86	13.30	85.26
Indonesia	0.56	0.92	1.07	2.22	3.67
Japan	26.91	38.25	47.31	56.85	66.78
Korea, Rep. of	3.18	6.88	14.02	23.44	26.82
Malaysia	1.52	2.00	2.20	2.99	4.96
Philippines	0.96	1.34	1.73	2.85	6.45
Singapore	0.43	0.85	1.09	1.63	2.75
Thailand	1.84	2.20	1.98	2.34	3.06

Source: International Telecommunications Union data.

By dramatically accelerating the sharing and diffusion of scientific knowledge, advances in telecommunications and connectivity will do more than increase the rate of catching up by countries able to build a strong base of technical skills. Their active participation in international scientific discourse is likely to feed creativity and to enlarge the contribution of East Asian economies in pushing the frontiers of knowledge outward. Japan's—and to a lesser extent Korea's and Taiwan's (China)—success in generating innovations is well established, as evidenced by patent data (figure 1.3). In the high-tech areas Japan remains a leader in consumer electronics and game consoles, for example.[3] It has achieved early successes in wireless telephony introduced by NTT DoCoMo, which in a matter of years has built up a subscriber base of more than 40 million customers. Anecdotal evidence indicates significant gains by China in a number of fields, including lasers, biochemistry, electronics, and materials, aided by globalizing processes that are drawing Chinese researchers into the first tier of scientific endeavors. These processes include the widening use of the Internet; the researchers' greater regional and trans-Pacific mobility; and the establishment of research facilities in China by multinational corporations (MNCs), such as Motorola, Philips, and IBM.

FDI and Production Networking

FDI combined with advances in supply chain management and logistics services is resulting in a networked geography of technology transfer and production that more fully harnesses the comparative

Figure 1.3 U.S. Patent Grants, Selected East Asian Economies, 1995 and 2000

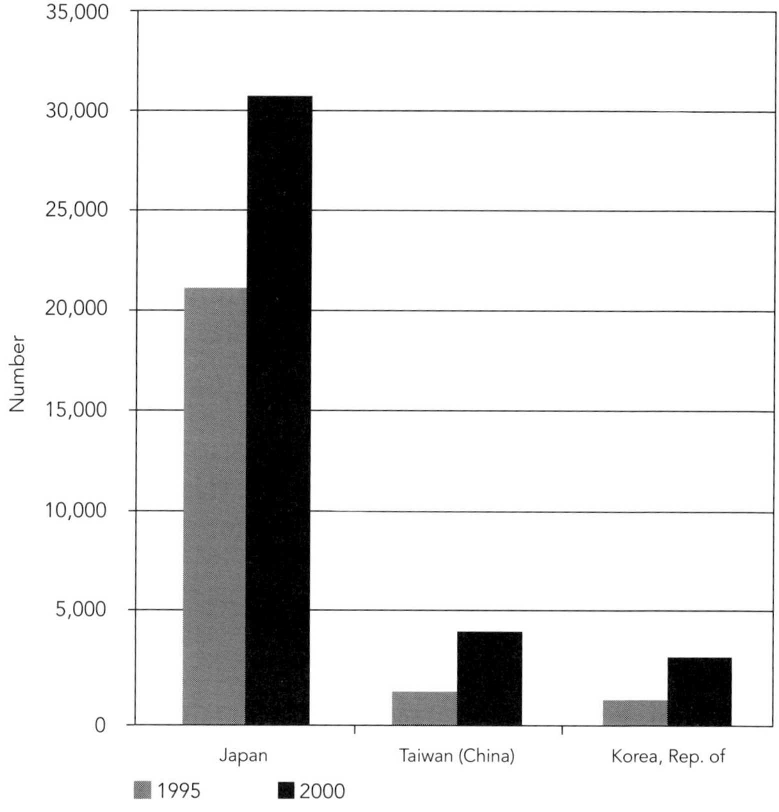

Note: Shows utility (invention) patents.

Source: U.S. Patent and Trademark Office database.

advantages of individual economies, or rather, of key urban areas within national economies.[4] A slicing of the value chain, the dispersal of production to maximize cost competitiveness, and business-to-business (B2B) dealings have been aided by the scaling down of trade barriers and by the use of ICT, which is dramatically lowering transaction costs associated with paperwork, ordering, fulfillment, tracking, payment, and even clearing customs. Countries such as Singapore pride themselves on the paperless efficiency of their ports and on the speed with which goods can be processed at points of entry. In addition, production networking and the ever finer subdivision of the production chain are also being propelled by the falling costs of air shipping time-sensitive goods (Hummels 2001),[5] as well as by the growing expertise of courier services such as UPS, and of intermediaries such as Li and Fung that can design, order, assemble, and deliver goods to a final buyer (Magretta 1998).[6] East Asia's manufacturing capability, which is concentrated in key urban regions, has a hand in this, but production networking as it is now evolving would be inconceivable without the great leap in telecommunications, Internet services, and air transport capacity.[7] Unless reversed by a widespread return to protectionist policies, the stage is set for a tightening of regional interdependence. This, in turn, could enhance the growth-inducing benefits of further regional trade reform, financial market linkages, informal—and eventually formal—institutional harmonization, and exchange rate policy cooperation.

Thus the resumption and persistence of rapid growth in East Asia rests on a new model that relies on the spread of facilitative institutions, the industrial and research initiatives that promote innovation, the effective deployment of ICT to build stronger knowledge economies that foster urban clusters and tap the full potential of international production networks, and a host of trade and regulatory reforms that can create a more integrated regional economy. Successful economies will be those that are both open and that have cultivated the innovative bent, institutional resilience, and growth momentum needed to deflect or absorb shocks (Easterly, Islam, and Stiglitz 2000).[8]

The manifold acquired strengths of the East Asian economies provide the springboard for future development. These include, most notably, their high rates of saving, relative abundance of human capital resources, manufacturing capability, and worldwide industrial reputation. In conjunction with strong export demand, these strengths facilitated the V-shaped rebound seen in 1999–2000. They can be the foundation for a new growth trajectory, and they provide some insurance that the changes promoting longer-term prosperity—if widely shared—will be implemented, but they offer no guarantees, and bad policies could easily plunge more countries in East Asia into a prolonged spell of low growth. Indeed, international experience suggests that consistent rapid growth is the exception. The dominant tendency is for rapidly growing countries to lapse back to slower rates of expansion (Easterly and others 1993; Temple 1999).

EAST ASIAN DEVELOPMENT: ROUND TWO

Just a decade ago the model of development that enjoyed the widest currency in East Asia was an amalgam of the Japanese and Korean models (see, for instance, Woo-Cumings 2001). The recent financial crisis and Japan's stagnation throughout the 1990s called into question the relevance of this recipe as a prescription for future economic growth in the region. The rest of this study examines how East Asia can capitalize on its achievements to date and the momentum of the past several decades to take full advantage of the opportunities presented by the growing services- and knowledge-based economy.

Chapter 2 provides a backdrop to the future growth outlook in the region by sketching how the role of the state needs to shift from a relatively dirigiste approach toward industrialization to one that strengthens market institutions and promotes activities that generate knowledge spillovers. The chapter also shows how the pattern of regional trade and capital flows could reinforce governments' efforts to enlarge the contribution of technology. The chapter then highlights some of the constraints to future development, namely, macroeconomic instability; rising inequality associated with technological change, globalization, and inadequate safety nets; and tensions related to Japan's economic weakness and China's growing economic and strategic presence in the region.

Chapter 3 examines innovation from three angles: the macroeconomic, the firm level, and the transnational. The chapter starts by looking at macroeconomic and sectoral policy that influences investment, R&D spending, and the training of technical personnel with the requisite skill levels. It then concentrates on business management, firm turnover, and the clustering of businesses in urban networks. Finally, it explores how the national business environment is modulated by international links among clusters; circulation of knowledge workers among countries; FDI; and innovation in supply chains, which tie together producers and their buyers.

As we argued earlier, a dynamic and innovative economy needs supporting institutions and efficient service providers. Subsequent research into the 1997–98 crisis revealed that most East Asian economies need to strengthen their market and financial institutions and to raise the volume and efficiency of core business services. Chapter 4 assesses the institutional gaps, particularly in the financial sector, and the reforms of institutions and regulations that are needed for the growth of innovative services activities.

The first part of chapter 5 looks at the contribution of ICT to productivity growth, to innovative activity, and to business development. The chapter also discusses the main hurdles to the widening use of the Internet for business and research purposes. The chapter then describes how advances in telecommunications are supporting ICT and examines the importance of sound regulation for healthy development.

Chapter 6 turns to the external dimension of an innovative economy and focuses on the shifting pattern of FDI, the evolution of production networking, and the likely pace of economic integration. By affecting the degree of openness and market access for East Asian firms, these developments will determine the international market environment that for most East Asian countries has an equal bearing on the course of innovation-led growth.

Chapter 7 summarizes the case for the centrality of innovation for future growth in East Asia and weaves together the main policy strands defined in the earlier chapters.

NOTES

1. Regarding fiscal policy, Bayoumi (2001) contends that the fiscal stimuli lacked sufficient "real water" and were blunted by the weakness of the banking sector. The volume of spending channeled into construction may also have reduced the multiplier effect of government outlay on national income.
2. A related issue is how R&D spending is classified and how it is used. Where governments offer tax incentives, firms will classify some outlays that are only marginally related to research as R&D expenditures, and a significant share of what is classified as R&D is probably more akin to product testing or development.
3. The electronics games industry had estimated sales of US$50 billion in 2001, with Sony and Nintendo dominating the market, and the market is expected to grow to US$86 billion by 2006 (*Red Herring*, "The Game of War," October 15, 2001).

4. See Scott (2001) for recent thinking on global city regions and Hanson and Feenstra (2001) on the relationship between globalization and the development of urban areas as nodes in production networks.
5. Retailers can replenish their stocks of time-sensitive goods more frequently and order in smaller lots to lessen the accumulation of inventories.
6. UPS, for example, now maintains parts inventories at its airline hubs to conduct repairs under warranty for companies such as Dell. This enables PC manufacturers to better meet the needs of their clients (Kirby 2001).
7. The surge in airport building throughout East Asia is feeding the process. Airports in Bangkok, Hanoi, Singapore, Tokyo, and other cities are being expanded; new airports have been built at Kansai, Kuala Lumpur, Macau, Pudong, and Pusan; and many more are under construction, for example, China is planning to build 118 new airports over the next 15 years (*Far Eastern Economic Review*, "Flying High," May 10, 2001; *Flight International*, "Traffic Wars," February 20–26, 2001; *Oxford Analytica*, "Southeast Asia, Airport Rivalry," April 3, 2002).
8. The incidence of shocks has certainly risen since the 1980s, although they seem unchanged in severity and the likelihood of contagion appears no greater (Bordo and Murshid 2000; Bordo and others 2001).

CHAPTER 2

THE NATIONAL AND REGIONAL DEVELOPMENT CONTEXT

The shift from an accumulation-based model of growth to one that relies more on technological change will be shaped by the broader policy environment—national as well as international—and by a number of long-term trends. This chapter discusses the state's role in initiating and implementing economic reforms and creating a climate that is friendly to innovation. It also notes the implications of regional integration, globalization, and the changing salience of major economies in the region.

INDUSTRIAL RESTRUCTURING AND THE NEW FACE OF POLICY

If innovation and efficiency are to be the drivers of growth, then the state's role in framing industrial strategy in East Asia needs to reconfigured. The role of industrial policy in this region needs to be re-examined for three reasons. First, for most East Asian economies, particularly the middle- and higher-income ones, mobilizing additional resources is no longer a top priority, because the availability of capital has ceased to be the binding constraint it once was.

Second, industrialization by way of large, state-sponsored, but privately-owned corporations or by public entities themselves has exhausted its potential. Markets are now mature enough to coordinate industrial decisions at least as well as, if not better than, the state can. Aggressively pushing exports of manufactures arouses resistance from importing countries, and the policy may be approaching the stage of diminishing returns for those East Asian economies where gross exports equal half or more of GDP. The kind of dirigisme practiced by several East Asian states had a hand in accelerating industrialization in the 1960s and 1970s and exports later, but after some early successes, the increasing complexity of the economy blunted its effectiveness (Yusuf 2001). Now government direction is associated with the misallocation of resources; the sheltering of sunset industries; the worsening of corruption; and an industrial structure favoring large, often highly leveraged, conglomerates (Porter, Takeuchi, and Sakakibara 2000).

Third, the state-guided approach to development failed to insulate governments from capture by powerful interest groups. In several economies public bureaucracies initially sustained a measure of "embedded autonomy" (Evans 1995), but this eroded in the 1980s and 1990s with the comingling of government and business interests that led to the spread of corrupt practices and, in a few countries, to rampant crony capitalism. As a consequence, resources were misallocated and banks were systematically looted by owners and debtors, accumulating liabilities that now burden taxpayers (Hutchcroft 1999). Research by Kaufman, Kraay, and Zoido-Lobaton (1999); Mauro (1995); and Wei (2000) reveals the costs of corruption and of rent-seeking activities in the form of reduced productivity and growth (corruption slows growth by raising transaction costs and uncertainty and by discouraging FDI).

State guidance of industrial development and efforts at promoting knowledge spillovers did yield some successes. They widened Korea's industrial base in the 1970s, and in the 1980s in Korea and Taiwan (China) they were responsible for introducing high-tech activities, such as the semiconductor and computer parts industries (Mathews and Cho 2000; Perkins 2001). However, similar efforts to build automobile and other industries in Indonesia (Aswicahyono, Basri, and Hill 2000) wasted large sums and created sectors with political voices that continue to lay claim to public resources, and after 30 years of protection Indonesia's automobile sector has a negative rate of productivity growth (Okamoto and Sjöholm 1999).

Although industrial policy as practiced in the recent past is rightly on the wane, the economies of a technologically dynamic East Asia will continue to demand highly competent and capable bureaucracies that can cope with complex regulation issues and that enable rapid technological change by promoting activities that generate spillovers and providing the framework for a competitive business environment. Those East Asian countries such as Japan, Korea, and Singapore, which have meritocratic systems in place for recruiting able individuals, pay them competitive salaries, and offer attractive career paths, need to ensure that they retain these policies and adapt to changing governance arrangements. Other economies need to build bureaucratic capability, not necessarily following a single model, but as in Singapore and Taiwan (China), going beyond the formal government structure to create task forces or statutory boards to achieve specific ends (Evans 1998).

The developmental energies of the state could also keep accelerating the ongoing, piecemeal restructuring of industry throughout the region. Such restructuring is helping to create leaner, more competitive, and financially resilient industrial systems, and this change is affecting both the public and private sectors. China, Indonesia, and Korea, for example, are privatizing publicly owned firms, and these countries are now prepared to consider majority foreign ownership in key sectors. They are also closing some loss-making public entities that cannot be salvaged. Moreover, the governments' willingness to curtail financial support for private firms and to reshape the public sector have also led to a substantial and potentially far-reaching shakeout of private industrial organizations. Korean *chaebol* are under pressure from the government, public opinion, the market, and foreign investors with rising stakes in local businesses to focus on their core businesses or risk being liquidated by their creditors. The demise of Daewoo, despite the prolonged rearguard action by the company, its unions, and its banks to save it, testifies to the strength of market forces. The magnitude of Daewoo's debt (US$74 billion) and the management practices leading to this debt buildup serve as a warning of how much damage can be wrought when market and regulatory vigilance is relaxed.[1]

Elsewhere firms and banks are seeking alliances; are being taken over by foreign companies, for example, Natsteel Electronics, one of Singapore's leading producers of semiconductors, has been acquired by Flextronics; or, as in Korea, Malaysia, Singapore, and Thailand, are being required to merge by the authorities to form, apparently, more optimally sized units. Even in Japan, the decade-long recession has triggered a change in industrial policy and organization that is likely to prove irreversible. The network of relationships among the government, politicians, banks, businesses, and workers has been subjected to public criticism and is being partially unstitched. The immediate effect has been to weaken *keiretsu* relationships and lifetime employment obligations,[2] to increase foreign shareholdings, and to weed out some of the weaker firms. However, the longer-term consequences are likely to reach deep into Japan's economy and society as the manifest weaknesses of Japan, Inc. are forcing bureaucrats, firms, and most important the public to scrutinize the key interrelationships, to acknowledge their drawbacks, and to consider alternative ways of doing business.

Restructuring of the economy is proceeding along several different axes. Samsung Electronics, for example, is 40 percent foreign owned, and shareholders' views now count. Even Malaysia is ready to sell part of the state-owned PROTON automobile company in the interests of gaining technology, capital, and global reach. Similar trends are apparent in the transport, power generation, and utility subsectors, all of which have been opened to foreign investment. In China thousands of small and medium state-owned enterprises have been divested, and the government is prepared to sell its stake in some of the larger state-owned enterprises if buyers are forthcoming.

The shift away from industrial policy and public ownership and toward foreign acquisition of firms and banks is a welcome one, and this shift is prompting a number of associated changes in the areas of banking, accounting, corporate governance, and company law, all of which will strengthen market institutions and redefine the role of the state. The pull of inertia remains strong, however, and a marked reluctance to let market forces determine outcomes persists, especially when large companies such as Hynex (formerly part of the Hyundai group) in Korea and major banks, as in Japan, are faced with painful choices to merge with foreign partners, to restructure their operations, or to face liquidation as their credit runs out.

The 1997–98 crisis has driven home the need to create banking sectors that are independent, efficient, profitable, and innovative. In time this could revolutionize the relationship between governments and banks, several of which (in Indonesia, Korea, and Thailand) were taken over by their governments after the crisis. The crisis pushed governments to eschew directed lending, a prominent feature of the

East Asian model, which is responsible for a sizable share of the nonperforming loans (NPLs) weighing down bank portfolios and limiting the supply of credit to potential entrants. The crisis also clearly underscored the need for strict adherence to capital adequacy rules, which had been largely implemented throughout the region by 2001, and begin the inevitably time-consuming processes of privatizing state-owned banks; improving corporate governance, accounting standards, rules of disclosure, and legal remedies; and monitoring bank performance using adequately trained public supervisors and private rating agencies.

The entire ongoing effort to recapitalize banks, clean up their loan portfolios, and dispose of their underpinning corporate assets has served to broaden the reform effort to include the business sector. As a result, governments are starting to address competition policy, including rules for mergers and takeovers, and relationships between banks and their corporate customers. Ultimately, it will be the depth and durability of these institutional changes, which in several instances exist only on paper, that will decide whether East Asian development acquires a new dynamic appropriate for the early 21st century.[3]

CONTEXT FOR REFORM IN EAST ASIA

In the past the economic change in East Asia was associated with the growth of trade; FDI; and more recently multilateral and bilateral agreements governing trade barriers, corporate law, and intellectual property rights. Collectively these are increasing East Asia's global integration and are continually raising the extent of intellectual agreement about the gains that can result from openness and about ways to improve market functioning. By participating more extensively in international trade and seeking to enlarge the share of FDI, East Asian countries have adopted market-based rules and lowered tariff and nontariff barriers since the mid-1980s (figure 2.1).

Trade, Foreign Direct Investment, and Regional Networks

The desire to attract FDI has also contributed to industrial restructuring by increasing foreign penetration.[4] This has accelerated since the

Figure 2.1 Trade Barriers, Selected Country Groups and China, 1984–87 and 1994–97

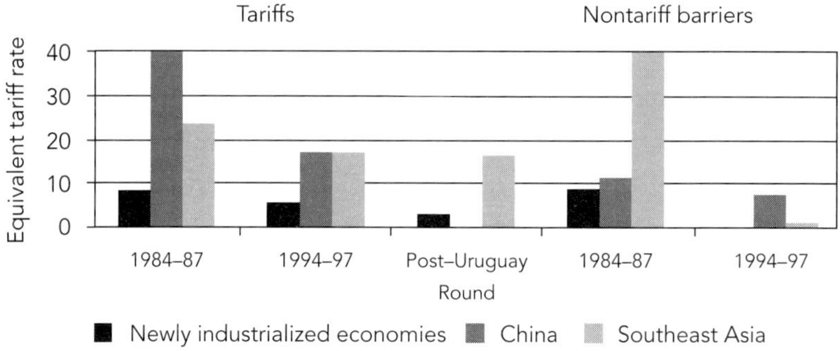

Note: As China did not join the World Trade Organization until 2001, no post–Uruguay Round tariff rate applies to its imports.
Source: Dowling and Ray (2000).

1997–98 crisis. Although countries such as Malaysia seek to defer lowering tariffs on certain imports, such as automobile parts, the region as a whole remains committed to freer trade (A New Front 2002; Southeast Asia 2002); however, alongside multilateral reform, economies in the region have moved toward bilateral treaties and regional agreements that could divert trade. The bilateral treaties being negotiated, even by Japan, are a response to regional trade agreements springing up in the Americas and Europe and to the temporary stalling of multilateral negotiations post-Seattle. While the bilateral agreements could become building blocks to freer multilateral trade if they adhere to World Trade Organization (WTO) rules and eliminate any trade barriers included in bilateral agreements for all trading partners in a stipulated period, engender regional support for particular issues, and serve as models for broader agreements, they could also divert East Asia away from arguably more fruitful multilateral initiatives (East Asia 2001).

For the past three decades trade, FDI, portfolio flows, and technology flows contributed to East Asia's prosperity by reinforcing the push provided by factor inputs, and their importance could increase in the next phase of development. Pressure from competing imports, for example, could raise the productivity of manufacturing industries (Lawrence and Weinstein 2001 showed how import competition has had a stronger effect on total factor productivity [TFP] in Japan and Korea than export growth). Furthermore, as countries build up their skills base, the technological diffusion from FDI and productivity gains could be magnified. Similarly, high-tech products and services will require expanding export markets to reap productivity gains and attract FDI (Choudhri and Hakura 2000; Parker and Lee 2001). It is this conviction, further buttressed by the advances in ICT, that is likely to sustain reform.

Six economies—China, Indonesia, Malaysia, the Philippines, Singapore, and Thailand—absorbed almost the entire flow of FDI to the region (90 percent), but what is notable is the scale of intraregional FDI—60 percent—most of it originating from Japan and the four newly industrializing economies (note that much of the US$64 billion in FDI in Hong Kong [China] flowed out to China, tightening the links between the two economies). This reflects the increasing dependence of Japanese, Korean, and Taiwanese firms on their East Asian affiliates for intermediate products. Thus for Japanese firms the share of East Asia in affiliates' total procurement and total sales rose from 51 and 29 percent, respectively, in 1986 to 55 and 32 percent in 1995. Other East Asian economies have begun procuring more from the region as well as exporting more to Japan and to each other (Parker and Lee 2001; Urata 2001). Aside from intraregional FDI, global production networking also attracts a large volume of FDI from outside the region.

With prosperity so firmly rooted in the external sector and with industrial development, as well as technological advances, paced by inflows from abroad, FDI inevitably leaves a strong imprint on the economy. In a matter of years foreign investors have acquired more than 40 percent of all shares on the Korea Stock Exchange. As a consequence policy, institutions, and attitudes are more exposed to demonstration effects emanating from trading partners, with Japan and the United States in the forefront. As long as Japan offered an alternative economic model of development and the international environment was hospitable to authoritarian regimes, institutional and policy convergence toward a Western model could proceed at a leisurely pace. East Asia could pursue its own brand of development policies and business practices and cultivate distinctive "Asian" value systems. These aspects of the East Asian model are now losing their appeal, and not just because the relative attractiveness of the U.S. model for the business community has risen (Rozman 2002). With globalization, pressure to institutionalize the tightening of international links through bilateral and multilateral agreements has increased. These agreements inexorably nudge countries to implement reforms that more firmly entrench the institutions of a market-based system and that strengthen competitiveness through adherence to formal rules (though smoldering resistance remains, most recently visible in Korea and Thailand, and the threat of a backlash against globalization cannot be dismissed).

Observers differ in their opinions about the degree of institutional convergence occurring or likely to occur. Some such as Ohmae (1990) perceive the coming of a borderless world manifesting increasing homogeneity. Others see a process of hybridization at work as countries selectively borrow and adapt institutions while maintaining their distinct identities. Still others feel that East Asia's successful business models, labor market institutions, and social relationships are resilient and will ride out the shocks of globalization with only minimal changes (Berger and Dore 1996). We believe that cultural borrowing and hybridization, plus some evolution, accounts for past successes in Japan and the United States, and that East Asia would benefit from approaching reform in this spirit.

The pace of change in East Asia, parts of South Asia, and Latin America depends in no small part on the institutional infrastructure supporting globalization and regional integration. This infrastructure comprises rules governing interaction among countries in many spheres, most notably political and economic. It is sustained by such bodies as the WTO, the World Bank, the International Monetary Fund, the International Labour Organisation, the Bank for International Settlements, the United Nations Development Programme, and others operating at the global level, together with bodies such as the Asian Development Bank and the Association of Southeast Asian Nations (ASEAN) that operate on a regional scale. Participation is "owned" by governments, which give the organizations their legitimacy and determine what authority they will have.

This infrastructure is instrumental in shaping thinking on policy and underpinning global integration through trade and capital flows. Although many barriers to trade in East Asia remain, they are much sparser than they were 15 years ago. Multilateral agreements and certain bilateral trade pacts are lowering barriers, which affects a host of other policies. Particular groups find that demanding special treatment is becoming harder and governments find that granting special treatment is more difficult when formal commitments curtail specific types of interventions. By participating in international agreements, governments can more easily deflect pressure from domestic interest groups. Policy reversal also becomes much less likely.

While global integration has progressed furthest in the sphere of trade, and the WTO/General Agreement on Tariffs and Trade rounds have probably contributed more to globalization than any other institutional developments, by altering the content of key policies, trade liberalization has influenced the tenor of other institutions and induced change toward increasing openness, enhancing market competition, and protecting intellectual property rights. An entire cohort of policymakers is now in place that views competition, openness, and global integration as intrinsic to development, and while they face resistance from often quite powerful groups, the dissolution of regional and multilateral agreements and the dismantling of international institutions seems unlikely. Countries in East Asia and other regions will change at their own pace, but in every instance the trends point in the same direction.

The change sweeping through East Asia over the past decade is likely to persist for another important reason: the international institutional infrastructure is only the visible part of a much more elaborate, albeit less formal, mesh of relationships that brings together policymakers, business people, members of professional groups such as lawyers and accountants, journalists, and opinion makers of all stripes. As a result, a continuous exchange of opinions and views takes place, feeding policies and institutions, both national and international. East Asia's dense and proliferating trading links mirror an equally rich and complex system of relationships binding transnational communities drawn from state bureaucracies, academic institutions, and the large pools of knowledge workers and business people.

Networks of nongovernmental organizations are also becoming an active part of these communities. Personal contacts vitally supplement electronic communication, and this mix of commentary, observations, and exchanges is then amplified and diffused by the media.

East Asia is an ethnically and culturally heterogeneous region, but following the lead of the Chinese diaspora, bureaucrats, business people, and academics have been remarkably quick to coalesce into informal groups that facilitate the circulation of information, ideas, and opinions on the central issues confronting the region.

Role of Macro Policies, Social Safety Nets, and Key Economies

Three counterdevelopments could slow or reverse the tendencies sketched out here. We will note their importance without tracing their likely effects, as to do so is well beyond the scope of this study. These are the region's macroeconomic policies; the sharing of the benefits as well as the burdens of the changing economic order; and the future role of the region's two major economies, China and Japan. Given the large literature that exists on each of these issues, a few observations must suffice (for a more detailed discussion of issues related to inequality and safety nets, governance and corporate restructuring see World Bank forthcoming).

Macroeconomic stability and competitiveness are ultimately a function of governance, and countries such as China, Indonesia, and the Philippines face many difficult choices in this area. These difficulties are compounded in open economies, where exchange rate fluctuations can have adverse, economywide effects. The debate on whether to fix or float exchange rates and on the use of inflation targeting under a regime of flexible rates, while instructive, has failed to define clearly the choices individual countries face. On this subject policymakers will have to learn by doing, using early warning indicators and international coordination mechanisms to minimize risks.

A widening of inequality is a distinct possibility, although as yet the evidence is equivocal (figure 2.2). Globalization is one factor affecting income distribution;[5] others are technological advances that benefit knowledge workers and the changing demographic profile of some East Asian economies.[6] These will compound existing regional income divergences that are already a source of tension in several East

Figure 2.2 Inequality, Selected East Asian Nations, Selected Years

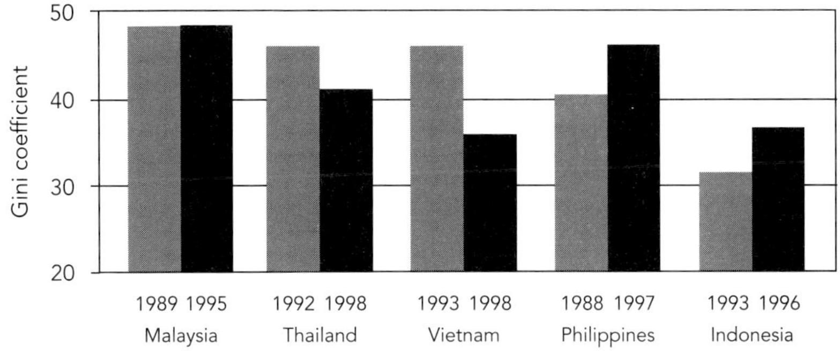

Note: For comparison, the Gini coefficient for China took a value of 40.3 in 1998.
Source: World Bank, *World Development Indicators,* various years.

Asian economies. The winners are likely to be geographically mobile skilled workers, who will enjoy access to better paying job opportunities. However, migration from the interior to coastal cities will also benefit the unskilled in countries such as China and Vietnam.

Unlike the OECD countries, with the exception of Japan and Singapore East Asian economies have allocated few resources for intraregional or intragroup transfers. Poorer regions are mainly left to fend for themselves, and individual households rely to a considerable degree on self-insurance and their extended families. Under more democratic political regimes, rising incomes and openness will probably entail either a significant upheaval of public finances to cover the costs of government-mediated transfers or public regulations to support the private provision of insurance. If East Asia follows OECD trends, governments may need to raise and channel a large volume of resources into transfers, especially if tackling intracountry inequalities becomes a political imperative in countries such as China and Indonesia. This has implications not just for tax and expenditure policies, but also for the development of financial markets to absorb social insurance funds efficiently. Rising transfer payments have disincentive effects and impose deadweight losses that detract from growth. Deeper pools of capital and more effective financial markets, however, will facilitate the entry of firms and innovation, as discussed in chapters 3 and 4.

Aging populations in China, Japan, and Korea will generate demand for larger transfers for social security and expenditure on medical benefits. Recent forecasts prepared by the OECD for its members convey a sense of how these costs could rise, and such costs range from 15 percent of GDP in the United Kingdom in 2050 to 35 percent of GDP in Denmark, with most of the countries having to devote 25 percent of their GDP to this purpose. Moreover, in the East Asian economies people in older age groups are acquiring the political weight to demand a shift in the composition of public expenditures, first, to ameliorate the risks arising from greater economic openness and from the industrial restructuring now reducing the size of the public sector, and second, to supplement private provision for pensions and health care (Garrett 1998; Iverson and Cusack 2000; Rodrik 1998).

The age profile of Asian countries raises other issues. Bloom and Williamson (1999) showed that up to a quarter of East Asia's prior growth could be explained by the rapid increase in the work force, which acted as the source of the region's dynamism, entrepreneurship, and higher savings. Such expansion has ended in Japan, and will begin to taper off first in Northeast Asia, and later in Southeast Asia. Thus starting with Japan, the region will gradually lose its demographic growth bonus. So long as the labor force continues to increase, however, the work of Beaudry and Green (2001) suggests that countries could experience more rapid absorption of technology and higher rates of employment, but slower rates of wage increase. Two decades from now, demographic effects that result in a slowed increase in the size of the labor force, rising average age of workers, declining rates of saving, and higher social security payments could erase the current growth advantages from this source. Japan will have to cope with this situation by the end of the decade (Adams and Gangnes 2001; Mason and Ogawa 2001). Nevertheless, a trend reduction in growth is by no means inevitable, and could be offset by further technological change and by equipping older people with fresh skills and extending their working lives,[7] along with rapid moves to set up fully financed pension schemes. Employing an aging work force productively through lifetime learning and suitable incentives will be a major test for Northeast Asia, starting with Japan.

During the latter part of the 20th century two countries exercised the greatest political, economic, and social influence on the development of East Asia: Japan and the United States. Overall, the United States has been, and for the foreseeable future is likely to remain, the more influential of the two, but Japan's economic links with the rest of Asia, supported by economic diplomacy and official assistance, have decisively affected industrialization, not least through FDI and associated trade flows, infrastructure development, and technology transfer. Furthermore, other nations have widely imitated aspects of the Japanese economic model, based on their view that it was more suited to East Asian societies. However, as figures 2.3 and 2.4 show, Japan's declining economic prowess has markedly affected its economic relationships with other East Asian economies via trade FDI and credit flows. At the same time Japan's ability to project an alternative model of growth has also waned.

In the second half of the 1990s, East Asian economies and the United States were contending with the emergence of China as a

Figure 2.3 Japan's Declining Influence in East Asia, Selected Years

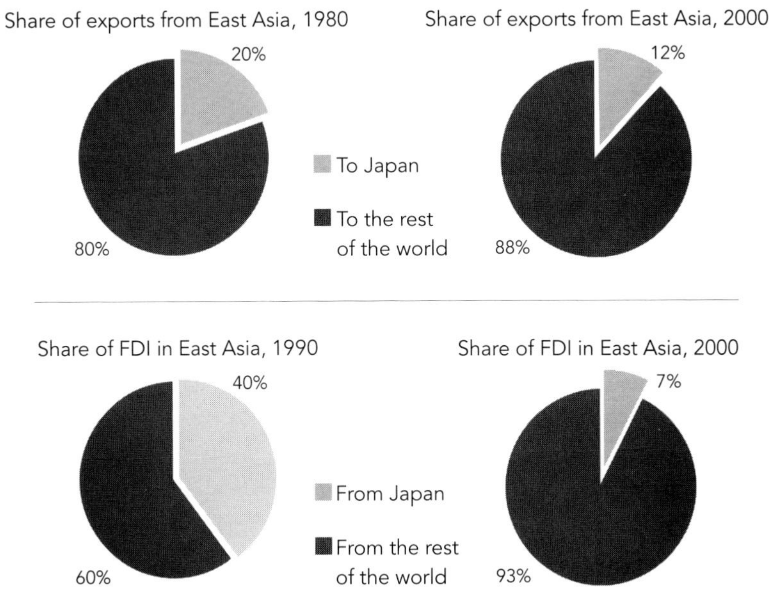

Note: FDI = foreign direct investment. FDI excludes Hong Kong (China).
Source: JETRO (1996, 2001); International Monetary Fund data.

Figure 2.4 Allocation of Japanese Bank Lending to East Asia, 1990 and 2000

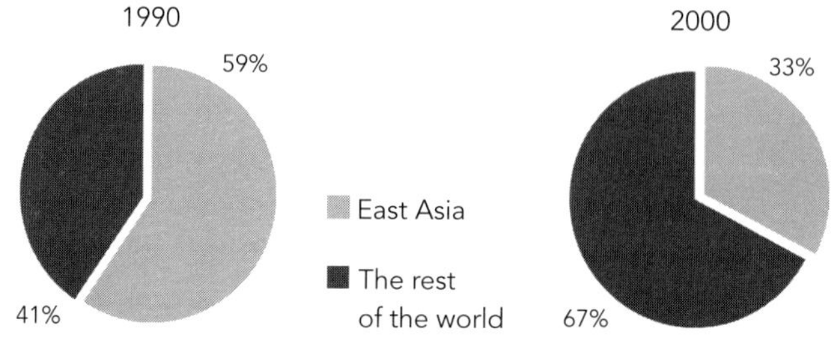

Source: Callen and McKibbin (2001).

fierce competitor in the sphere of trade, a magnet for FDI, and a regional power whose concerns—and claims in the South China Sea—must be factored in by all other parties. China's economic weight and political presence will surpass that of Japan in 15 to 20 years and will pose a serious challenge to that of the United States. This transition could be an exceedingly delicate one, and will involve major adjustments by all countries in the region, including China. Given its size and gathering industrial competitiveness, China's neighbors will need to scramble to retain an edge. Many industries in Japan will also become susceptible to competitive pressure from China. China's expanding military power will further complicate the geopolitical situation in the region and could heighten perceptions of a strategic threat among certain circles in the United States. One possible scenario is a pooling of economic interests that leads to a mutually advantageous integration of countries in the region, with China displacing Japan as the main engine of growth (Enough for Everyone 2002). We explore the possibilities for such integration in chapter 6. Other less positive scenarios cannot be ruled out, however.

How East Asia integrates and how countries work together to coordinate their policies and institutions so as to sustain growth with stability will become clearer over the coming decade. Throughout this period Japan will remain, at least in size, East Asia's dominant economy, and its economic performance and leadership will affect regional integration and growth. Meanwhile, now that China has acceded to the WTO and is beginning to implement the agreed on terms, its trading and other links will intensify. A rapidly growing and more open Chinese economy that enlarges market opportunities in East Asia could be advantageous for the other countries in the region (Lardy 2002; Ianchovichina, Martin, and Fukase 2000), but this depends on how competition and coordination evolve and on how East Asian countries diversify their comparative advantage through measures to stimulate productivity and innovation in leading sectors (A Panda Breaks 2001).

Since the crisis, East Asian countries have made some difficult choices, but even harder ones remain to be made if the region is to embrace a new dynamic and loosen the grip of political and institutional rigidities. Japan's attempt to restructure its banking industry during the 1990s and China's 20-year effort to reform its state sector and banks are but a few examples of institutional inertia and the capacity of large, inefficient industries to mobilize political support to resist change for long periods, even in the face of severe market pressures. Those East Asian economies that defer institutional reforms and are slow to restructure their industry will see their dynamism ebb. Foreign capital and the advanced export industries will move elsewhere. Southeast Asia had a warning of this in 1999–2001. Countries willing to change policy direction can use their capacity to mobilize domestic resources, their elastic supply of human capital, their reputation in export markets, and their participation in international production networks to enter a new phase of rapid growth. The virtuous spirals of tomorrow will have a different sectoral focus than those of yesterday and will be powered by innovation and increasing allocative efficiencies throughout the economy. These are precisely the kinds of opportunities that East Asia, because of its history of economic achievement, is well positioned to grasp.

NOTES

1. A billion is 1,000 million.
2. On balance, Japanese firms have avoided major layoffs that would have disrupted established labor practices. Instead they have absorbed weakening demand by hiring fewer young workers and by transferring employees to subsidiaries (Kato 2001). Nevertheless, the number of employees on regular contracts providing for full-time employment over an indefinite period fell from 77 percent in 1996

to 72 percent in 1999, and nonstandard work arrangements are becoming increasingly common (*Oxford Analytica*, "Japan: Labor Market," March 1, 2001).

3. The United States took close to five decades, starting in the 1880s and under the prodding of British investors in railway bonds, to establish institutions requiring the disclosure of financial information, the auditing of accounts, the strengthening of minority shareholders' rights, and the monitoring of industrial concentration (Bordo, Eichengreen, and Irwin 1999). Even today, U.S. regulatory agencies and courts struggle to cope with the volume and complexity of the workload generated by financial regulation and antitrust policies, not to mention the problems posed by the esoteric nature of new business activities associated with the ICT revolution. The U.S. savings and loan crisis during the early 1980s demonstrates how difficult it is for regulators to deflect overtures from their clients and to limit forbearance. Thus the East Asian economies face a considerable challenge in meeting the political and administrative costs of transforming corporate governance, legal systems, and business cultures to comport more closely with global norms when benefits will obviously be slow to materialize. All the countries are struggling to raise their institutional standards, if only to remain competitive in a globalizing world.
4. The developing countries received US$240 billion in FDI in 2000. Of this total US$141 billion went to developing East Asia, of which $41 billion went to China (UNCTAD 2001).
5. Although global inequality has risen over the past two centuries, Lindert and Williamson (2001) showed that globalization as such may not be the culprit, and that other factors account for the increasing divergence.
6. See, for instance, Behrman, Birdsall, and Szekely (2001), who show that reforms in Latin America are affecting inequality more through technology than through trade.
7. Boersch-Supan (2001) analyzed the German experience and underlines the significance of further education in offsetting the effects of aging through increased productivity.

CHAPTER 3

THE WARP AND WEFT OF INNOVATION

Throughout the 1970s and 1980s, a consensus existed regarding the primacy of factor inputs, especially capital, as the principal determinants of growth, with total factor productivity (TFP) providing a small, but steadily expanding, share of the impetus. More recently the contribution of TFP to past East Asian growth has been extensively debated. According to some estimates, the growth of TFP in some of the most rapidly growing economies was negligible (table 3.1). Although others have contested this extreme position, without minimizing the ingenuity of firms throughout East Asia in assimilating and adapting new technologies, most estimates show that the proportional share of TFP in East Asia (excluding Japan) is still well below that observed in the industrial countries.[1] The results of such analyses, while they leave some methodological and econometric questions unanswered, clearly indicate that technological assimilation, innovation, and gains in productive efficiency based on an accumulation of skills and tacit knowledge are among the principal vehicles for potential future growth (Easterly and Levine 2001; Robertson 2000; Temple 1999).

The growth potential inherent in technological change scarcely needs reaffirming. It is central to growth theory, and the empirical documentation is both voluminous and convincing. What we lack is a reliable means of translating a widely shared aspiration into a self-sustaining process. In other words, economies or firms seeking to harness their future growth to technological advances must still rely on trial and error. However, research is reducing the element of chance, while at the same time revealing the complexity of successful innovation systems. In this chapter we present what are arguably the

Table 3.1 Estimates of TFP Growth, Selected East Asian Economies, Selected Years (percent per year)

Economy	Young (1994, 1995), 1966–90	Adjusted Young estimates (1994, 1995), 1966–90[a]	Collins and Bosworth (1996), 1960–94	Sarel (1997), 1978–96
China			4.6[b]	
Hong Kong (China)	2.3	2.4[c]		
Indonesia	1.2[d]		0.8	1.2
Korea	1.7	1.3	1.5	
Malaysia	1.1[d]		0.9	2.0
Philippines			–0.4	–0.8
Singapore	0.2	1.0	1.5	2.2
Taiwan (China)	2.6	1.9	2.0	
Thailand	1.5[d]		1.8	2.0

Note: TFP = total factor productivity. The column heads show the publications and the years they covered.

a. Adjusted Young estimates use the revised factor share weights with capital assumed to have a weight of 0.35.

b. 1984–94.

c. 1966–91.

d. 1970–85.

Source: Crafts (1998).

necessary elements of an innovation system appropriate for East Asian economies. These range from national-level policies to impart macroeconomic stability, protect intellectual property, increase research expenditures, enhance the supply of skills, and reduce the entry barriers for firms to the emergence of clusters that support local and global networks with global links, further strengthened by ICT and the building of international supply chains.

Innovation will be spearheaded mainly by firms making decisions shaped by the overall business environment. The universe of innovation at the beginning of the 21st century looks quite different from what it was a decade ago. This is not because the tempo of innovation has accelerated substantially, although product cycles have shortened, the speed of commercialization has increased, and the volume of patents granted for software is much larger. More significant is the shift in the composition of innovation: where it is done and how it is done. Of the four main types of innovation—product, process, service, and transactional—ICT has enlarged the role and penetration of the latter two types. Innovation increasingly stems from research in universities and firms concentrated in clusters that feed off knowledge spillovers from the diverse activities and intellectual energies generated by networks. Its cost and complexity demand that innovation be done cooperatively, both locally and internationally, while ICT has reduced the cost of doing so.[2]

Research on industrial and emerging economies reveals no single and clearly superior means to achieving greater innovativeness. Many different factors appear to contribute, and varying mixes of these factors can give good results. Two findings deserve emphasis. First, innovation depends on private and public measures across a broad front and not just on increased R&D or on skill development, although both of these are necessary conditions. Second, innovativeness does not automatically guarantee rapid growth. Japan remained capable of great innovativeness in certain manufacturing subsectors during the 1990s—although the growth of this capacity slowed relative to the 1980s—without this being reflected in either its productivity statistics or its growth (Branstetter and Nakamura 2002; Posen 2001).[3] This chapter examines the range of interrelated factors driving innovation by focusing on eight proximate determinants of innovation, namely:

- The building of R&D capital
- The business environment, including ease of entry by firms, level of competition, and protection of intellectual property
- The effectiveness of the education system in producing an adequate supply of skilled and technical workers
- The links among businesses, universities, and public and private research institutes that stimulate innovation and its commercialization
- The interaction among firms and agglomeration economies in industrial clusters
- The extent of technology generation and absorption by firms through their own R&D, licensing, FDI, assistance from lynchpin buyers in a production network, new equipment purchases, and support from equipment or component suppliers
- The degree of access to an international pool of professionals and to centers of excellence in East Asia and the West
- The development status of production networking, supply chain management, and logistics.

For a more in-depth discussion of these determinants, see World Bank (forthcoming).

ROLE OF THE BUSINESS ENVIRONMENT

East Asia's past economic performance relative to that of other developing regions highlights the significance of the business environment as a necessary condition for rapid, outward-oriented industrialization. The business environment is a broad term, but for our purposes it refers to macroeconomic stability, openness, effective public policy management, and a reliance on market institutions to achieve development objectives. Combined with judicious regulation, these factors induce businesses to make long-lived investments and to innovate and strive after competitiveness in domestic and foreign markets. Several East Asian economies—with Hong Kong (China), Korea, Singapore, and Taiwan (China) being among the foremost—have created attractive business environments (table 3.2), and most maintained the fiscal and balance of payments discipline essential for containing macroeconomic imbalances through much of the 1990s. Although this discipline weakened in Korea and Thailand prior to the crisis, macroeconomic stress indicators have been restored to normal.[4] Most East Asian economies have welcomed FDI, while also

Table 3.2 Business Environment Rankings, Selected Economies, 2001–02

Rank	Economy	Rank	Economy
1	Finland	14	Denmark
2	United States	15	Switzerland
3	Canada	16	Iceland
4	Singapore	17	Germany
5	Australia	18	Austria
6	Norway	19	Belgium
7	Taiwan (China)	20	France
8	Netherlands	21	Japan
9	Sweden	22	Spain
10	New Zealand	23	Korea, Rep. of
11	Ireland	24	Israel
12	United Kingdom	25	Portugal
13	Hong Kong (China)		

Source: World Economic Forum (2001).

promoting exports. In recent years they have been reducing nominal tariffs on imports, a step that can stimulate industrial productivity, because import competition forces out inefficient firms and induces those that remain to raise their productivity (Lawrence and Weinstein 2001). Furthermore, increased trade with technologically advanced countries can promote productivity through the importation of embodied and disembodied technology, although large countries are the main beneficiaries (Coe, Hoffmaister, and Helpman 1997; de la Potterie and Lichtenberg 2001).[5]

Building R&D Capital and Intellectual Property

In chapter 2 we noted the rise in R&D expenditures in several East Asian economies and the pace of innovation as displayed by patent statistics. While spending on research does not ensure innovation or rapid growth rates, such spending is a necessary condition. In the absence of an adequate volume of R&D outlay a country will most likely not ascend the technology ladder. The experience of the OECD countries, especially that of the United States, suggests that private and social returns from R&D can be substantial. Private returns have been estimated in the range of 10 to 20 percent, with social returns ranging from 20 to 60 percent (Griliches 1992). If 25 percent is the median social rate, then a permanent increase in R&D spending equivalent to 2 percent of GDP could raise growth by 0.5 percent. A more conservative estimate by the OECD points to a 0.05 to 0.15 increase in output for every 1 percent increase in the stock of R&D. The evidence also shows that more of the R&D in the upper-income countries is used to push the technology frontier outward, whereas, predictably, in the middle-income countries it assists in technology assimilation (OECD 2001a). Furthermore, decentralized research activities seeking to derive codifiable findings from an existing body of knowledge yielded more fruitful outcomes in terms of usable results in the middle-income countries. Advancing basic science, methodology, or tacit knowledge generally calls for a strong accumulated base of knowledge and a critical mass of skills that favors the advanced countries with long track records in research (Feldman and Lichtenberg 1997).

Thus the empirical work to date indicates the high potential value of investing in R&D. When the conditions are right it can lead to a flow of innovation that promotes growth, but as the experience of Japan in the 1990s again suggests, such innovation must be broadly based and supported by a mix of demand and institutions, such as an intellectual property regime (IPR), that permit innovation to feed into growth. With the exception of Japan, Korea, and Singapore, the other economies have yet to move beyond a rudimentary and weakly enforced IPR, which, as in the case of Taiwan (China), can affect FDI inflows into the software industry and domestic initiatives to develop packaged software. This influences domestic innovation in the longer term and the transfer of technology from abroad, especially in the ICT sector.[6] Once the industrializing East Asian economies begin marketing their own innovations, IPRs will become increasingly important as a safeguard against piracy in foreign markets.

IPRs have many variants, and given its stage of development, each country must design a regime that keeps its own interests in the forefront. Now that several East Asian economies are signatories of the WTO's Trade-Related Agreement on Intellectual Property Rights, which sets a minimum threshold, the process could accelerate. For most the task is large and urgent. It involves translating a formal intention into viable domestic institutions that send clear signals, provide the appropriate incentives, and build as well as effectively harness the legal infrastructure to protect ownership rights. The increasing importance of innovation in the ICT sector and of trade in ICT products has drawn more attention to the issues pertaining to intellectual property. It has also revealed the gaps in regulatory capability and legal infrastructure more starkly, not just in East Asia, but also in the United States and European countries (see figure 3.1 for a subjective ranking of these institutions). East Asian countries such as Japan, Malaysia, and Singapore are tackling both competition and intellectual property concerns on the legislative plane, as well as at the practical level of enforcement, but overall, progress toward more robust IPR regimes is slow.

The Education System as a Fulcrum of Research

The supply and quality of skills available influence the search for new technology; the monitoring of information about scientific discoveries around the world; and the assimilation of relevant local technology,

Figure 3.1 Opinions as to Whether Intellectual Property Is Well Protected, Selected Economies

(7 = strongly agree, 1 = strongly disagree)

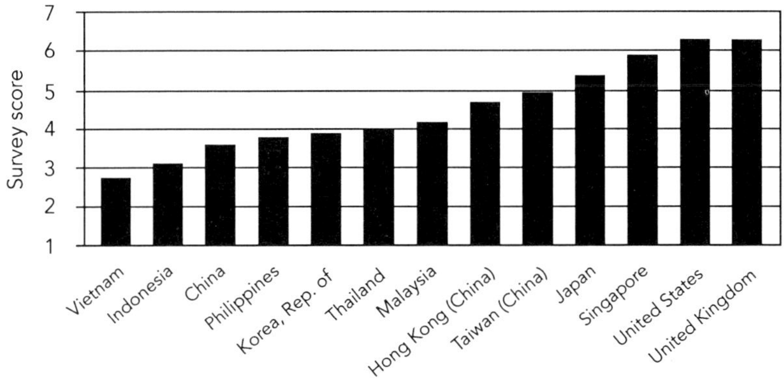

Note: The score reported is the mean assessment of a survey of an economy's business people.
Source: World Economic Forum (2000).

whether from the spillover effects of FDI, from supplying original equipment manufacturers, from imports of capital equipment, or from licensing. The key to absorbing technology, a task that generally rests on a country's indigenous R&D effort, is the availability of human capital and the readiness to fully master new products and means of production (Forbes and Wield 2000; Goto and Odagiri 1997; Hobday 1995; L. Kim 1997; Lan 1996; Lau and Higuchi 1999).

The endogenous growth literature views human capital as providing the push for longer-term advances through new ideas arising from formal R&D and from other informal processes of innovation (Romer 2000; Temple 2001). This is in line with the findings of labor economists, who have estimated private returns of between 5 and 15 percent for a year of extra schooling. Initially attempts at confirming an equivalent level of social return from education were unsuccessful, but more recent work, which takes full account of externalities, suggests that the macroeconomic effects are equal to the private benefits and account for one-fifth or more of the growth in gross output (Temple 2001).

Table 3.3 Enrollment Ratios, Selected East Asian Economies, 1996 (percent)

Economy	Secondary enrollment ratio	Tertiary enrollment ratio
China		6
Hong Kong (China)	71	
Indonesia	42	11
Japan	98	41
Korea	97	68
Malaysia		12
Philippines	60	29
Singapore	74	39
Thailand	56	22

Sources: UNESCO (1999, table 8; 2000, table 6); World Bank (1999); World Bank World Development Indicators database.

Most East Asian economies have already achieved high literacy rates, and the supply of human capital has been associated with rapid growth in the past (see table 3.3 for data on secondary and tertiary enrollments). However, investigators have frequently questioned the association between levels of schooling and growth (Bils and Klenow 2000; Easterly 2001; Pritchett 2001). Research now leans toward the quality of the education imparted rather than its mere volume, the scale of tertiary education, and the degree to which pedagogical techniques inculcate creativity among students. Hanushek and Kimko (2000) have strongly argued the case for quality, using cross-country analysis to trace its effect on economic growth. The importance ascribed to quality and depth of schooling is growing steadily for another reason as well. As the volume of knowledge in each field increases, the time needed to acquire the expertise to make creative or innovative contributions expands, to as much as 10,000 to 20,000 hours in some areas of science and mathematics.[7] Solving Fermat's Problem, for example, required command of more than half a dozen subfields of number theory, each highly evolved and arcane. As the frontiers of knowledge advance, the children who might contribute to tomorrow's advances must acquire mastery over many more facts and techniques than in the past, while also developing a capacity for creative thinking.

A greater appreciation for educational quality than in the past echoes throughout East Asia. Experiments in moving from rote learning to discovery-oriented approaches are taking place in Japan, Korea, and Singapore, alongside the extensive introduction of very young children to computer equipment and the Internet.

Korea proposes setting up special schools, similar to China's key schools, to nurture the scientific talent of gifted youngsters (Grooming a Science 2001). China, meanwhile, encourages competition between schools by giving legal recognition to the private schools that currently train 7 million primary and high school students (China Moves to Encourage 2001). Research in the United States suggests that increased expenditures will make little difference to performance outcomes, although smaller classes can influence results by permitting teachers to give individual children more attention. In Japan and Korea older teachers are reluctant to acquire computer and Internet skills, and are therefore unable to help students derive the maximum advantage from new equipment and technology. Stronger incentives and retraining could yield superior outcomes, and Korea is attempting to refresh its pool of teachers by lowering the retirement age. Countries could also augment the supply of teachers by persuading those who recently acquired doctorates in science and mathematics to spend some time teaching (How to Produce 2000).

For East Asian economies with effective lower and middle school systems that deliver good test results, the next step is to produce more scholars with high-level skills and to move schools up several notches in quality to heighten pupils' creativity and computer literacy without sacrificing the schools' current good attributes in the areas of science and mathematics skills (table 3.4).[8]

Much more ground must be covered at the high school and tertiary level, because at these levels education systems in most of East Asia are mediocre and uncompetitive at best.[9] Only a few elite institutions—such as the Korea Advanced Institute of Science and Technology, set up in 1975, and the Hong Kong University of Science and Technology—consistently produce high-caliber graduates. The initiatives East Asian and Western universities are taking to build alliances and establish joint programs are promising, because they import educational techniques and adapt them to local environments, something that the overseas training of thousands of East Asians has failed to bring about. Many of the leading schools in Australia, France, the United Kingdom, and the United States now have joint programs or other arrangements

Table 3.4 Science and Mathematics Achievement Scores at Age 14, Selected Economies

Economy	Mathematics average achievement	Economy	Science average achievement
Singapore	604	Taiwan (China)	569
Korea, Rep. of	587	Singapore	568
Taiwan (China)	585	Hungary	552
Japan	579	Japan	550
Netherlands	540	Korea, Rep. of	549
Canada	531	Netherlands	545
Finland	520	United Kingdom	538
United States	502	Finland	535
United Kingdom	496	Canada	533
Thailand	467	United States	515
Israel	466	Thailand	482
Indonesia	403	Israel	468
Philippines	345	Philippines	345
International average	487	International average	488

Source: Science, "Third International Mathematics and Science Study," December 8, 2000.

with universities in Japan, Korea, Malaysia, and Singapore. This is an important step in globalizing knowledge, especially tacit knowledge, and in developing institutions to govern and encourage the production of new knowledge. East Asia is at the early stages of this task, however, and just as resistance impedes industrial and financial reform, education systems will also change slowly.

Few universities in East Asia can impart effective research skills, and those that can are located in the principal cities. This has a localizing effect on knowledge generation and promotes technology-based clusters in these cities. A local supply of higher-level skills in conjunction with market competition induces firms to invest in research. Recognizing that research is the key to future advances in important industries, governments in such countries as China, Japan, Korea, and Malaysia are investing in tertiary-level education, encouraging R&D, and funding government research institutes. Table 3.5 shows how these investments are increasing the supply of professional skills, patents granted (by the U.S. Patent and Trademark Office), and high-tech exports, particularly in Korea and Singapore.[10]

Table 3.5 Indicators of R&D Effort and Outcomes, Selected East Asian Economies, Selected Years

Economy	Scientists and engineers in R&D, per million population, 1985–95	Number of patents granted, 1996[a]	High-tech exports as a percentage of manufacturing exports, 1997
China	350	46	21
Hong Kong (China)	98	88	29
Indonesia		1	20
Japan	6,309	23,052	38
Korea, Rep. of	2,636	1,493	39
Malaysia	87	12	67
Philippines	1,299	4	12
Singapore	2,728	88	71
Taiwan (China)		1,897	
Thailand	119	11	43
United States	3,732	61,107	44

Note: R&D = research and development.

a. By the U.S. Patent and Trademark Office (utility patents).

Sources: World Bank (1999); *Taiwan Statistical Data Book* 1999; Council for Economic Planning and Development, China; www.uspto.gov.

Taking their cue from trends in the United States and Europe, more recently East Asian universities have also become more actively involved in commercial research. Starting with consulting activities, they are expanding into contract research, a path followed by the Massachusetts Institute of Technology starting in the late 19th century under the leadership of a faculty committed to a practical engineering education and with close ties to local industry (Lecuyer 1998).[11] Some universities are now venturing into self-financed research, which the institutions hope to capitalize on by way of patents or through new start-ups. Licensing income at U.S. universities amounted to US$700 million in 1998, compared with US$12.7 million in Japan (Japan Acts to Speed 1999). Faculty from the University of California have founded fully one-third of the world's biotechnology companies (Is the University-Industrial Complex 2001).[12] In Japan new government legislation similar to the technology transfer provisions of the Bayh-Dole Act in the United States is beginning to encourage this tendency, but many hurdles remain, for example, limits on the amounts universities can receive from private donors, how the money can be disbursed, and what it can be used for (University Industry Cooperation 2000).

Many of the genome research institutes in China have been spun off by academic and government research institutes, forcing them to be more financially independent by capitalizing on their research findings. Alongside this, investment by private companies in university-based research, particularly by industrial country pharmaceutical companies with large research budgets, has increased, mostly in the West, but now also in East Asia. This trend worries some faculty members, who fear that it will divert universities from teaching and basic research and dilute their autonomy.

Industrial Organization and Management

In the current economic milieu macroeconomic regulation and skill development alone cannot sustain a virtuous spiral of productivity, innovation, and growth. As East Asian companies have begun to enter high-tech areas and to compete not just on the basis of price, but also of technology, service, and speed of response, management quality has emerged as a major determinant of further success. Most firms in East Asian economies are family-owned and closely managed by family members.[13] This has its advantages, especially for small firms. Financing, changes of direction, and decisionmaking are all made easier, and staff loyalty is more likely to be assured. The achievements of family enterprises in Hong Kong (China) and Taiwan (China) testify to the initiative and nimbleness of family firms, especially in manufacturing fields in which technology is stable. Several large family-dominated companies in Korea and Taiwan (China) have performed remarkably well, and many have honed their management skills through formal training at some of the most prestigious Western business schools. Moreover, many of the larger family-run firms and their affiliated banks can mobilize "patient money" to finance significant innovations that can take years to achieve commercial success. The Corning Company in the United States is an example of a firm that throughout its history has emphasized innovation and backed it with patient investments (Graham and Shuldiner 2001).

However, the managerial skills and organizational structures adequate for competing in standardized product markets are often not suitable for companies that must compete on the basis of innovative capacity. When business conditions are fluid and product cycles are short, a company environment that favors conformity and the readiness to follow orders rather than excellence and initiative can be a serious hindrance. Family-owned businesses frequently possess hierarchical structures, and these are likely to place strong curbs on managerial activism and excellence. They may offer no strong financial incentives for employees to excel and no mechanisms for weeding out poor performers. Cautious managers eager to please owners by meeting or exceeding performance targets are unlikely to suffuse the organization with a culture that nurtures innovation, even if goal orientation and energy levels are high. Moreover, such management will not be constantly alert for new ideas from within the company that may disrupt the smooth running of the business, and may also show limited initiative in seeking continuous feedback from other market participants (such as venture capitalists) on emerging possibilities to be tapped or in entering potentially fruitful strategic partnerships with other companies that might require determined, coordinated efforts to share knowledge, both tacit and formal, and to locate such functions within the organization (Dyer, Kale, and Singh 2001).

The new generation of owners and managers that is taking over as business founders begin to retire could change the tenor of managerial practice; however, the motivation to change is more likely to come from tougher competition from foreign firms and new entrants, which can become a conduit for better managerial practices (Asian Capitalism 2000; Pulling Away 2000).

Firm Turnover

The entry of new firms and the maturing of those able to keep up the tempo of commercially viable innovations and to emerge as effective competitors by acquiring new management and organizational skills will be critical for East Asian competitiveness. Ease of entry and growth of firms to medium or large size is not commonplace in developing countries because of regulatory barriers (in China, for example, interprovincial, and even intercounty, barriers still pose a significant handicap); weak entrepreneurship; labor market constraints; limited organizational skills; unwillingness to dilute family ownership; poor infrastructure; and insufficient capital, especially risk capital. In China exit barriers sustained by supervising bureaus with the help of banks keep loss-making state enterprises alive, which dampens competition and diverts capital that more efficient producers could have used. Banks guided by signals from governments have also enabled troubled private firms to limp along in Indonesia, Korea, and Malaysia. Research on Taiwan (China) shows that the turnover of firms—entry and exit—has contributed to the changing mix of industry, technological gains, and advances in productivity because of the differential between those entering and those leaving (Aw, Chen, and Roberts 1997).

The leading East Asian economies are notable for their wide dispersion in relation to the scale of entry barriers to domestic firms. These include the time and resources expended on meeting registration requirements as well as labor, environmental, and other regulations. Barriers are lowest in Hong Kong (China) and Singapore and highest in Indonesia and Vietnam (Djankov and others 2000). At least for small and medium firms, exit barriers are low. Large private and state-owned firms, however, use their leverage with governments and banks to defer breakup or liquidation, which may help explain the productivity differentials between the United States and China, Japan, and Korea in several major manufacturing and services subsectors (Baily and Zitzewitz 1998; McKinsey and Company 2001). Korea and Singapore have sought to lower the transaction costs of setting up enterprises by minimizing regulatory and licensing requirements, especially for technology-intensive firms and those whose products have export potential. Efforts to keep down entry barriers in these countries extend to providing serviced land, industrial extension, and research grants; reducing labor market rigidities; and augmenting the supply of credit to smaller enterprises. Other East Asian economies, such as China, Malaysia, and the Philippines, have not attained the same level of regulatory efficiency or labor market flexibility, but have shown initiative by creating special economic zones with minimal entry restrictions, high-quality infrastructure, and on-site services to attract foreign investors. Penang and the Multimedia Development

Corridor in Malaysia and Subic Bay in the Philippines are examples of such zones.

In China, township and village enterprises (TVEs) compose a vast and more lightly regulated enclave within the larger economy. Even though the TVE sector has undergone significant consolidation since 1998 with a concomitant decline in employment from a peak of about 130 million, TVEs still employ close to 90 million workers and are responsible for 40 percent of China's exports (Lin and Yao 2001). The growth of TVEs was almost inadvertent, and occurred because administrative and fiscal decentralization gave lower-level governments the latitude and incentives to create a favorable microeconomic environment for business within a relatively rigid planned economy. Becker (2000, p. 68) quotes Deng Xiaoping as saying to Yugoslav visitors:

> Generally speaking, our rural reforms have proceeded very fast, and farmers have been enthusiastic. What took us completely by surprise was the development of township and rural industries. All sorts of small enterprises boomed in the countryside, as if a strange army had appeared suddenly from nowhere. This is not the achievement of our central government. Every year, township and village enterprises achieve 20 percent growth. This was not something I had thought about. Nor had the other comrades. It surprised us.

As yet, most East Asian economies have only taken the first steps toward institutionalizing a competitive business environment by defining and implementing specific laws. While several have formally embraced competition policy, the elaboration of rules and their enforcement by a court system equipped to handle cases involving mergers, predatory pricing, collusion, and monopolistic behavior is in its infancy. In addition, little attempt has been made to date to harmonize such policies among countries.

CLUSTERS: THE SPATIAL DIMENSION TO INNOVATION

While the previous section dwelt on the importance of the macroeconomic environment and the enabling institutional architecture, an equally significant driver of innovation is the nature of the municipal environment and how it contributes to the emergence of directly networked clusters of firms, the transmission of knowledge, and agglomeration economies. Porter (1998, p. 5) defines a cluster as

> geographic concentrations of interconnected companies and institutions in a particular field. . . . They include suppliers of specialized inputs, components machinery and services. Clusters also often extend downstream to channels and customers and laterally to manufacturers of complementary products. . . . Finally many clusters include governmental and other institutions.

The proximity of firms to one another generates the productivity boost associated with clusters. The traditional benefit to firms of proximity to others—namely, reduced transportation costs between and among suppliers and purchasers—has become less important over time, principally because of improvements in domestic and international transportation infrastructures that have reduced per unit shipping costs. In the United States these have fallen nearly tenfold since the 1980s and, on average, now amount to just 1 percent of the final retail price of most products (see The Box that Launched 2000). Recent empirical research has pointed to other benefits of proximity, each of which offers not just the possibility of one-off cost reductions (as in the case of shipping costs), but the potential to accelerate the rate of innovation and productivity growth. These benefits include the following:

- Large numbers of proximate firms engaged in similar economic activities are likely to attract specialized workers and professionals, resulting in the development of a "thick" urban labor market. Not only does this deeper pool allow firms to find better employment matches for their specific needs, but it also allows for the transmission of tacit knowledge between firms as employees move from firm to firm. World cities such as London derive some of their success from providing specialized services sector firms with the large supply of skills they need to meet the great increase in outsourcing by MNCs and smaller companies.
- Large numbers of proximate firms can sustain a considerable pool of specialized service suppliers that can customize services to meet purchasers' needs. Without a large potential market for specialist services, only generic service suppliers will find it profitable to establish operations in a city. Such clustering also generates demand for upscale office and housing facilities, which in turn gives rise to

demand for other service providers that can maintain and upgrade these facilities and cater to the needs of high-income occupants.

- Proximity to suppliers and consumers is important when deciding whether and how to upgrade products and services. Such collaboration between firms and their suppliers and between firms and their customers is becoming the norm in high value added manufacturing.
- Proximity to firms in related but distinct industries can generate positive spillovers, as innovations in an industry provoke other firms to re-evaluate their own commercial practices.
- Proximity to large, axial foreign firms or to universities and research institutes generates the potential for knowledge spillovers. Large foreign firms tend to be demanding purchasers, requiring constant improvements from suppliers, and often encouraging the latter to collaborate in innovation and to share best practices. With respect to academic institutions, in addition to the traditional benefits of training students, universities provide local firms with opportunities to commercialize new findings, often in partnership with researchers.

Each of these arguments had been advanced well before the late 1990s (see, for example, the well-known research of Jane Jacobs, Alfred Marshall, and Edwin Mills). Only recently, however, have rich datasets been assembled to assess and confirm the empirical importance of each of these factors.[14] Unsurprisingly, then, these findings have led to a reassessment of the growth potential of clusters, cities, and urban regions more generally. As Leamer and Storper (2001, pp. 3–4) observe:

> [R]outine coordination of standardized intellectual or physical tasks can be done with markets that can be extended geographically with communication technologies. But complex and unfamiliar coordination of innovative activities requires long term relationships, closeness and agglomeration. . . . [T]he successful transfer of complex and un-codifiable messages requires a kind of closeness between sender and receiver that the Internet does not allow. . . . It is a medium that may help maintain relationships but does not establish deep and complex contacts.

Because knowledge is their lifeblood, clusters thrive on the density of informal networks made possible by proximity and further reinforced by new communications technology. This helps build a special type of social capital—horizontal relationships—and trust that induce the circulation of knowledge and are the basis of good governance within producer networks. The social capital that serves as the glue for Silicon Valley in California or Silicon Fen in Cambridge in the United Kingdom has little in common with what animates a dense civil society. Silicon Valley networks facilitate productive interactions among individuals, firms, educational institutions, financing houses, policy instruments, and other entities. In their analysis of U.S. clusters, Cohen and Fields (1999) found seven principal interactors: the great research universities; U.S. government policy, in particular, defense-related research was of vital significance; venture capital firms; law firms; business networks; stock options; and thick labor markets. More broadly, social capital also determines municipal governance and the supply of community services to firms. For example, the city government of San Jose, an agglomeration at the head of Silicon Valley, collaborates with existing area firms and helps new firms acquire testing facilities, laboratory space, and business services.

Clusters come in many varieties. We focus on the large metropolitan variants that bring together a mix of industries and services and contain firms of varying sizes, but clusters can also be more modestly scaled and consist mainly of small networked firms, as in northern Italy, Brazil, and India. Clusters can also be of the hub and spoke variety, in which activity revolves around a few large firms and their suppliers (Markusen 1996). Certain special economic zones in East Asia consist of the branch plants of MNCs plus components manufacturers. China and Korea have clusters that are anchored by a major state enterprise, such as an automobile or steel making firm, with numerous subcontracting affiliates.

Single industry clusters, for example, the telecommunications cluster in Finland, generate localization economies arising from specialization and focus that extend to suppliers, labor markets, infrastructure, and logistics. They have their own dynamic and are capable of rapid growth. We are more persuaded by research optimistic about the prospects of the large, multifaceted agglomerations that stimulate intellectual spillovers. We see many significant innovations arising from the intersection of different disciplines and technologies, and believe that ICT will help catalyze even more interdisciplinary activity. Furthermore, innovative clusters are also likely to be performing well with respect to other indicators, such as exports and employment (Department of Trade and Industry 2001).

Clusters differ in the quality, variety, and nature of the relationships they induce among producers, and spillovers seem to be related to the size and depth of a cluster,[15] the specialization of the labor pool, and the mix of producers within a cluster. Innovation and the commercialization of new technologies is disproportionately concentrated in clusters in a particular field (Porter 1998). For example, the Washington, D.C. clusters are specific sources of innovation in ICT and biotechnology; London leads in areas such as business services and finance; while Austin, Phoenix, Portland, and San Jose lead in electronics and software (Cortright and Mayer 2001; Markusen and others 2001). In some of the industrial subsectors productivity is aided by strategic interaction between firms, often through buyer-driven supply chains, as well as suppliers of components, producer services, and now ICT services.[16] Such interaction, which embraces the provision of venture capital, research, design, marketing, and other services, is most effective in a compact coastal area well served by the full panoply of transport and telecommunications services.

Only certain choice urban locations have the attributes conducive to cluster formation, and a good deal of research is being devoted to identifying these attributes. They range from the quality of municipal institutions and governance; to the caliber and research intensity of local universities; to the climate and the quality of the cultural amenities,[17] housing, and schooling available (van den Berg, Braun, and van Winden 2001). Humphrey and Schmitz (2000) correctly point to governance as contributing to the competitiveness of clusters; their upgrading through strategic investments; and, most important, to their repositioning in the race to stay ahead.

Most clusters started in an area favored by history and tradition with the appearance of a cluster engine, that is, a major university or research institute, a dynamic firm, or equivalent MNCs. Singapore, for example, brought in MNCs through the government's incentive regime and a stream of measures to supply skills and infrastructure targeted at these global firms' needs. The result has been that firms in the Singapore-Johore cluster have been able to move up the technology ladder (Mathews 1999). In other research, however, Mathews (1997) showed that governments can plant the seed for a cluster through direct action, such as by setting up a free trade zone and then making it grow through well-timed interventions.

The Baden-Wuerttemberg model of technology development and diffusion from Germany is an early example of how public initiative can create a multilayered system of institutes and research clusters that can work with private companies to meet a hierarchy of needs, ranging from identification of technological needs to adaptation, customized development, original research, and training. The system consists of the Steinbeis Foundation, which runs more than 100 technology transfer centers, often in cooperation with a nearby technical college, university, or research institute carrying out basic or applied research. Complementing the transfer centers adjacent to universities are technical schools linked to between 10 and 20 firms closely associated with the universities. Support in the areas of natural and engineering sciences, jointly funded from private and public sources, is provided by Fraunhofer institutes. The institutes provide specific contract-based technology transfer and development services, mainly to large companies. Lastly, local chambers of commerce, supported by levies on companies, are responsible for educating, training, and organizing work groups in key areas such as biotechnology, laser development, and software. This multipronged system has helped secure Baden-Wuerttemberg's industrial leadership in Germany and has sustained the dynamism of Germany's several industrial clusters (Cooke and Morgan 1998).

Hsinchu Park in Taiwan (China) was the outgrowth of deliberate government policy. Starting with the creation of the Industrial Technology Research Institute in 1973, the government founded Hsinchu Park in September 1979 explicitly on the model of Silicon Valley. The government then set up the United Microelectronics Corporation, which launched the electronics industry. The major advance, however, occurred when the semiconductor industry embarked on the so-called Very Large Scale Integration phase in the mid-1980s. Again, this was triggered by government initiative by requiring that the Industrial Technology Research Institute obtain technical capability through Chinese-American firms in Silicon Valley. This was followed by a joint venture with Philips to form the Taiwan Semiconductor Manufacturing Corporation to fabricate silicon wafers. Philips not only transferred Very Large Scale Integration technology, but also its cross-licensing agreements with other companies, enabling the corporation to avoid intellectual property rights disputes. The success of the Taiwan Semiconductor Manufacturing Corporation initiated Hsinchu Park's virtuous spiral.

The striking feature of such recent developments, especially the growth of leading-edge industries and services, is their tendency to concentrate in just a few localities. A small number of clusters in the United States—around Boston, Chicago, Los Angeles, New York, San Jose, Seattle, and Washington, D.C.—and in the United Kingdom—Cambridge, London, the southeast, the west Midlands, Scotland, and Wales—account for the bulk of the high-tech industry in those countries (Markusen and others 2001; Department of Trade and Industry 2001). The same is true in Japan and in other East Asian countries. Once they have taken root, and if the area sustains its attractions,[18] the cluster pulls in other activities and solidifies its advantages.

As noted earlier, the high-tech clusters with the brightest prospects depend on large, diversified, and efficient labor markets. They must draw and retain people with the mix of skills that firms in the area require and be a magnet for mobile and discriminating knowledge workers (Dumais, Ellison, and Glaeser 1997). A successful cluster accumulates and continuously refreshes human capital. Penang's past success in attracting electronics-producing MNCs to Malaysia indicates how incentives, good governance, infrastructure, the environment, and a flexible labor force can combine to yield success. Its current struggle to retain the companies that have made Penang their base and to attract new ones underscores the competitive nature of the regional environment and the importance of building tertiary-level institutions to train workers in the requisite skills. The Malaysian authorities and the Penang municipality have worked hard to build the requisite university departments, and they are now ready to bring in professionals from overseas, but because a scarcity of skills continues, more MNC capital is flowing elsewhere, most of it to China and Korea (see All Wired Up 2000; Kotler and others 2002; chapter 6 in this volume). The skills clusters need include those provided by specialty service entities, for example, firms that supply legal, headhunting, equipment leasing, accounting, investment banking, and venture capital services. All these together compose the ecosystem that makes a cluster a world-class player.

In the lower-middle-income countries such as China, clusters are at an early stage and have yet to develop the full range of activities that contribute to virtuous spirals, although the Pearl River Delta region is well served by Hong Kong (China), while clusters in Beijing and Shanghai increasingly have access to a wide range of services. More venture capital is becoming available in most East Asian economies, but research facilities and their links to business are both weak, and they have few ties with clusters in Japan, the United States, and Europe. If clusters are centers of growth, then understanding better how they might be created and managed in individual countries is a matter of great significance for the future (see table 3.6 for a ranking of the perceived role of clusters by economy).

Although government pressure on the corporate and research sectors backed by generous financial incentives can create an agglomeration of establishments devoted to research, the spillover effects of such deliberate action can be slow to materialize, moreover, clusters are often slow to acquire depth and to draw in the large MNCs that can lend momentum to a cluster and help link it more tightly to world markets (Survey of Cambridge 2001). Both Tsukuba Science

Table 3.6 Perceived Role of Clusters, Selected East Asian Economies

Economy	Ranking
Finland	1
United States	2
Germany	3
Singapore	4
Taiwan (China)	5
Japan	8
Hong Kong (China)	11
Korea, Rep. of	17
Malaysia	25
China	28
Philippines	35
Thailand	38
Vietnam	39
Indonesia	46

Note: Business people in 50 economies were asked to assess the extent to which they agreed with the following statement: "Clusters are present in most international industries and include not only suppliers, but specialized institutions such as university research programs and training providers." The mean response for each economy was calculated. The lowest possible ranking is 50.
Source: World Economic Forum (2000).

City near Tokyo and the Daeduck Science Park in Taejon City in Korea were the outcome of state directives, incentives, and infrastructure building. Both now host a large number of research establishments; in the case of Daeduck 12,000 scientists and technicians work in 60 centers. But whereas in the case of Hsinchu Park a few government initiatives spawned a cluster of industries, the much more ambitious efforts in Japan and Korea failed to induce networking among the transplanted or newly created research centers and local industry or, at least until recently, the entry of new start-ups to feed off the research done in the parks (Asia's High Tech Future 2000; Castells and Hall 1994; Shin 2001).

LOCAL-GLOBAL NETWORKING

Clusters crystallize the new economics of industrial development on a municipal, or at most a regional scale, where the region might embrace a number of contiguous centers that are all part of a local network. The Singapore-Johore region is one example, with Singapore serving as the hub. Another is the Hong Kong (China)-Pearl River Delta region, which comprises several somewhat specialized clusters, including Foshan, Dongguan, Guangzhou, Shenzhen, and Zhuhai (Yusuf and Wu 1997). Many of the firms in these clusters were initially launched by entrepreneurs from Hong Kong (China), who began moving their factories out into the Pearl River Delta area to take advantage of cheaper labor (Enright, Scott, and Dodwell 1997). Now the individual clusters concentrate on production and depend on Hong Kong (China) for management, marketing, consultancy, finishing, quality control, testing, certification, and shipping services—an efficient division of labor (Berger and Lester 1997). These networks are sufficiently diverse to internalize spillovers, but are also compact enough to capitalize on the benefits of proximity.

The successful high-tech clusters, whether in East Asia, the United States, or Europe, have a local-global characteristic that is likely to be increasingly significant. Even lower-technology clusters producing buttons, cutlery, or frames for eyeglasses, whether in China or Japan, must be alert to changes in tastes, designs, and technology. High-tech clusters are no longer self-sufficient. Instead firms are continuously acquiring, observing, or seeking alliances with firms in other clusters. Moreover, a trend toward production networking among clusters, frequently mediated by MNCs, distributes various activities in accordance with changing comparative advantage. Hsinchu Park outside Taipei and Silicon Valley are virtually coextensive because of multiple interfirm associations and the ceaseless movement of people to and from each location (Saxenian and Hsu 2000). This global dimension of clustering is now critically important for governments and firms.

The overseas Chinese network, whose members are estimated to have an annual income of US$700 billion (not including Taiwan [China]), has long demonstrated the utility of informal, close-knit arrangements in the East Asian milieu.[19] It provides entrepreneurship, implements sanctions, deters opportunistic behavior, and generally supplements weak legal systems in individual countries. In addition, its members provide marketing information, matching, and referral services. This latter aspect of the network is declining in importance, however, especially for standardized products, as the information intensity of economic relationships increases, better communications technology becomes available, contract enforcement is put on a more sound footing, and firms become part of international production networks in which formal market-based relationships begin to displace informal ties (J. E. Rauch 1999a, 1999b). However, for new or differentiated products the Chinese network can still be valuable for exchanging information and leveraging marketing skills (Rauch and Trindade 2002).

GLOBAL CIRCULATION OF KNOWLEDGE AND OF KNOWLEDGE WORKERS

The localization of knowledge goes hand in hand with the international mobility of knowledge workers and the need for leading universities and research institutes to maintain global connections if they are to attract the best talent, stay abreast of the latest advances, and forge the alliances now intrinsic to cutting-edge research. While investment in universities and in building research capacity is undoubtedly necessary, East Asian countries have discovered that this alone does not result in research that generates marketable innovations and pushes development in desired directions. Research universities in East Asia need to establish links with institutions in the main research clusters in Europe, Japan, and the United States so that they can tap into the large pools of knowledge that sustain the world's main techno-industrial clusters. This is an integral part of knowledge networking in a world in which a high proportion of research skills remains concentrated in not much more than two dozen locations worldwide. Lucky (2000, p. 262) observes that

> In their influence on how science is transacted, the Internet and World Wide Web have had the greatest impact of any communications medium since possibly the printing press. The telegraph, telephone, and wireless were not different in concept from the postal system, except that the modern technologies were so much faster. The postal system, telephone, and telegraph are also one-to-one topologies, connecting a single user to another single, predesignated user. On the other hand, radio and television are one-to-many topologies for the broadcast of a small number of common channels to a great many receivers. The Internet and Web are something else entirely. The beauty and power of these new media are that they allow the formation of spontaneous communities of unacquainted users. Their topology is neither one to one nor one to many, but rather many to many. They allow the sharing of information in textual, graphic, and multimedia formats across these communities, and they empower users within these communities to build their own applications. It is this empowerment of the periphery that has opened the floodgates of innovation to millions. In all previous communications technologies the ability to innovate and craft new systems and applications was confined to a small number of industrial engineers who tended the centralized intelligence and functionality.

ICT is helping boost networking by diasporas of professionals, in particular, African, Chinese, Indian, and Latin American. In the 18th and 19th centuries the transfer of industrial technology from the United Kingdom to the United States and Western Europe depended on the movement of skilled workers (Jeremy 1981; Landes 1980). The experience of the 1980s and 1990s underscores this finding: the international movement of human capital is enormously fruitful in generating new knowledge and remains a major conduit for transferring both codified and tacit knowledge. Such migration is linked to trade liberalization and to some easing of curbs on immigration in OECD countries (Globerman 2000). Japan, for example, will need to import 30,000 skilled and professional workers to meet its requirements over the next five years.

Nowhere is the role of foreign-born science and engineering professionals more apparent than in the United States.[20] The results of a study published in 1999 show that "individuals making exceptional contributions to S&E [science and engineering] are disproportionately drawn from the foreign born; individuals making exceptional contributions are also disproportionately foreign educated both at the graduate and undergraduate levels" (Are the Foreign Born 1999). Twenty percent of all those employed by the ICT sector in the United States are foreign born (Devan and Tewari 2001).

These flows lead to the concentrations of researchers in particular locations needed to promote usable research. They are responsible for the vitality of linked clusters within and between countries, as well as for the fruitfulness of collaborative research. Almost 40 percent of the companies in Hsinchu Park near Taipei were cofounded by at least one returnee from the United States (Valley of the Deals 1998). More than 320,000 mainland Chinese went overseas to study between 1978 and 1999, double the number that went abroad during 1872–1978, complementing substantial flows from Korea, Malaysia, and Taiwan (China). This was a large outflow from a fairly small pool of people with some tertiary-level skills. The brain drain is now being compensated for in part with brain gain, however, as 110,000 people have returned to their home countries. The trend in return migration as China develops is positive, aided by active recruitment by Chinese research bodies such as the Chinese Academy of Sciences (China's Leader Commits 2000; Scientists with Business Flair 1998). In several other countries, including India, Korea, and the Philippines, a small percentage of those leaving intend to return (figure 3.2).

The continuous circulation of researchers among universities and research facilities in the United States is also a notable vehicle for human capital augmentation, for cross-fertilization, and for the dissemination of research. Similarly, the links established between U.S. West Coast clusters, Hsinchu Park near Taipei, and facilities near Seoul have begun to integrate research in those two economies with U.S. research. In large part this is due to the circulation of researchers, FDI, and the increasingly coextensive nature of the research in certain fields on both sides of the Pacific.

Figure 3.2 Likelihood that the Well Educated Will Remain at Home, Selected Economies

(10 = the most likely to stay at home)

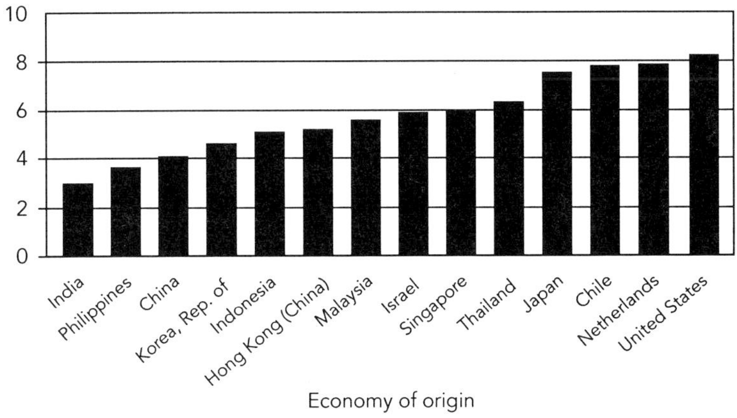

Source: International Institute for Management Development; *Economist* (July 10, 1999).

RESEARCH AND INNOVATION BY FIRMS: THE GROWING FDI DIMENSION

Analyses of research expenditures suggest that an accumulation of effort and findings at the local level provides a springboard for fresh research results. Before countries can effectively assimilate knowledge from overseas or begin to advance the research frontier, a base of R&D and a capacity to innovate in ways that add to the stock of knowledge are necessary conditions (Fagerberg 1994; Parente and Prescott 2000). While research in universities and in government and private institutes makes a major contribution, in East Asia and across the world a dominant portion of applied and basic research is done by firms. IBM, for example, accumulated the largest number of patents during 1993–2001, receiving 3,454 in 2001 alone, and companies such as Lucent, NEC, Canon, Micron, and Motorola are significant innovators (Economic Bust 2002). An analysis of innovation in East Asia (Hobday 1995) showed that the slow accumulation of technical skills, the mastery of manufacturing techniques, and the assimilation of design and testing capability provided a base for research capacity, as demonstrated by the generation of patents by firms in Korea and Taiwan (China).

Setting up laboratories has become easier with the advent of new physical technology and equipment, and firms in high-tech areas find that investing in such facilities is advantageous. The increasing need to compete on the technology plane is also prodding firms in other sectors to undertake R&D. Firms' research efforts generally correlate with exports, patents, new products, and profitability. The mobility of human capital and bidirectional investment in high-tech industries have helped to unify local and international pools of research skills to some extent, making it possible for Korea and Taiwan (China) to enhance the productivity of their research efforts significantly (table 3.7).

Debate about the extent to which FDI contributes to innovation in the host countries persists; the findings to date are equivocal. Investment by MNCs does bring with it more advanced technology to the benefit of production network members, and foreign-owned firms are likely to have an edge over comparable local firms because of advantages in efficiency and product design (Bartelsman and Doms 2000; E. Kim 2000). Initially, FDI flows were mainly from the United States to East Asia. Starting in the 1980s, sizable flows of Japanese FDI spread throughout Southeast Asia and began to establish industrial beachheads in the United States. More recently some of the smaller East Asian economies, such as Korea (see Lindblad 2000 for a review of Korean investment in Indonesia), Malaysia, Taiwan (China), and Thailand, have begun investing throughout the region, while Korea and Taiwan (China) invest selectively in the United States as well. A substantial portion of this investment is by MNCs, which are actively engaged in promoting and coordinating research in a number of countries and are becoming increasingly energetic in fully exploiting research inside and outside the organization (Zanfei 2000). By dispersing production facilities to take full advantage of cost differences, the benefits of proximity to markets, and the advantages of observing or tapping into research in the destination country, investment by MNCs and others is tightening the production as well as the research links throughout the Pacific region. Producers can thus exploit scale, scope, and network economies, depending on the type of industry and the extent of knowledge spillovers. This also makes producers footloose and ready to shift production to minimize costs.

Table 3.7 Patents Filed, Selected Economies, 1968–97 and 1992–97

	Patents per year		Patents per capita		Annual growth rate (percent)	
Economy	**1968–97**	**1992–97**	**1968–97**	**1992–97**	**1968–97**	**1992–97**
Asian Tigers						
Hong Kong (China)	39	95	0.7	1.5	12.5	9.6
Korea, Rep. of	443	1,989	1.1	4.4	27.7	27.9
Singapore	22	83	0.8	2.6	16.5	10.3
Taiwan (China)	554	2,006	2.8	9.3	33.8	15.7
Group of Seven						
Canada	1,525	2,401	6.1	8.1	3.4	5.5
France	2,423	2,896	4.5	5.0	1.9	0.5
Germany	6,338	7,250	9.8	8.9	2.3	2.4
Italy	937	1,197	1.7	2.1	2.8	–0.4
Japan	13,226	23,847	11.5	19.0	8.4	2.8
United Kingdom	2,547	2,494	4.4	4.3	–0.2	3.1
United States	46,913	66,325	19.8	25.2	1.6	5.3
Other						
Finland	214	438	4.5	8.6	8.6	10.0
Israel	234	577	5.3	10.2	10.1	13.3
Ireland	35	6	1.0	1.7	6.8	5.5

Source: Trajtenberg (1999).

FDI is also a necessary complement to the movement of human capital, the emergence of clusters, the transfer of technology, and the cementing of interfirm links, whether through purchase or the formation of alliances. The flow of capital into high-tech industries in Korea and Taiwan (China) parallels the reflux of highly trained nationals to these economies from the industrial countries (L. Kim 2000). Many companies now have an industrial presence in both the United States and East Asia, having either invested directly or established alliances with local firms. These links are transmission belts for capital, technology, and skills. LG Electronics of Korea, for example, together with other local firms, has R&D laboratories in Tokyo; Sunnyvale, California; Chicago; Germany; and Ireland.[21] These laboratories monitor new developments, engage in research on the frontier, and help build strategic alliances (L. Kim 2000). More important, they have created an international innovation system that is linking research capabilities formerly localized among the key clusters. The development underlying a global innovation system is the growing community of knowledge workers, many of whom have been trained in elite universities in the West and in East Asia. These individuals share values, communicate in English, and have comparable skills. Travel and ICT make research a joint international activity, even where knowledge remains somewhat localized or circulates mainly between clusters.

The move to partially liberalize capital flows during the 1990s has energized the nascent global innovation system by allowing budding high-tech clusters to begin to realize their full potential, as in Bangalore. Available local skills would have gone unutilized had the capital not arrived with new technology to trigger and expand market prospects. FDI, along with other kinds of investment, has begun to galvanize education systems in recipient countries by providing funds, as in China and India, but also by revealing the full extent of opportunity as, for instance, in Malaysia.

Throughout East Asia, the entry of FDI into high-tech sectors and some initial successes with clusters have induced policymakers and business firms to think harder about human skills. If innovation and productivity are going to be the keys to growth, as many are coming to realize, then the human capital to operate on the frontiers of global technology is essential. The flow of capital to Ireland, Israel, Korea, Taiwan (China), and now India indicates that the attraction is human resources, increasingly those equipped to exploit ICT. FDI is bringing technology to these countries, but with the expectation of generating more technological advances that can be dispersed to the country of origin and elsewhere.

LOGISTICS AND SUPPLY CHAINS

Globally networked cluster arrangements are a fairly recent phenomenon, spawned by advances in logistics and supply chain management that enable the move to a global plane through lowered warehousing costs, lean manufacturing, and just-in-time delivery. In the absence of such advances, regional market integration through the subdivision and dispersion of production processes would not be cost-effective, nor would businesses be able to meet the test of timely delivery of products to buyers. The new economic geography has greatly raised awareness of the effects of transport costs on trade. The elasticity of trade volume with respect to distance is –1 to –1.3, thus when distance is doubled, trade can be cut by one-half to two-thirds. Overall, trade volumes seem to be sensitive to transport costs, with an elasticity of –2.5, implying that a doubling of costs reduces trade by 80 percent. The reduction in transport costs and improvement in supply chain management is advantageous for East Asia, but the time sensitivity of some goods has led to a geographic relocation of production that brings suppliers closer to users, such as the shift in U.S. imports of apparel from East Asia to Mexico and the Caribbean countries (Abernathy and others 2001; Hummels 2001), a process that has been reinforced by the preferential treatment of imports from the Caribbean region.

Supply chains in East Asia are still relatively inefficient compared with those in Europe. On average, distribution and logistics account for 12 percent of the free on board price of steel in East Asia, as against 4 percent in Europe (Dhawan and others 2000; Henderson, Shalizi, and Venables 2000; Hummels 2001). In East Asia freight costs account for 8 percent of the total value of inputs, compared with 14 percent for Sub-Saharan Africa and 4 percent for the industrial countries (Pedersen 2001). Thus the growth of e-commerce will depend on parallel advances in logistics to realize its full potential benefits. Notably, the biggest gainers from e-commerce include the courier services, such as UPS and Federal Express, which respond with the speed and innovativeness desired by the new breed of businesses and their clientele.

The decline in transport costs stems from technological improvements, such as larger container ships capable of carrying 6,000 20-foot-equivalent-unit containers (TEUs) rather than the former maximum of 4,500. These improvements have both lowered transport costs and widened the range as well as the convenience of services available to producers (Cullinane and Khanna 2001).[22] The ease, flexibility, and speed of multimodal services has increased substantially. Better transport infrastructure, exemplified by the highly efficient ports and airports of Hong Kong (China), Korea, and Singapore, have also contributed to the rapidity of freight movement and allow firms to distribute their production optimally. In 2000 Hong Kong (China), the second busiest airport in the world, handled 2.3 million tons of cargo.

The new airport at Sepang could help boost the ability of Malaysia's Multimedia Development Corridor to attract businesses. Many high-tech products are shipped by air, and the rising efficiency of long-range cargo aircraft enables production networks to embrace much larger geographic regions. With the massive expansion of courier services and the growth of domestic trunk networks in China and Malaysia, for example, firms in those countries are now able to move key consignments speedily among customers. Even the mid-size centers that are nodes in the East Asian production system depend on transport service providers for rapid delivery of parts and shipment of components for further assembly or sale. Additional benefits for all users derive from the ties between domestic and international shippers, which further enhance flexibility, provide door-to-door service, and reduce costs.

Superior logistics capability allows companies to revamp their supply chain management to ensure the smooth movement of goods from the producer to the final user. It also allows assemblers and the big retail chains to squeeze out the maximum cost savings by rationalizing when and where they buy products and how they organize production. The use of e-procurement to gain access to a wider range of supplies, to check the status of transactions and resolve problems with purchase orders, and to charge back is becoming an additional means of minimizing costs (e-businessadvisor.com, "Optimize Your Supply Chain," June 2002). In the highly competitive East Asian market, supply chain management in networked arrangements can make a significant difference to profits. This has created a role for a new kind of intermediary that manages the supply chain for the final buyer or customizes production arrangements. Among East Asian companies that have made a name for themselves in distribution and process technology, Li and Fung of Hong Kong (China) is preeminent. It handles a wide array of information-intensive services for its 350 customers, extending from product development and sourcing to logistics. Using ICT to bring the entire supply chain online, Li and Fung has made dispersed manufacturing—the company works with 7,500 suppliers in 26 countries—a fine art, shortening and cheapening product delivery cycles, reducing inventory costs, and revolutionizing supply chains (Dhawan and others 2000; Magretta 1998).

Two factors help expedite the networking of clusters using modern systems of logistics orchestrated by sophisticated supply chain management. One is the strategic behavior by port owners, shippers, and airlines. Port owners, for instance, are investing in and entering into alliances to improve the flow of traffic and to encourage the clustering of businesses around port facilities. Singapore Port has invested in ports in Venice and Genoa, while Hutchinson, which runs Hong Kong Port, has acquired equity in Thamesport and Shanghai Port (Lakshmanian 2001). Rotterdam Port collaborates with rail and trucking companies to provide efficient multimodal services to ensure prompt delivery. Sizable gains remain to be made by harmonizing standards for surface transport and entering into more flexible airline alliances, but regional arrangements are making some headway.

The second factor is the capacity to elaborate and exploit ICT to the fullest. Without advanced ICT and widespread computerization, the sprawling production networks that enfold the main East Asian production centers would be unimaginable. Equally difficult to achieve would be the intricate interrelationships among producers and suppliers for the numerous steps that go into the assembly of a final product. ICT has made possible the efficient management of far-flung operations as well as allowing companies to mesh logistical operations. Paperless processing of freight consignments, including customs clearance, involves computerized sorting and dispatching. It has slashed costs at airports and ports and permits precise scheduling that greatly reduces inventory holdings.[23]

These developments have been and will remain an important source of cost savings and productivity gains, but they also necessarily reduce overall logistics costs and ratchet up the pressure on producers. Transport outlays as a share of GDP have not diminished. While the direct transport component has diminished, the share of other value adding logistics services has risen (Pedersen 2001). Being part of a production network that leverages the spillovers arising from major clusters such as Silicon Valley or Singapore-Johore is now more critical for companies that want to participate in the global marketplace. Such participation also increasingly demands state-of-the-art supply chain management. Inevitably companies taking this route must regularly upgrade their computer hardware and ICT software to hold onto their competitive advantage. With the spread of e-business and the emergence of e-marketing hubs, the role of ICT will move increasingly to center stage.

CONCLUSION

The growth of a knowledge economy is a phenomenon of much consequence for both East Asia and other parts of the world. The knowledge economy has two important characteristics relevant to our discussion. First, it places universities and other high-level training institutes at the core of development and associates achievement with the quality of knowledge workers. Second, for the foreseeable future—until ICT greatly improves the efficiency of distance education—knowledge generation and its commercial use are likely to be localized (Cooke 2000; Jaffee 1989; Jaffee, Trajtenberg, and Henderson 1993). By reinforcing the gains from networking, agglomeration economies, and the advantages of face-to-face contact in the provision of many producer services, particularly finance, this localization will continue to favor the few clusters that can combine several essential ingredients.

The modern production system is being subdivided into a number of elements, the most important of which are research, design, key producer services, manufacturing, component supplies, marketing, and after-sales service. Clusters bring all these elements together in different combinations; however, the globalization of production is leading to a concentration of specific activities in particular clusters. Manufacturing has gravitated more to East Asia, for example, along a gradient that situates high-tech activities in Taiwan (China) and less technologically sophisticated activities in China, Malaysia, and Thailand.

One interesting example, symptomatic of the changes afoot, is the production of computer disk drives, which has been partitioned and distributed around the Pacific Rim in line with the outsourcing strategies of MNCs and the evolving comparative advantage of East Asian economies. Seagate, the largest manufacturer of hard disk drives (HDDs), has dispersed its production around the world. According to Gourevitch, Bohn, and McKendrick (2000, pp. 304–05): "[A] single component may be worked on in five countries and across two oceans, while Seagate is building it up through its value chain." The company develops products at seven locations in the United States and in Singapore and assembles the HDDs in China, Malaysia (Penang, now being scaled down and production being redistributed following Seagate's acquisition of a rival's facilities in Ipoh), Singapore, and

Thailand. Heads for the HDDs start with wafer fabrication in Northern Ireland and the United States, which are cut into bars and assembled into head gimbals in Thailand. Printed circuit cables are made in Thailand, while the printed circuit boards are assembled in Malaysia, Singapore, and Thailand. All this is done in synchrony with component suppliers such as Komag, also in Malaysia, which makes thin film disks. Seagate is the largest nongovernmental employer in Singapore and Thailand.

As the world edges closer to a global production system, eventually the system will likely be anchored in a few clusters within city regions. This is not just because of centripetal pressures arising from networking and agglomeration economies, but also because of first-mover advantages and the imperatives of geography. If the preference is for a coastal location with good access to markets, an adequate water supply, and a pleasant climate, the options narrow rapidly.

The problems that surfaced in the Silicon Valley area during 2001 drew attention to the importance of a high-quality physical infrastructure for a cluster's success. Silicon Valley capitalized on the lavish spending on power, water, transport, and sewerage facilities in the early postwar decades. These lowered entry barriers for industry and contained production costs, while at the same time supporting a quality of life few other areas in the United States could match. Inadequate attention to this infrastructure, plus increasing population density, has pushed up congestion costs and led to power shortages that in early 2001 threatened to shut down parts of the valley (The Real Trouble 2001).

This chapter has sketched a new dynamic of technological change that puts it into a global context. Innovation is now a cooperative, cross-national activity concentrated in a number of interlinked clusters. The bridges between these clusters consist of flows of capital, knowledge workers, and trade and firms' transnational operations. ICT advances contribute to connectedness at many levels. No government or firm can avoid this reality, certainly not in East Asia. For countries—and firms—to grow by dint of innovation and productivity gains, the approach to innovation must have both a local and a global dimension. At the local level, the innovation system will rest on the strength of the education system and the capacity to bring together the ingredients that make clusters thrive. The global dimension consists of the degree to which the country can participate in the traffic in FDI, human capital, and the commerce of ideas.

At the close of his magnificent and opinionated work on the wealth and poverty of nations, Landes (1998, p. 517) concludes:

> If we learn anything from the history of economic development it is that culture makes all the difference. On the other hand, it does not stand out alone. . . . Because culture and economic performance are linked, changes in one will work back on the other. In Thailand, all good young men used to spend their years undergoing a religious apprenticeship in Buddhist monasteries. This period of replenishing was good for the spirit and soul; it also suited the pace of traditional economic activity and employment. That was then. Today, Thailand moves faster; commerce thrives; business calls. As a result young men spiritualize for a few weeks—time enough to learn some prayers and rituals and get back to the real material world.

The experience of the leading economies of East Asia, such as China, Japan, and Korea, suggests that a culture that is open to ideas, but is also successful in conserving core values, is most likely to thrive in a world where knowledge is a dynamic force permeating and modifying virtually every aspect of existence. This kind of mix makes social stability possible, even as it promotes a vibrant intellectual discourse fruitful in both its reflexive assimilation of outside ideas and its unique contribution to the traffic in innovation.

A hundred and fifty years of Japanese history nicely delineate the fine balance that can be struck between conservation and openness, as well as the need to modulate this balance to allow for increased global integration. The state-orchestrated drive toward modernity and the cooperative effort that took Japan to the frontiers of technological achievement was astonishingly well suited to a country catching up with the industrial front-runners. In today's complex, knowledge-intensive, globalized environment, the earlier cultural balance is less suitable, and Japan's economic stagnation over the past decade sends a signal to other East Asian economies. The role of the state in directing technological catch-up is much diminished, although by no means over. Increasingly, technological advance rests with researchers spurred by a highly competitive environment that rewards excellence, and it depends on large, research-oriented corporations; universities; and private financiers willing to support research. East Asian economies, particularly Japan, have excelled at team-based research calculated to maximize steady incremental gains, but they have not shown the sharp competitive edge, the hard-nosed peer scrutiny, and the aggressive individualism that can regularly yield breakthrough technologies.[24] For the several Northeast Asian countries wanting to carve out a lucrative place near the frontiers of technology, the challenge will be to introduce this shift in culture without disrupting other desired relationships.

NOTES

1. In the process of refining measures of TFP the methodology used has come under sustained scrutiny, and its many shortcomings have been detailed at length (Felipe 1999; Pack 2001; Rodrigo 2001).
2. See chapter 1 on technological alliances. The contrasting experiences of the PC and hard disk drive industries in Taiwan (China) suggest that only some technologically intensive industries concentrate in clusters. Small, cooperatively networked Taiwanese producers of PC platforms can still thrive, but producing hard disk drives requires small manufacturers to establish relationships with the four firms—Seagate, Maxtor, Fujitsu, and Hitachi—that control 80 percent of the industry's output (Hung 2000).
3. Low productivity during the 1990s was partly responsible for Japan's slow growth, and perhaps the problems the financial system was facing prevented the commercialization of some research findings.
4. These so-called stress or vulnerability indicators include the state of current account balances, foreign currency reserves held by central banks, public sector deficits and indebtedness, short- and long-term external debt, and financial sector balance sheets (Goldstein, Kaminsky, and Reinhart 2000).
5. De la Potterie, van Pottelsberghe, and Lichtenberg (2001) also show that FDI is a greater source of technology acquisition when less technology-intensive countries invest in countries that are more technology intensive, but far fewer spillovers arise from FDI by research-intensive countries in countries that are less research intensive.
6. In most East Asian economies scientists generally derive little financial reward from innovations, and their property rights are weakly defined or enforced. One example is Shuji Nakamura, the developer of the blue light-emitting diode. He received ¥20,000 from Nichia Corporation for his patent, which has contributed ¥2 billion to the company's profits (*Financial Times*, "Japanese Scientist Sues for His Share of Profit from Blue LED," August 24, 2001).
7. Howe (1999) noted that among champion chess players, outstanding musical performers, or exceptional mathematicians, finding outstanding individuals who had not already achieved high standards prior to reaching adulthood is unusual.
8. Compared with an average of 3,805 scientists and engineers per 1 million people in such industrial nations as the United States, Malaysia and Thailand have

121 comparably qualified persons per million people (Persaud 2001). In an effort to build problem-solving and critical thinking skills and to encourage students to be more creative, Singapore introduced the Thinking Schools Learning Nation Program in 1997. In 1999, content in all subjects was reduced by 10 to 30 percent to give students more time to think around a subject. This, and possibly the openness introduced by ICT, might change the work-intensive, grade-oriented culture, but it will take time to feel the effects, and the consequences of ICT on education have yet to be clearly understood (*Far Eastern Economic Review*, "Thinking Out of the Box," December 14, 2000).

9. Lee (2001) points to the "sorry state" of secondary and tertiary education in Korea, where students' performance and foreign language skills taper sharply in higher age groups. He ascribes this to a poor academic environment; inadequate facilities; insufficient pay for teachers, which affects teacher quality; tight regulation of secondary education (as in Japan); and weak competition between schools. Korea is second only to the United States in the number of college graduates per unit of population, but educational quality remains a concern (*Science*, "Korean Science and Technology," August 7, 1998).

10. In the U.S. context Romer (2000) has argued that government policy that enlarges private sector demand for scientists and engineers without attending to the supply is basically misguided. He calls for increased attention to enhancing the supply response through programs that increase the numbers of such professionals coming into the market. Rodriguez-Pose (1999) distinguishes between regions that are innovation prone or innovation averse. He notes that heavy investment in R&D can spur growth, but may not necessarily do so, because research does not lead inevitably to innovation and gains in productivity. For that to occur a region must be open to ideas and not subject to strong social filtering of ideas. Moreover, regions with labor market rigidities, an aging work force, and scarce skills that experience the outmigration of able individuals will tend to be less innovative.

11. Stanford also adopted a proactive policy toward local development by creating the Stanford Research Institute to do its own research and to assist firms, inviting local companies to enroll employees in its Honors Cooperative Program, and creating the Stanford Industrial Park (Cohen and Fields 1999).

12. In the United States university-business collaboration was facilitated by a series of legislative actions that highlight the role governments can play in removing barriers inadvertently put in place by past actions. The Bayh-Dole Patent Act of 1980 permitted government agencies to grant exclusive licenses for inventions made with agency funding. This was followed in the same year by the Stevenson-Wydler Act encouraging university-business collaboration, while the National Cooperative Research Act of 1984 reduced the risk of antitrust action being taken against companies engaged in cooperative research. This was reinforced two years later by the Technology Transfer Act, which provided specific incentives for cooperation between national and other laboratories (Branscomb, Kodama, and Florida 1999). These legislative initiatives are being replicated across the Pacific, and other actions taken by European countries are also being emulated. The flow is in both directions, however. Technology development partnerships instigated by the Japanese government in the 1950s and 1960s are becoming commonplace as

research costs mount and the advantages of interfirm sharing become more apparent. Moreover, the involvement of suppliers in the design and development of parts—brought to perfection in Japan—is widely emulated. This and the transcontinental dispersal of research laboratories by large firms is intrinsic to the new globalized style of distributed and decentralized technology developments.

13. Family ownership is generally pervasive worldwide; however, where the legal environment offers few safeguards to minority shareholders, family control and management of firms is especially marked (see Burkart, Panunzi, and Shleifer 2002).

14. Estimates of the extent of spillovers between firms located close to one another can be found in Cicone and Hall (1996) and Henderson (1999), among others. Glaeser and others (1992) and Harhoff (1999) provide estimates of the importance of citywide labor markets for firm productivity. Adams (2001), Audretsch and Stephan (1996), and Mansfield and Lee (1996) provide three of the best empirical examinations of the effects of proximity to academic institutions on firm start-ups and performance. The *Economist* ("Press the Flesh, Not the Keyboard," August 24, 2002, p. 50) notes: "For companies whose lifeblood is creativity, personal contact matters even more. Silicon Valley was born from long nights spent drinking in the now-defunct Wagon Wheel bar in Mountain View, California, where the early geeks and semiconductor executives thrashed out technical glitches over beers."

15. The advantages of cluster size and density are most apparent in the case of Silicon Valley, which has more than 7,000 electronics and software firms and tens of thousands of workers whose lives revolve around the high-tech industry. Supporting these firms are more than 600 venture capitalists and a university system that graduates more engineers than any other region in the United States. This does not include the thousands more who immigrate to the region. Black and Henderson (1999) rightly emphasize, however, the disincentive effects of rising housing prices, lengthening commuting times, and hence wage costs as clusters grow in size. These costs must be offset by the scale of agglomeration economies.

16. Firms surveyed in the Singapore-Johore area attached the highest importance to local links with suppliers, subcontractors, and customers that also promoted technology transfer. Local courier services, banks, and venture capitalists were also rated high, as was the quality of the physical infrastructure and the favorable business environment (Konstadakopulos 2000).

17. A flourishing cultural environment attracts skilled people to a city and generates large revenues. In New York, for instance, museums, art galleries, and other cultural centers are the source of US$10 billion in direct and indirect earnings for the city.

18. These attractions depend on investments in power, the transport infrastructure, and housing. They also rest on maintaining the livability of the environment. In all these respects Silicon Valley has allowed its advantages to erode.

19. A distant but still sizable second is the Indian diaspora, with an annual income of US$160 billion (Devan and Tewari 2001).

20. The United States approved some 81,262 petitions for H-1B visas between October 1999 and February 2000. Half of these were for computer-related

occupations, and about 16 percent were for individuals with science and engineering degrees. In 1997–98, 4,092 Indian-born professors were teaching in U.S. universities, and 33,900 Indian students were enrolled in 2,579 U.S. universities. According to the American Association of Physicians, 35,000 of its members are of Indian origin and 14 of every 100 researchers in U.S. pharmaceuticals laboratories are from India (Panagariya 2001).

21. The difficult years following the 1997–98 crisis have prompted some Korean companies to sell off their large-scale integration facilities overseas, however, increasing their dependence on memory chips and jeopardizing their long-term viability.

22. Further advances in shipping technology are on the way that will result in cargo vessels capable of traveling at 38 knots. These new vessels, powered by jet engines and with sharp bows and concave bottoms, would carry 1,400 containers (*Economist*, "How to Shrink the World," August 4, 2001).

23. Computerized tracking relies on radio frequency and other tags and has helped to reduce cargo theft, a problem amounting to US$30 billion to US$50 billion worldwide and US$10 billion in the United States alone. Companies such as i2 use software to handle inventory; Bolero standardizes cargo documents and exchanges ownership online; and shippers such as UPS run smart warehouses with computerized stacking, tracking, and cross-docking facilities that speed flow and ensure quick and accurate delivery (*Asian Wall Street Journal*, "UPS Delivers Logistics to Asia," April 25, 2001; *Financial Times*, "Supply Chain Management: Survey," October 25, 2000; *Financial Times*, "Supply Chain Management: Survey," June 20, 2001).

24. One of the most prolific research centers in the world is the Angen Institute in Toronto. It owes its success to the stern philosophy of its director, Tak Wah Mak, who is determined to attract and promote the best scientific talent by demanding excellence and ensuring that the research in the institute passes the most rigorous scrutiny by peers (*Science*, "Toronto's Science Jewel," May 21, 2001). The absence of such standards, competition, and demanding scrutiny by peers is regularly decried as the cause of innovative slack in Japan and Korea (Lim 1999; *New York Times*, "Hypothesis: A Scientific Gap. Conclusion: Japanese Custom," August 27, 2001).

CHAPTER 4

FINANCIAL AND BUSINESS SERVICES

East Asia will remember the last third of the 20th century as the heyday of manufacturing. The prosperity of all these emerging economies was built on manufacturing prowess, first of light consumer goods, then of a wide range of intermediate goods. More recently this prosperity has been based on the manufacture of electronic products and capital equipment. East Asian producers penetrated markets throughout the world, consolidated a reputation for quality and delivery, and acquired a knack for incremental innovation, transforming a handful of the region's economies into some of the premier trading nations in the world.

For some of the lower-middle-income countries, manufacturing will remain the leading sector in the coming decades, with services gaining in importance. For the middle- and higher-income economies, however, the key drivers of growth and employment will be financial, design, management, ICT, advertising, marketing, logistics, and other business services. In a matter of years such services are likely to be the principal sources of employment, innovation, and exports. This trend is already apparent in Hong Kong (China): the share of manufacturing share shrank from nearly 30 percent of GDP in 1985 to only 8 percent in 1998, while the share of services rose by more than 90 percent (Kueh 2001). Japan and Singapore are moving in the same direction. The prices that the newly industrializing economies'—Hong Kong (China), Korea, Singapore, Taiwan (China)—exports command in the United States began falling before the crisis, suggesting that the manufacturing-dominated model had begun to exhaust its competitive potential. Increasing the profitability and market performance of higher-technology manufactured goods is coming to depend on how they are bundled together with value adding services that enhance their utility while contributing to the profits of the supplier.[1]

Among business services, those related to ICT receive the greatest attention because of their relationship with knowledge-based activities. From a modest base the scale of ICT-enabled services has grown immensely since the early 1990s, and even from the soberest perspective, their longer-term potential appears to be vast (though realizing this potential is another matter). Their contribution to East Asia's growth over the next 10 years—and possibly longer—is, however, likely to be overshadowed by "old economy" services such as banking, finance, accounting, marketing, and insurance. Nonetheless, these services too will be making greater use of ICT because of rapidly multiplying synergies. Developing these services to the fullest is the low-hanging and long-neglected fruit in East Asia.

This chapter first focuses on the reforms of banking and finance subsectors, which will strongly influence East Asia's medium-term growth by channeling funds to the most promising and innovative segments of the economy. It then discusses some of the opportunities inherent in other business services intrinsic to the new dynamic.

THE BANKING SECTOR: CRISIS AVOIDANCE, MACROECONOMIC STABILITY, AND GROWTH

The crisis that brought so much of East Asia to its knees in 1997 was primarily financial, and the persistent weakness of the banking sector—which remains despite the closure of insolvent institutions, the recapitalization of viable ones, and the transfer of NPLs to asset management companies—and of finance companies, which are responsible for intermediating a large share of the region's vast household savings, principally accounts for the continuing fragility of economies such as Japan, Korea, and Thailand. The banking sector has been central to East Asia's development, because under state guidance it served as the main financier of rapid industrialization. In the absence of other alternatives, and for the sake of security, most households deposited their savings in banks, finance companies, or postal savings accounts. These in turn funneled the resources into industry, real estate, and the public sector, frequently at the government's behest. The slow broadening of financial markets, a pattern observed throughout the developing world (and earlier in the industrial countries as well), further inhibited by the inadequacy of both regulatory oversight and legal protection for investors and creditors, has sustained the primacy of banks. In Korea, for example, half of all corporate borrowing in 1997 was from banks. In Thailand such borrowing was close to three-quarters between 1992 and 1996. Malaysian corporations raised 40 percent of their funds from banks and finance companies, the same as in Singapore. Only in Taiwan (China) did corporations rely on banks for less than a quarter of their financing because of the economy's relatively more developed equity and venture capital market (Deckle and Kletzer 2001).

The experience of industrial countries suggests that the banking sector's dominance in East Asia will diminish, as it already has in Taiwan (China), but that it will do so gradually, depending on the speed at which other segments of the financial industry mature. In the meantime, however, the dependence on bank lending can exacerbate the risk of financial crises (see Krueger and Yoo 2001 for a discussion of lending by Korean banks to *chaebol*, many in weak financial shape, and the evergreening of *chaebol* debt by the banks). Analyses of events leading up to the crisis in Indonesia, Korea, and Thailand indicate that deteriorating bank balance sheets resulting from the incautious (principally overseas) borrowing and lending practices of recently deregulated banks and finance companies contributed substantially to the perception of fragility that triggered the huge outflows of capital in 1997 and 1998 (Haggard 2000).

Following the lifting of curbs on overseas short-term borrowing and the easing of entry barriers on banks and finance companies, banks in Korea and Thailand accumulated large volumes of NPLs because of imprudent lending, sometimes at the urging of the government and major shareholders, and because of speculative real estate development, which resulted in asset price bubbles. Korean banks, among others, also invested in risky Russian and Latin American debt instruments. Such lending was financed in part by unhedged, short-term borrowing from overseas banks, which, equally unwisely, were ready to lend without factoring the appropriate risk premium into the interest rates they charged. The process continued as long as it did because of the pervasiveness of moral hazard. Domestic banks, their depositors, and their overseas creditors were ready to believe that East Asian governments would hold fast to their exchange rate pegs, which had remained in place for several years, and would underwrite bank debts should any of the banks become insolvent. This mind-set was compounded by the pervasiveness of inept credit assessment and risk management in each of the three worst affected countries, casual accounting procedures, and lax regulatory oversight. After years of coddling and exploitation by governments and by influential shareholders, banks, much like their clients, had been lulled into believing that implicit government guarantees absolved the banks of responsibility for managing prudential risk, even after the introduction of financial liberalization.

When confidence was tested by the scattered failures of banks and finance companies in Korea and Thailand, the reluctance of governments to bail out the affected entities, the widespread awareness of currency and maturity mismatch problems, and the poor quality of bank and finance company portfolios triggered a massive flight of domestic and foreign capital (Ito 2001; Mishkin 2000). This led in turn to currency crises, which administered the coup de grâce to indebted banks and highly leveraged companies (Kaminsky and Reinhart 1999; Mishkin 2000). Where financial liberalization and exchange controls had proceeded cautiously and the banking system had already been subjected to a round of reforms or was better regulated, as in the Philippines, Singapore, and Taiwan (China), banking systems suffered less severely. Likewise where capital controls, large reserves, and a strong balance of payments contained capital flight, as in China, insolvent (but not illiquid) banks have continued to limp along (see, for example, Lardy 1999, 2001).[2]

Developing business services is a long-term priority for East Asian countries. The urgent task for the near term, however, is for governments to divest banking and corporate assets acquired after 1998 and to ensure the sound footing of their banking systems. This process will help expedite the strengthening of accounting, legal, and other services. It will also pave the way for a reform of corporate governance. Restructuring is a priority, and not just for the four countries worst hit by the crisis, where the cost of bank recapitalization ranges from 19 to 30 percent of GDP (World Bank 1999).[3]

China, Japan, and Taiwan (China), all of which suffered from the enormous extent of the crisis, must also redouble their efforts to address long-standing banking problems (Taiwan: Banking Burdens 2000).

Stalled Banking Reform Slows the Entry of Dynamic New Firms

Banking reforms should be given priority for many reasons. Foremost among them is the robust causal link running from financial development to growth and the shifting composition of economic activity toward service providers and innovative firms, both of which require funds to expand their activities.

These two arguments, among others, underlie the well-established empirical finding that after controlling for a number of other variables, including education, political stability, and openness, a strong positive relationship is apparent between several measures of financial development and subsequent economic growth (Levine 1997; Levine, Loayza, and Beck 2000; Speigel 2001). Furthermore, improving the functioning of financial systems enhances growth by widening firms' access to stock markets and increasing stock market liquidity (Levine and Zervos 1998). Causality tests have begun to show that this is more than just a correlation as, for instance, in Korea, financial development leads to growth (Choe and Moosa 1999).[4] The availability of financing and the range of financial instruments do not passively respond to demand from the real sectors. Financial development impinges on growth, directly and indirectly, through higher investment/GDP ratios and greater trade flows (Bekaert, Harvey, and Lundblad 2001).

In any market economy, a competitive and well-regulated financial sector is a critical determinant of allocative efficiency. In the United States, for instance, financial markets, banks, and venture capitalists continuously scrutinize and validate investment decisions and firm performance. The excessive significance attached to stock market valuation has the drawback of overemphasizing short-term profits to the occasional detriment of longer-term development strategy, but it also helps explain the high productivity attained by virtually all industrial subsectors in the United States, most of which are pacesetters for the rest of the world.

The absence of comparable financial markets in most East Asian countries has made banks the principal source of funds for growing firms. As argued in the last chapter, productivity growth and innovation are determined in part by the entry of new firms and the growth of existing ones, and these latter firms rely on bank lending and what little venture capital is available to finance their expansion.[5] In East Asia such expansion is being constrained by banks, whose capital has been eroded by the accumulation of NPLs. Without prompting from regulators, banks are reluctant to lend and are inclined to employ any available funds to prop up struggling borrowers with what they think are reasonable prospects. An unreformed banking system acts like a tax on the more dynamic sectors of the economy.

A distinct and important argument is that the underdevelopment of the banking and finance institutions in much of the region has hobbled the evolution of corporate governance, which determines the effectiveness of the oversight of banks' principal borrowers, that is, the firms. Put another way, the laws and conventions that dictate the accountability of a firm's managers have a large bearing on how much they are willing to borrow and, by implication, on the longer-term viability of the bank or banks that lent them the funds. Although our focus here is on the banking system's role in corporate governance, broader analyses of corporate governance reform and its effects on firm restructuring in East Asia can be found in Mako (2001) and OECD (2001b). These examine, among other points, the desirability of buttressing the rights of stockholders with respect to managers, of debt holders in relation to stockholders, and of minority stockholders in relation to majority stockholders.[6]

In some European countries, and to a lesser extent in Japan, investment banks can substitute for market surveillance over the performance of companies. Bank representatives sit on company boards in Germany, Japan, Italy, and the Scandinavian countries and exercise oversight in relation to decisionmaking. This has proven to be a weak substitute for legal protection of shareholders' rights (as provided by customary law in the United Kingdom, for example), but it can partially address agency problems (La Porta and others 1999). In most East Asian economies, banks have failed to fulfill an agency function. In the 1970s and 1980s, by directing bank lending and appointing senior bank managers, not infrequently from the ranks of retired public employees, many East Asian governments undermined bank autonomy; sheltered banks from competition; and discouraged banks from adopting efficient loan evaluation, credit assessment, provisioning, and information management practices. More recently, because governments in Indonesia, Korea, and Thailand have renationalized insolvent banks and taken over the reins of management, banking independence has received another setback from which it will need to recover by way of carefully orchestrated divestiture by the state (on average, state-owned banks are less profitable than privately owned banks, according to La Porta, Lopez-de-Silanes, and Schleifer 2000). Such a process will entail good governance, fiduciary responsibility, and efficiency in lending. Corporate ownership of banks and cross-shareholdings link banks with their corporate clients, which then exercise influence over lending decisions. This is a further constraint to bank autonomy and to the efficient allocation of funds.

Finally, the urgency of domestic banking reform is compatible with the long-term goal of opening the capital account. Economies with large, adequately capitalized, effectively managed, and well-regulated banks have proven to be much less susceptible to shocks, even when their capital markets were globally integrated. Both Hong Kong (China) and Singapore experienced considerable difficulty during the recent financial crisis, but they avoided the extreme disruption experienced in Korea and Thailand. Nevertheless, before robust banks will have time to emerge, the case for opening the capital account is likely to be qualified; a sizable program of research is examining the factors that determine the sequencing of banking and capital account reform.[7]

Direction of Reforms

Reform and restructuring of the banking sector will be decisive in two respects. First, it will determine the course and pace of financial liberalization in countries at different stages of development, from Japan at one end of the spectrum to China at the other. All the East Asian economies confront the same global parameters, including continuing integration of national financial markets; probable small, near-term gains from further liberalization; and large reform-induced inflows of capital that, if improperly managed, can increase the likelihood of banking and currency crises. Easing restrictions on the entry of banks and finance companies and removing restrictions on lending and exchange transactions can produce significant shocks as investors reallocate their portfolios, and these shocks may in turn trigger speculative lending. Against this background note that many controls have already been dismantled, and that open economies find it difficult to insulate themselves from capital flows—not even China can do so. In addition, some evidence points to the absence of increased equity market volatility following the opening of markets. Over the long term, even if it does not do much good, financial liberalization does little harm either (Bekaert 1999, 2000; Mishkin 2000; Thurbon 2001; Wyplosz 2001).

The second reason that banking reform is crucial is that bank reforms have a bearing on other areas, such as accounting, the legal system, and corporate governance. More broadly, banking reforms also influence the course of institution building in sectors such as telecommunications and ICT.

Banking reform in East Asia has a long history punctuated by a series of minor crises culminating in the major financial and currency crisis of 1997–98. Current reform efforts focus on the following four areas:

- The autonomy of central banks and bank supervisors
- The cleaning up of bank portfolios and recapitalization
- The prudential systems and their enforcement
- The consolidation of banks and the joint provision of financial and nonfinancial services.

Autonomy of supervisory agencies. For more than a decade, policymakers and legislators have argued about the advantages of autonomy for central banks and the regulatory agencies responsible for different facets of the financial sector. Research points to the efficacy of central bank autonomy and to the autonomy and accountability of key supervisory agencies in promoting sound monetary policy and financial stability, and this view is gaining widespread currency (Quintyn and Taylor 2002). Countries such as China, Japan, and the Philippines have moved toward giving their central banks a larger role, though they have all stopped short of granting them the kind of autonomy enjoyed by the Federal Reserve Bank in the United States or by the Swiss central bank. Such autonomy derives from the fixed term of the bank governor, the governor's accountability to the national legislature, and the central bank's budgetary independence. The push for autonomy acquired new momentum following the 1997–98 crisis; however, this slackened rapidly in the Southeast Asian countries, which have seen an erosion in the independence of central banks and an increase in the politicization of decisions (Southeast Asia 2002).

In the years leading up to the crisis banking laws in East Asia were not updated, and regulators did not put in the requisite effort to put prudential systems on a par with international standards.[8] Bank regulators and supervisors generally did not have the authority to credibly perform their functions as required by law or, as in the United States, to take prompt corrective action when problems were uncovered. A shortage of skilled supervisors further constrained regulatory bodies. Inadequate laws and regulatory slack meant that loan classification was generally lenient, and provisioning for loan losses was inadequate. In the absence of strict limits on exposure to high-risk sectors or individual borrowers, banks drifted into trouble relatively easily. Moreover, limited disclosure requirements made it difficult for supervisors to determine when capital adequacy ratios were being breached or to anticipate serious problems. Assessing the health of banks was rendered doubly problematic when valuation procedures permitted banks to overstate their assets and when rules for loan classification and provisioning allowed earnings to be exaggerated (Brownbridge and Kirkpatrick 2000; Deckle and Kletzer 2001).

Improvements are occurring within the region, however, and efforts under way in the European Union (EU) to assess the relative advantages of a single financial regulator as against different regulatory agencies for the various market segments provide a basis for a considered choice (EU Financial Regulation 2001). Both Japan and Korea have taken a lead in this regard, with other countries, such as Indonesia, beginning to follow suit. This is by no means a linear process, because giving a regulatory agency the mandate to remedy banking system weaknesses puts it at odds with well-connected vested interests. Reformers are having to fend off pressure from such interest groups throughout East Asia.[9] Early successes in dealing with problem cases demonstrated that credible commitment to transparent rules and a reputation for probity contribute to regulatory capability. Regulators not only confront a degree of hostility from the industry they are attempting to restructure and reform, but must also contend with unavoidable changes in signals from their political masters, who are sensitive to pressure from the business elites, the overall state of the economy, and the timing of election cycles. Measures affecting the accountability of regulators, better-informed voters, and the rise of e-governance should enlarge the amount of information available to the public (Keefer 2001). Furthermore, as the financial sector matures and deals increasingly with global integration, the value for the industry of stringent regulatory oversight and cross-border cooperation will become more urgent.[10] For most East Asian economies, delay in coming to grips with regulation is costing them dearly.

Bank balance sheets and capital adequacy. Following the examples of Mexico and the United States, East Asian economies have created asset management corporations (AMCs) to take over and dispose of banks' NPLs.[11] Such AMCs are now operating in China, Indonesia, Japan, Korea, Malaysia, Taiwan (China), and Thailand, and they are charged with selling assets worth billions of dollars. Korea's Asset Management Corporation and Malaysia's Danaharta have enjoyed some success in selling assets, but they and their counterparts in China, Indonesia (Indonesian Bank Restructuring Agency), and Thailand have had little effect on corporate governance. Some East Asian countries such as China have also begun capitalizing banks using budgetary resources or bond financing. At considerable current and long-term fiscal cost, the region's banks are being restored to health, but having injected the capital, governments are also keen on selling the banks to leading investors who will infuse management skills, broaden the range of services, and encourage innovation. Korea has permitted the takeover of Korea First Bank by Newbridge Capital, and foreign investors have also acquired banks in Thailand. Another approach, which is being implemented in Japan, Malaysia, Singapore, and Thailand, is to merge mid-size banks into larger, potentially more internationally competitive entities.

Political pressure in China, Japan, Korea, Thailand, and other countries favors rolling over NPLs to avoid a wave of bankruptcies, with their attendant political costs and deflationary effects. The Daewoo debacle in Korea inhibited attempts to tackle other major problem cases, such as Hyundai Securities and Hynex, and to quickly dispose of the firms to strategic investors such as Micron. Moreover, undercapitalized or insolvent banks, with little of their own capital at risk, have no reason to do so. By avoiding this harsh medicine, however, countries further jeopardize the recovery of their banking sectors; by keeping failing businesses alive they divert resources from more profitable uses (Posen 2001).

Banking reform, if rigorously implemented, will send the signal that management, whether of banks or of corporations, is accountable and that East Asia will not tolerate fraud on the scale practiced by Daewoo. However, cleaning up the balance sheets is only half the story; recapitalizing banks and consolidating them into viable units is the second and equally important half. This effort is under way across East Asia. The cost is staggering, and constitutes a major strain on the budgets of countries such as Indonesia, Japan, and Thailand. In China the cost of writing off the NPLs on the books of the four major state banks and of raising their capital/asset ratios to Basle standards could reach 60 percent of GDP.[12] Inevitably, it will be tackled in several stages (Lardy 1999, 2001), but restoring the health of the banking system is so central to future development that delay is an even less viable option. Japan's recent experience makes this abundantly clear.

Prudential systems and their enforcement. Prudential systems encompass a variety of key rules. Although risk-adjusted capital adequacy guidelines receive prominent notice, the utility of such guidelines depends on other rules covering auditing and disclosure. Banking problems in East Asia are related in no small measure to nontransparent accounting practices and the criteria used for determining whether loans are nonperforming. In many instances regulators and shareholders were in the dark about the true financial condition of banks during 1996–97. Not infrequently, senior management was also ill informed as a result of backward information systems and monitoring techniques, which remained unchanged in the absence of pressure from competitors, shareholders, or regulators.

Although regulators are now beginning to press banks to keep a close watch on key ratios, credit risk management, provisioning against NPLs, and earnings, this effort will require validation through reformed governance as is tentatively being initiated in Japan, Korea, and Thailand. Aside from giving voice to minority shareholders and groups representing shareholders, unwinding cross-shareholdings, and radically circumscribing government demands on the banking system, the reform of prudential systems also calls for a different mix of board directors, with the appointment of more external directors on fixed terms who are able to wield authority in corporate environments dominated by the owning families and their associates. One side benefit of unwinding cross-shareholdings is the greater availability of credit to firms that do not belong to bank-affiliated conglomerates. Ultimately, the tenor of governance may only change when competition becomes fiercer, foreign banks acquire a larger say, and foreign standards of governance become the norm.

Complementing these reforms are other institutional changes, which if implemented could help further reduce the possibility that banks will once again accumulate NPLs on the same scale or that governance reforms will fail to enhance accountability to shareholders. Both involve legal developments. The first requires strengthening bankruptcy laws and defining procedures for liquidating assets and sharing the proceeds among creditors. The second relates to judicial institutions.

In economies such as China, Taiwan (China), and Thailand, ineffectual bankruptcy laws have hindered banks from taking aggressive action to deal with NPLs and have given undue protection to debtors.[13] This needs to change, but as Thailand's experience since 1998 shows, modifying decades-long practices takes time (Overholt 1999). Business culture adapts gradually and only under duress (for an examination of the hurdles presented by East Asian business culture and Asian values, see Backman 1999; and on the state of the courts in Indonesia, see Praying for Rule 2002). If the pressure eases, as it did in several countries between 1999 and 2000, change slows or is reversed. What is more, courts can be equally recalcitrant when it comes to implementing new legislation. Indeed, the significance of legal development is considerable, and extends beyond issues of bankruptcy, foreclosure, and disposal of collateral. Court systems will determine whether corporate governance begins to converge toward institutions comparable to those of the industrial countries.

Table 4.1 Legal Protection for External Financiers of Firms, Selected East Asian Economies

Country	Shareholder protection	Creditor rights	Accounting standards
Japan	4	2	65
Korea, Rep. of	2	3	62
Malaysia	4	4	76
Thailand	2	3	64
United States	5	1	71

Note: For shareholder and creditor protection measures, the scale is from 1 to 5, with a score of 5 corresponding to the strongest protection and 1 to the weakest. For accounting standards the higher the measure, the higher the standard. The United States has such a low ranking on creditor rights for various reasons: it permits automatic stay on assets, allows unimpeded petition for reorganization, and lets managers keep their jobs in reorganization (La Porta and others 1998).
Sources: La Porta and others (1998, 1999).

Only after they have the backing of a court system capable of enforcing a market-based framework of corporate laws will minority shareholders gain effective voice; launch class action suits inducing firms, for example, to submit properly audited reports;[14] and begin to influence management. Table 4.1 presents a recent ranking of legal protections available to investors in selected East Asian economies and the United States and shows room for improvement in Japan, Korea, Malaysia, and Thailand along almost all dimensions.

Consolidation of banks and joint provision of services. In the years leading up to the crisis, bank regulators in several East Asian countries, notably Indonesia and Korea, eased licensing procedures for banks and finance companies. This resulted in an increase in numbers, reducing franchise value and encouraging risk taking, while at the same time raising the burden on regulators. Since the crisis, and in line with trends elsewhere, virtually all the East Asian economies—including Taiwan (China)—have sought to consolidate their banking industry through measures to support mergers or closures of banks and finance houses (table 4.2). From 1999 to 2000 the Korean Financial Supervisory Commission closed 10 commercial banks and 2 out of 30 merchant banks. Consolidation is also under way in Malaysia and Singapore. In March 2002 the Bank of Thailand merged the Siam City

Table 4.2 Financial Restructuring, Selected East Asian Economies

Action	China	Indonesia	Rep. of Korea	Malaysia	Thailand
Initial government response					
Liquidity support, US$ billions (% of GDP)	Not disclosed	21.7 (18%)	23.3 (5%)	9.2 (13%)	24.1 (20%)
NPLs					
NPL/total loans, % (date)	About 40	58.8 (11/00)	17.9 (9/00)	23.3 (6/00)	26.5 (12/00)
NPL/total loans, after transfer to AMCs, % (date)	About 10	23.9 (11/00)	12.3 (9/00)	15.3 (12/00)	17.7 (12/00)
Provisioning as a percentage of NPLs (date)	Not applicable	76.0 (11/00)	63.1 (6/00)	40.7 (12/00)	39.0 (9/00)
Financial distress resolutions					
Bank closures	1 commercial bank	70 out of 237	12	0	1 out of 15
Closures of other financial institutions	About 200 financial institutions	0	More than 200	0	59 out of 91 finance companies
Mergers	Multiple credit cooperatives, 2 banks, and trade and investment companies	9 nationalized banks with 4 state banks	9 of 26 banks absorbed by other banks	50 of 54 banks merged into 10 anchor groups	3 banks and 12 finance companies
Banks temporarily nationalized	0	4	4	1	4
Bank recapitalization strategies					
Use of public funds	Injected Y270 billion and transferred Y1.4 trillion to AMCs	Issued US$67.8 billion of bonds	Injection of US$50 billion	Injection of US$1.3 billion by Danamodal	Injection of US$13.7 billion by state
Majority foreign ownership of banks?	Allowed, but not for domestic currency operations	1	1 sold with majority stake, 6 sold so that foreign owners hold significant stakes	13 foreign banks hold 30% of commercial bank assets	4 completed, 2 pending

Note: GDP = gross domestic product; NPL = nonperforming loan; AMC = asset management corporation.

Source: World Bank (2001).

Bank and the Bangkok Metropolitan Bank (Thailand, Bank Consolidation 2002). As the market becomes more competitive, such consolidation makes sense, not least because it enables banks to diversify their portfolios. Moreover profits increase with size, and larger banks are better at attaining risk-adjusted capital adequacy ratios (Reynolds, Ratanakomut, and Gander 2000). Consolidation of banks and the impetus to supply insurance, brokerage, leasing, credit card, investment, and other services also stem from narrowing profit margins in traditional lines of business. Despite competition from other providers of such services, banks find conditions favorable for such efforts because of economies of scale and the use of ICT. Banks also find that their name brands and large client bases give them an edge over new Internet starts. Physical facilities, too, still confer some advantages over purely online providers (Online Finance 2000).

This process of consolidation and heightened market contestability from local and foreign service providers is in its early stages, but it promises to gather momentum. The potential for innovation and better overall performance is there, but the risks are also increasing, as noted in chapter 2. The incidence of crises has risen in part because of the interwoven nature of the global financial system (De Swaan 2000). The presence of extremely large, diversified financial institutions places additional burdens on regulators. They must be alert to collusive practices and pricing, conflicts of interest, excessive risk taking, and exposure in specific markets. Permitting such large entities to fail is much more problematic than allowing smaller banks to go under and constitutes a moral hazard to be monitored with care (Mishkin 1996; Mishkin and Strahan 1999).

Banking reform is proceeding at varying speeds in virtually all the East Asian economies, and in some instances has been ongoing for close to two decades. As East Asia attempts to reinvigorate its growth, accelerating financial development will be an obvious policy option. With ICT and the possibilities created by consolidating financial institutions, the gains could be larger than in the past, and the costs of delaying bank reform and restructuring will be even greater. As indicated earlier, strengthened regulation must parallel financial change, but as Levine, Loayza, and Beck (2000) have pointed out, financial development depends on the quality of legal and accounting services, a point we explore later. The emergence and spread of venture capital are critical for an era in which technological change is bound to speed up.

Venture Capital in East Asia

The renaissance of venture capital in the United States and Europe is closely associated with the emphasis on commercializing innovative products and services (see World Bank forthcoming). Since the start of formal venture capital investing in 1946, the amounts invested worldwide have risen, increasing from US$100 million in 1965 to US$48 billion in 1999 (Kenney and Florida 2001). Venture capitalists are the handmaidens of an innovative economy, because they provide professionally managed, equity-like financing for young, growth-oriented companies (Hellmann 2000). Although the bulk of venture capital is in the United States, primarily in the Silicon Valley region, East Asia is attracting a trickle of American, Japanese (especially trading companies branching into venture capital), and European companies, for example, Warburg Pincus, Softbank, and Deutsche Bank. Some countries, such as China, Malaysia, and Singapore, are promoting home-grown venture capital from the public sector, for instance, Walden International and H&Q. While not significant in the near term, this development will promote the growth of technology-intensive firms that stimulate local innovation in the long run.

Currently, most venture capitalist activity in East Asia is in Hong Kong (China), Singapore, and Taiwan (China).[15] In part, this is because innovation-driven entrepreneurship is concentrated in these locations and because of government activism. However, these three economies also provide venture capitalists with the institutions that permit exit by way of an initial public offering or a merger with a larger company. Either option calls for well-developed capital markets, a business-friendly environment, and listing rules hospitable to launching initial public offerings and to mergers and acquisitions.

Venture capitalists are active in Taipei because of its institutions and multistranded links with Silicon Valley, and because, much like the San Francisco Bay area in the 1950s and 1960s, the region around Taipei has the large firms, wealthy individuals, and accumulated skills and experience that provide the soil from which venture capitalists spring (Kenney and Florida 2000). Elsewhere, true venture capital activity is in its infancy. Unlike the United States and Europe, where venture capital is concentrated in a few high-tech sectors that hold promise of large gains in market capitalization and earnings, venture capital in most East Asian countries is distributed across a number of traditional and new sectors. Moreover, because of the tight hold of families, the venture capitalist rarely provides the inputs—technical and managerial guidance, contacts, networking skills, and strategy ideas—associated with venture capitalism in the West. Families are reluctant to sell their shares in firms. Thus much of East Asia is still not ready for venture capital in the institutional sense, and such institutional preparation must precede less critical, but easier steps, such as setting up a second NASDAQ-style stock market.

SALIENCE AND COMPETITIVENESS OF BUSINESS SERVICES

The benefits of financial development increasingly extend beyond its contribution to macroeconomic stability and the efficient intermediation of resources to industry. Currently, exports of services worldwide, direct and indirect, are about one-fifth of total trade and are growing faster than trade in manufactures. By 2001 international trade in services had reached US$1.4 trillion. Between 1990 and 1998 real global merchandise exports rose by 6.8 percent per year, while the growth rate for services was 8 percent. Financial services constitute a major component of the business services now coming to dominate East Asian economies in terms of employment, value added, and share of GDP. They also attract a significant percentage of inward FDI.

For export-oriented economies, competitive financial and other business services can become a major source of earnings from direct exports (see table 4.3, which shows the still relatively modest share of exports of services by East Asian economies).

In addition, because services are increasingly large inputs into the production of manufactures, every country now runs a large trade balance in indirectly utilized services. Using input-output tables to compute the direct and indirect trade in services, Urata and Kiyota (2000) found that Singapore and Taiwan (China) run a net surplus in services (incorporated in manufactured exports). In contrast, China, Japan, Malaysia, and the Philippines run net deficits in services. Although

Table 4.3 Trade in Services, Selected Economies, 1987 and 1997 (share of services in total exports)

Economy	1987	1997
Hong Kong (China)	22	58
Philippines	6	37
Singapore	6	30
Thailand	4	22
Korea, Rep. of	3	16
Malaysia	2	16
Japan	4	14
Indonesia	2	11
United States	9	25
Italy	8	23
United Kingdom	10	23
France	11	22
Germany	4	13

Source: Hardin and Holmes (1997).

Japan is a net exporter of wholesale retail and transport services, overall it emerges as a net importer of embodied and disembodied services.

The cost competitiveness of banking, ICT, marketing, accounting, transport, and legal and other services influences the competitiveness of final goods. In the industrial countries, producers of high-tech items are gearing up to sell bundles of manufactured items and services to their customers, and because of the fierce competition in the market for manufacturers, differentiated services tailored for each customer can be a much larger source of profits than manufactured products alone. Companies such as IBM, Sun Microsystems, and General Electric derive most of their profits from the services they sell along with their computers, servers, and airplane engines. In the case of IBM, much of its growth and market capitalization comes from services (Getting the Most 2001). Boeing, General Motors, Dell, and Hewlett-Packard-Compaq are moving in the same direction, with General Motors banking on telematic services provided to its automobile buyers generating a sizable slice of future profits (Can Compaq Escape 2001; Driving the Info Highway 2001).

In the industrial countries intense competition in the retail banking market has sharply trimmed profit margins. Thus banks must reduce their costs; rely more on online banking; and diversify into credit card, real estate, trust, and investment services, which offer greater scope for innovation. Supporting such moves is a large cohort of people approaching retirement who demand a host of personalized services. Thus far, most of the increase in banking has been in electronic transactions, which in Asia, North America, and Western Europe and have now surpassed paper-based ones (figure 4.1).

The era of online services provided by banks and other suppliers is less than a decade old, and many untapped possibilities remain as new demands are created and met. With Internet access via PCs and generation (G) 2.5, and eventually 3G, wireless gadgets on the rise, a new era of service provision is opening up (see chapter 5). The opportunities are immense, but they are greatest for those who establish new, widely adopted platforms and protocols that quickly capitalize on network economies and who invest in communications infrastructures.

Figure 4.1 Electronic versus Paper Payments, Selected Years

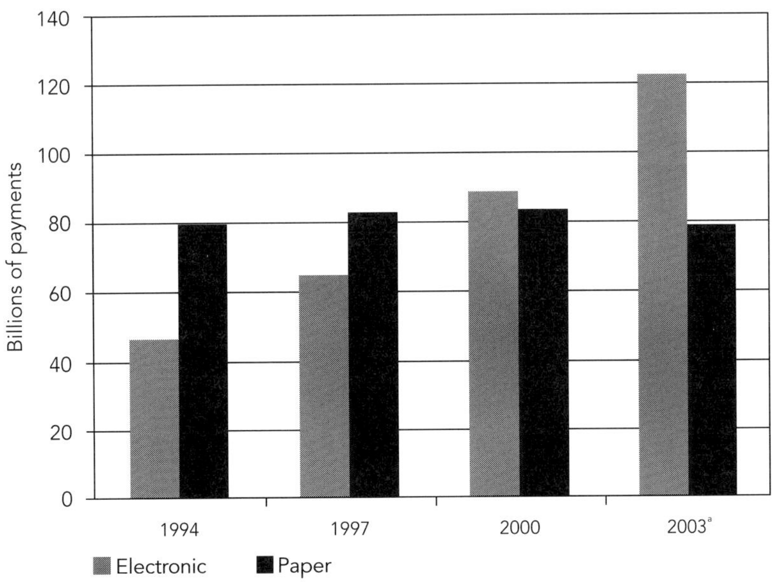

a. Projected.

Source: Teixeira (2000).

Ease of entry, a competitive environment, and integration with the world economy are the keys to a dynamic services sector, including the kind of financial industry that East Asian economies need as they enter the 21st century. This confronts policymakers with difficult choices. Banks and other providers of business services have traditionally been sheltered from external competition, and internal regulations have generally buffered them from domestic competition as well. Invariably the threat of having to face foreign suppliers elicits a strong negative response that politicians cannot easily ignore. But the status quo will prove untenable. The share of business services in GDP and their contribution to the efficiency and innovativeness of other industries is large and growing larger. Hence future growth depends on rapid gains in the competitiveness of the services sector—in terms of quality, timeliness, and convenience—and the liberalization of trade in services. A survey of the business community in Hong Kong (China) indicated that business people view a freeing of trade in financial services as the highest priority, followed by other business services. We discuss how this might be accomplished on a regionwide basis in chapter 6.[16]

What is true of the banking and finance sector extends to other business services as well. East Asia has been slow to recognize the vital role of such services in promoting productivity, directly and through the manufacturing sector; in inspiring innovation; and in contributing to employment and exports. In the area of legal and accounting services, for example, international law firms provide advice to local and international firms on expanding their businesses, handling regulatory matters, managing their finances, and resolving disputes. They constitute an important force supporting a more rules-based business environment. Furthermore, law firms can tap expertise from colleagues both in major financial centers worldwide and in innovative clusters such as Silicon Valley, thereby helping East Asian firms to raise funds overseas as well as to keep abreast of the legal consequences of the latest developments in business strategy and technological change (see, for example, the description of China's expansion of legal services described in The Contender 2000). The cities with the most regional company headquarters and FDI are also those with the closest links to international law and accounting firms (figure 4.2). Hong Kong (China) is in the lead, but other cities have also entered the arena of globalized services.

Throughout the region, business services account for one-quarter to one-third of GDP, but remain relatively backward and inefficient, when they could be the equal of manufacturing industries. This can be traced in part to the still limited supplies of knowledge workers in many countries, such as China and Indonesia. The shortages of such workers are being reduced, but building a stock of experienced professionals will take time. Inadequate supplies of knowledge workers reflect past government inattention, except in economies such as Hong Kong (China) and Singapore, where governments have for some time consciously sought to groom service activities. Preoccupied with manufacturing, East Asian governments did not fully realize that the institutional environment for services is more complex than that for manufacturers, which at a pinch can be nurtured in enclaves. The bare-bones institutions adequate for manufacturing operations and the types of workers appropriate for the assembly line are both unsuited for the business services now at the leading edge of the modern economy. Much like high-tech manufacturing, the modern services economy is on a different technical and institutional plane.

Figure 4.2 Connections to Leading U.S. Law Firms, Selected Asian Cities, 1997

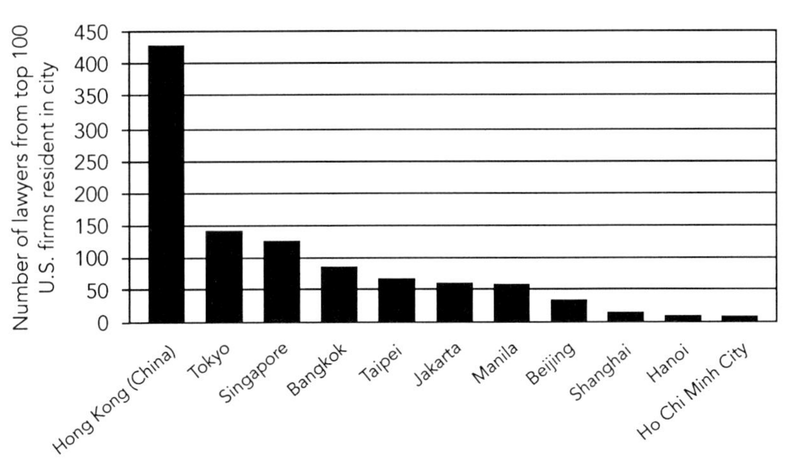

Source: World City Relational Database (http://www.lboro.ac.uk/gawc).

Both derive their impetus from inputs of skilled workers, large doses of ICT, continuous innovation, and international networking.

The 1990s altered the perspective on development for both emerging and industrial economies. At the beginning of the decade they still viewed the manufacturing sector as the engine of growth and the principal source of transformative (or disruptive) innovations. The share of services in GDP was large and growing, and they saw services as crucial in support of manufacturing, but industry remained in the forefront. For East Asian economies banking and finance greased the wheels of industry and commerce, but their role was subsidiary to that of manufacturing. Thus policy focused on creating and sustaining conditions supportive of manufacturing. Labor market and banking sector policies sought to supply industry with low-priced inputs, trade policies attempted to enlarge export markets, technology policies emphasized product and process innovation, and policies toward FDI sought to attract foreign capital to the manufacturing sector. East Asia has not abandoned this mix of policies, and for most countries the significance of manufacturing remains basically undiminished. However, a new, more broadly conceived approach to development is needed, and the winning combination will be a mix of manufacturing and services. Moreover, the productivity, profitability, and market penetration of manufactured goods are closely tied to the efficiency and innovativeness of service inputs.

FUTURE ROLE OF BUSINESS SERVICES

Three causes account for the increasing primacy of services. The first is the contribution of banking and finance to development beyond the mobilization of resources. The availability of risk capital is important to innovation, especially in ICT-sensitive sectors, because it promotes the entry of new firms and enables existing firms to commercialize new products and processes. A vast increase in trade in financial services has followed the liberalization of capital flows, and this in turn has given suppliers incentives to offer a wide range of new value adding services. In short, the financial sector is now at the core of a dynamic that entwines innovation and productivity growth.

A second underlying cause of the expansion in the services sector is the trend toward outsourcing services such as research, logistics, supply chain management, fulfillment, back office functions, and systems integration (see Barthelemy 2001 for a discussion of the risks of such outsourcing without carefully screening vendors and drawing up detailed contracts). Since the 1980s firms have found that buying-in many services previously done in-house is advantageous, because it allows the firms to concentrate on their core functions.[17] Such specialization enhances efficiency, and advances in ICT have made buying-in a more attractive and convenient prospect, as services can now be purchased wherever in the world firms find the lowest price.

The third underlying factor, the subject of chapter 5, is ICT. The impact of ICT on business services cannot be overestimated. Not only has ICT become a leading growth sector in its own right, but its role in other commercial activities has allowed the effects of its diffusion to be much more widely felt. It has both induced and supported innovation in other service areas, such as finance, advertising, marketing, logistics, and supply chain management, while at the same time making it much easier for firms to buy-in services and weave them together with other in-house and contracted activities. As noted earlier, for many manufacturing firms the abundance of new services lowers costs and allows them to offer customers a tailored mix of goods and services that commands price premiums.

For East Asia's economies, the beginning of the 21st century will almost certainly be remembered as the era in which services emerged as a leading component of a hybrid growth model. As this model takes shape in the coming decade, other economies will join Hong Kong (China) and Singapore in benefiting from the higher living standards created by services. Underpinning this development will be a change in the mind-sets of policymakers, who will move their countries' economies forward by improving market regulations and by encouraging improvement in the supply of skills and services that will define the tempo of growth for the foreseeable future.

NOTES

1. On the growth of services in East Asia, see Wirtz (2000), who underlines the significance of industrial services in East Asia. Profit margins in most manufacturing industries are modest, stable, or falling. After six years of record growth the automobile industry has seen no change in its profitability, hence companies like General Motors and Boeing are preparing to diversify into telematic and financial services that they can provide jointly with their main products (*Aviation Week*, "Boeing Widens Reach to Generate Growth," March 19, 2001; *Oxford Analytica*, "Auto Industry," April 6, 2001; *Red Herring*, "The New Thin Client," April 2001).
2. As Sicular (1998) has shown, however, and as is apparent from the large errors and omissions in the balance of payments accounts, capital flight from China is substantial and persists despite controls.
3. By comparison, the cost of bailing out U.S. banks at the time of the Great Depression in 1929–33 was about 3 percent of GDP, and the cost of resolving seven major banking crises worldwide between 1870 and 1913 never exceeded 5 percent of GDP. This provides a perspective on how steep the cost of not managing and regulating East Asia's banking systems effectively has become (Calomiris and Mason 2001).
4. Cross-provincial data from China also support the view that the efficient allocation of financial resources by the banking sector has a strong influence on growth, along with the ability of enterprises to raise funds by themselves (Liu and Li 2001).
5. Urata and Kawai (2001) provided empirical evidence for Japan that bank-directed credit slows down the entry of new firms, because funds are diverted to incumbent firms. This has the effect of reducing the incentive for unprofitable incumbents to exit the industry, and not surprisingly, the net entry of new firms into Japanese industries is now zero.
6. The change in corporate governance is especially noticeable in Japan, long a stronghold of stakeholder power. There the increased shareholder influence arises from the buffeting endured by the economy over a decade, the banks' unwinding of share portfolios, the pressure on companies to diversify sources of funding, and the increase in shares held by non-Japanese investors (from 4 percent in 1990 to more than 14 percent in 2001), who are more forthright in expressing their views and demanding a response from management (*Far Eastern Economic Review*, "Day of the Shareholder," September 13, 2001).
7. Moreover, cross-country experience during the 1990s suggests that a banking system sheltered from foreign competition and subject to the guidance of governments and corporate clients will not become autonomous and efficient in a relatively closed environment. Regulators operating in such an environment, with its powerful traditions and exposed to the demands of public agencies, politicians, and business interests, have difficulty making banks adhere to strict rules. Forbearance is the rule. A sheltered environment also negates the influence of other market entities—such as rating agencies, accountants, auditors,

financial media, and bank shareholders—from contributing to the level of market competition.

8. White (2001, p. 7) maintains that effective prudential regulation has the following components: "[A] transparent accounting system based on market value; adequate risk-based capital requirements that are based on the market value accounting framework and are forward-looking, sensible rules on risk limitations; insistence on the financial and managerial competency of owners and managers, a clear understanding that owners of insolvent institutions lose their investments; clear authority for intervention and enforcement of the rules; and adequate numbers of well-trained and well paid regulators."
9. Calomiris and Mason (2001, pp. 3–4) observe that "too many influential people simply have too much at stake to allow banking to be reorganized efficiently. Banks are only able to channel favors if they themselves are recipients of subsidies from the government, hence the need to preserve the banks' exclusive rights and the need to offer banks subsidized deposit insurance, subsidized purchase of bad loans, or subsidized capital injections. Crony capitalists will appeal for bank assistance on the basis of 'credit crunch' motive while in fact hoping to channel government assistance for banks into their own coffers. Thus the central goal of bank bailout policy is to design bank assistance to meet the legitimate goals of mitigating credit supply contraction for value creating bank dependent borrowers while minimizing the potential 'abuse of assistance.'"
10. De Swaan (2000) has doubts "whether the initiatives for cross border and cross sectoral cooperation can go far enough and fast enough in light of the globalization of the financial system. For example, the cooperation between independent supervisory bodies could result in conflicts of interest as well as overlaps or gaps in supervisory practices. Moreover differences between national supervisors in terms of resources, culture and legal interpretations could place serious roadblocks on the path to international harmonization or centralization of supervision."
11. Nevertheless, significant NPLs remain. As a percentage of total loans, the remaining NPLs in Indonesia, Malaysia, the Philippines, and Thailand were 48.7 percent, 19.5 percent, 17.4 percent, and 30 percent, respectively, toward the end of 2001 (see World Bank 2002 for details). In China Lardy (2001) states that central bank officials have reported that the four largest state-owned banks have NPLs equivalent to a quarter of the value of their loan portfolios.
12. The official estimates of the NPLs in the portfolios of China's big four banks are in the 30 percent range. Unofficial estimates put the ratio at 50 percent or more, with accumulation continuing (*Financial Times*, "China Survey," October 8, 2001).
13. Bankruptcy laws in some Southeast Asian countries, for example, are based on outdated commercial and corporate laws, enforcement by the courts is weak and unreliable, and the courts themselves are not free of corruption, which further reduces the laws' effectiveness (*Oxford Analytica*, "Southeast Asia: Bankruptcy Law," August 21, 2001). The low salaries of Indonesian judges is a problem, as is the extreme litigiousness of Filipino society, where business activity is constantly subject to nuisance and harassment costs. In mid-1997 a judge in a first-instance

court in Indonesia earned about US$380. By year's end this had shrunk to about US$160 (Backman 1999). Backman points out that enforcement of bankruptcy laws was the main problem in Indonesia, with the law invoked only four times in the cases of insolvent companies in the 10 years prior to 1994. In Thailand lengthy windup and liquidation procedures plus high court fees discouraged recourse to bankruptcy procedures. In Taiwan (China) the Bankruptcy Law and the Company Law are designed, interpreted, and enforced so as to protect owners from creditors and to avoid letting companies go into receivership. This is achieved by processes that delay the appointment of an external administrator and by giving the creditor no final say in the restructuring plan, by the reluctance of the oversight agencies to decide whether a company is salvageable, and by the ill-defined nature of the audit process (*Oxford Analytica*, "Taiwan: Restructuring Resistance," October 4, 2001).

14. Accounting firms must also be subjected to the discipline of strict rules and be held liable for connivance with corporate management and for gross oversight.
15. As of 2001, Singapore was second only to Japan in providing venture capital funding. The amount invested was US$379 million compared with US$634 million in Japan. The Singapore government's attempt to turn the island nation into a biotechnology hub has resulted in up to US$2 billion being provided to the government-backed Biomedical Sciences Group to invest in new start-ups and promising firms. This flood of money has also attracted other funds and drawn large pharmaceutical companies, such as Eli Lilly, Chiron, and Affymerix, to start research operations in Singapore (*Red Herring*, "Singapore Gambles Big with Biotech Payouts," September 15, 2001).
16. Such services could be liberalized multilaterally, of course, and Mattoo (2001) discusses the prospects for this.
17. There are limits to the efficacy of outsourcing manufacturing, however. Companies are finding out how to outsource advantageously, and are also discovering that sharing proprietary information with suppliers risks leaks to competitors.

CHAPTER 5

ICT: BEYOND THE HYPE

An influential body of opinion now maintains that the pace of development in the industrial and middle-income countries will be keyed to a range of general purpose technologies spawned by ICT. Although its contribution to growth in most industrializing economies has been limited to date, the untapped potential of ICT can scarcely be doubted. Countries that do not embrace ICT at many different levels risk jeopardizing export shares in current markets; entry into new export markets; flows of inward FDI; and gains from production networking, technology transfer, and knowledge sharing. ICT will also be responsible for the growth of myriad high value added services, and it has already begun to transform the organization of firms.

WHAT'S AT STAKE?

The reach of ICT extends well beyond the economic realm. The end of the 1990s saw the rudiments of e-governance materialize in those countries where Internet use was most widespread (see the chapters on trends in the United States in Kamarck and Nye 2002), and both telemedicine and distance learning crossed major thresholds. Observing these factors, many analysts are persuaded that ICT will be the 21st century equivalent of electricity and the automobile, slowly permeating virtually all aspects of life and raising living standards far into the future.

No doubt the U.S. experience in the second half of the 1990s has strongly colored both views on ICT and likely estimates of its role in the growth process. A slowing of the pace of growth in the United States relative to the second half of the 1990s could shake faith in the power of ICT to enhance productivity. Even so, the ICT revolution will spread, and countries that do not assimilate the new technologies will lag behind in critical respects and will not fully realize the gains from participating in the global economy.

The high expectations surrounding ICT derive mainly from the performance of the U.S. economy between 1995 and 2000 in three key areas: productivity growth, innovation, and improved business strategy. The U.S. experience can provide a lens for looking at East Asia. Thus in this chapter we first critically summarize the major findings of research on the United States, consider the relevance of these findings for East Asia, and offer a perspective on ICT penetration in the region. The second part of the chapter concentrates on how government regulation could lead to more rapid and efficient exploitation of ICT. The rest of the chapter is devoted to an analysis of the telecommunications sector, which paces the growth of ICT.

The "New Economy" in the United States

Between 1995 and 2000 the growth rate of American output per person was approximately 3.2 percent per year, well above the 1.9 percent per year that the American economy experienced between 1973 and 1990, and even higher than the 2.9 percent per year increase achieved during 1959–73 (Baily 2001). The difference between a 1.9 percent and 3.2 percent growth rate may seem small, until one appreciates that the former implies that output per person doubles in 37 years, while the latter implies a doubling of productivity in only 22 years. This fact alone calls for an assessment of the productivity acceleration and of whether it represents a phase shift from which to draw lessons that might apply to East Asia.

Determining the contribution of ICT to this growth performance is central to this debate (for an overview of this debate see Landefeld and Fraumeni 2001). Spending on ICT—including software, hardware, and communications equipment—undoubtedly rose considerably during the 1990s. During this decade firms in the United States increased their investment outlays by 19 percent a year in real terms, and by the end of the decade more than half of this investment was in

ICT. As a share of GDP, investment in ICT rose from 3 to 6 percent over the 1990s (Basu, Fernald, and Shapiro 2001). Other sources of demand were changing, too, however, clouding the picture. U.S. federal government spending fell during this period, a fall partially offset by increased state and local expenditures (Vatter and Walker 2001). Statistical tools have been used to disentangle these different effects, and we now turn to these findings.

Economists have employed growth accounting techniques to estimate the contribution to output growth of the greater use of the nation's productive inputs, such as capital, including ICT; labor; raw materials; and energy. Ideally these techniques enable us to see how much ICT has added to growth after taking into account the growth of the labor force, energy use, and other inputs into production. Initially these studies were conducted on data for the entire U.S. economy, and the principal findings are reported in table 5.1. In all but one study, the contribution to growth of computer hardware—one form of ICT—doubled after 1995. This is the first indication that the spread of ICT throughout the U.S. economy quickened the pace of American economic growth. It is perhaps not surprising that all economists agree with these findings. Analysis by Kiley (1999) suggests that computer hardware actually reduced growth every year (although at a slower rate after 1995), and Jorgenson and Stiroh (2000) found that investment in ICT has apparently not generated the spillover and networking effects that feed TFP. These disagreements reflect differences in the methods used to calculate actual inputs into

Table 5.1 Contribution of Computer Hardware to U.S. Output Growth, Selected Years

Study	Before 1995 (years covered)	Before 1995 (contribution, percentage points/year)	Since 1995 (years covered)	Since 1995 (contribution, percentage points/year)
Oliner and Sichel (2000)	1991–95	0.25	1996–99	0.63
			1996–98	0.59
Whelan (2000)	1990–95	0.33	1996–98	0.82
Jorgenson and Stiroh (2000)	1991–95	0.19	1996–99	0.49
Kiley (1999)	1974–84	−0.34	1985–98	−0.27

Sources: Authors.

production as well as techniques employed to adjust for inflation. The number of people currently employed, for example, is not necessarily a good proxy for the total amount of labor used in production in a given year, especially if the number of hours worked varies between years. Some variations in hours worked are recorded—and so can be taken in account—but no such records are kept for salaried workers. Making such adjustments is typically fraught with errors and controversy.

One objection to these economywide studies is that they do not allow for the differential effects of ICT in different sectors of the economy. For example, knowing whether ICT had a greater impact in manufacturing industries than in service activities, such as banking, is useful. An analysis of U.S. productivity growth indicates that ICT-related inputs were responsible for about two-fifths to one-half of the acceleration in productivity growth between 1995 and 2000 (table 5.2). This is likely to be an underestimate, because it neglects the 0.3 percentage point gain from capital deepening. The bulk of the

Table 5.2 Decomposition of Productivity Acceleration, United States, 1995–2000 Compared with 1973–95
(percent per year)

Category	Oliner and Sichel (2000)	Gordon (2002)	Jorgenson and Stiroh (2000)[a]	Baily (2001)
Labor productivity, nonfarm business	1.38	1.81	1.01	1.63
Cyclical effect	n.a.	0.40	n.a.	0.04
ICT capital	0.70	0.60	0.44	0.62
Other capital	–0.26	–0.23	0.09	–0.23
Measurement effects	n.a.	0.14	n.a.	n.a.
Labor quality	0.04	0.01	–0.23	0.00
Multifactor productivity	0.90	0.89	0.71	1.19
Computer sector multifactor productivity	0.31	0.30	0.31[b]	0.18
Other nonfarm business multifactor productivity	0.59	0.59	0.40	1.00

n.a. Not applicable.

Note: ICT = information and communication technologies.

a. Compares 1995–99 with 1973–95. Includes consumer durables and the farm sector.

b. ICT-related multifactor productivity.

Sources: Authors.

productivity growth stems from gains in the sectors producing industrial machinery (mainly computers) and electronic machinery (mainly semiconductors), but wholesaling and retailing also registered sharp gains. Other services and construction performed relatively poorly, and most of the "non-new" economy industries turned in an average performance, with that of the food sector being unusually bad (Nordhaus 2001).

Although Nordhaus's estimates of productivity increases are higher, his findings regarding the sources of productivity increases are not very different from those of Gordon (2002), who to date has estimated the smallest incremental returns from the spread of ICT. Gordon estimated that annual productivity growth in the United States from 1995 to 2000 was 2.86 percent, nearly double the 1.42 percent achieved from 1972 to 1995. Once a cyclical component of growth is removed (0.4 percent), however, the increase in trend growth is about 1.04 percent. After allowing for changes in measurement and labor quality, only 0.89 percent of the annual increase in the productivity growth rate needs explaining. Gordon ascribes this almost entirely to productivity growth in the durable manufacturing sector, with 0.30 percent contributed by technical change in computer hardware and 0.22 percent coming from technological acceleration in the rest of durable manufacturing. Only 0.07 percent can be traced to gains in productivity in the services sector, where much of the computer hardware is installed. However, when Basu, Fernald, and Shapiro (2001) corrected for cyclical savings using average weekly hours as a proxy for factor utilization and for adjustment costs, they arrived at an estimate for the contribution of technological gains to growth well above that implied by Gordon (2002) and close to that of Oliner and Sichel (2000). Basu, Fernald, and Shapiro found that for the private sector as a whole, the contribution of technology in the second half of the 1990s rose from 1.2 to 3.1 percent per year. More surprising, and contrary to some other findings, nonmanufacturing technological performance increased from 0.9 to 2.7 percent. Because this sector accounts for four-fifths of production, technology gains in the nonmanufacturing sector were responsible for 1.3 percentage points of the overall 2.9 percent advance in annual technology-related benefits for GDP growth.

Bear in mind that our understanding of sectoral productivity gains in the latter half of the 1990s is still evolving. Modification of the time series data in 2001 revised U.S. GDP growth in 2000 to 4.1 percent, down from the earlier estimate of 5 percent. Annual growth in labor productivity between 1996 and 2000 is now estimated to have averaged 2.5 percent and not 2.7 percent (A Miracle Revised 2001; United States 2001). Moreover, contrary to the opinion of Basu, Fernald, and Shapiro (2001), the majority opinion remains that productivity in the services sector still lags for three reasons.

First, the services sector accounted for the overwhelming part of the US$10 trillion plus U.S. economy in 2001, and the new investment in ICT was only a small share of the existing capital stock in the services sector.[1] (Recall that in the growth accounting framework, only increases in the stock of productive assets raise output. Investment adds to the stock of capital, and so affects growth through this channel.)

Second, some of the ICT investments may have only diverted demand from other services rather than generated new demand for services, thereby providing additional growth impetus. Projections indicate that by the end of 2002, business to consumer sales will reach US$39 billion, or about 2 percent of retail sales in the United States.[2] Some of those would probably have been made in the absence of ICT, and so the demand-stimulating effect of these technologies may have been quite modest to date.

A third reason ICT effects appear to be so small in the services sector is that growth accounting techniques do not include investments in difficult to measure intangible assets that complement the introduction of ICT. These intangible investments include outlays on training staff to use ICT and spending on organizational restructuring and the reorganization of decisionmaking power and incentives within the corporation. A recent analysis that incorporated these effects into U.S. aggregate data found that ICT had contributed much more growth than had been shown by other methods (Yang and Brynjolfsson 2000). The techniques used to take account of intangibles comprising knowledge, skills, and learning acquired by workers are very much in their infancy, but they suggest the need to factor in the indirect role of ICT (Blair and Wallman 2001).[3]

From these findings, arguing that ICT has transformed the U.S. economy in five years is difficult. Nevertheless, enough positive evidence exists (including continuing productivity growth during 2001, which buttresses the claim that the benefits of ICT are continuing to work their way through the system) to merit a closer examination of how ICT affects firms, adopting a bottom-up analysis in contrast to the top-down statistical analysis reviewed here. Such a bottom-up approach focuses attention on how ICT affects the way firms innovate and the rate of technical change, effects that are difficult to capture in the aggregate studies of economic growth discussed earlier.

Research results are now also available on how ICT is impinging on European economies and higher-income East Asian countries. These findings, summarized in table 5.3, suggest that the United States derived a significantly greater growth stimulus than European countries and Japan: 1.71 percent per year in 1995–2000 compared with 0.21 to 0.62 in Europe. However, countries with large and dynamic ICT

Table 5.3 Contribution of ICT Capital and TFP in ICT Production to Growth in GDP and Labor Productivity, Selected Countries and Years

Country	Years	Contribution of ICT capital to annual GDP growth (%)
Australia	1990–95	0.48 out of 3.4
Australia	1995–2000	0.68 out of 4.6
Canada	1990–95	0.30 out of 1.8
Canada	1995–2000	0.57 out of 4.2
Finland	1990–95	0.24 out of 0.7
Finland	1995–99	0.62 out of 5.6
France	1990–95	0.18 out of 1.0
France	1995–2000	0.35 out of 2.8
Germany	1990–95	0.30 out of 2.2
Germany	1995–2000	0.38 out of 2.1
Italy	1990–95	0.21 out of 1.4
Italy	1995–99	0.36 out of 1.9
Japan	1990–95	0.31 out of 1.3
Japan	1995–99	0.38 out of 1.1
United Kingdom	1990–95	0.27 out of 2.1
United Kingdom	1995–2000	0.48 out of 3.6
United States	1990–95	0.97 out of 2.6
United States	1995–2000	1.71 out of 4.4

Notes: ICT = information and communication technologies; TFP = total factor productivity; GDP = gross domestic product. All estimates refer to total economy GDP. All estimates on the contribution of ICT capital include software.

Source: van Ark (2002).

Table 5.4 Contributions of Computer Hardware to GDP Growth in the Republic of Korea and Singapore, Selected Years
(percent)

		Computer hardware's contribution	
Economy and years	GDP growth rate	GDP growth	Own growth rate
Korea 1980–95	7.9	2.54	39.1
Korea 1990–95	7.5	2.71	42.7
Singapore 1977–97	7.8	1.46	34.2

Note: GDP = gross domestic product.
Source: Pohjola (2000).

sectors, such as the Netherlands, Sweden, and the United Kingdom, have performed strongly, as have Korea and Singapore (table 5.4). In Japan, however, while a few leading companies with ICT-related products, such as Sony, Toshiba, NTT, Canon, DoCoMo, and Fujitsu, have continued to forge ahead, the effects of ICT on the economy as a whole were lower through the end of the 1990s.

The rest of East Asia also presents a mixed picture. Hong Kong (China), Korea, Singapore, and Taiwan (China) have large ICT subsectors and have rapidly embraced the use of ICT in governance and transportation, for example.[4] Internet connectivity is high and rising. As in the United States, the proportional contribution of computer hardware to growth is significant, but the full macroeconomic implications for TFP are still in the future. Most firms, even the largest, have yet to overcome the skill and organizational hurdles on the road to e-business. This finding was recently reaffirmed by a study (Dutta and Biren 2001) of the use of the Internet, which showed East Asian companies lagging in the use of ICT for marketing and customer relations (figure 5.1).

Impact of ICT on Business Strategy

How quickly ICT can be deployed and begin to raise productivity substantially will depend in part on how readily firms alter their organizations and strategies for innovation and customer service. They must, in essence, review their business models. Here the United States, with its ceaseless experimentation and prolific business schools, is very much the pacesetter. Accumulating evidence from corporations

Figure 5.1 Use of the Internet by *Fortune* Global 500 Companies

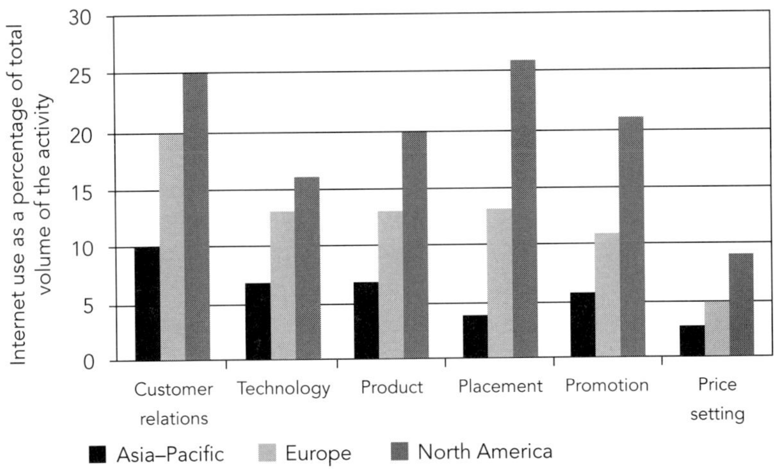

Source: Dutta and Biren (2001).

in the United States and elsewhere suggests that ICT will affect many dimensions of a firm's activities, making simple characterizations inappropriate at best and misleading at worse. A single business model of ICT adoption for followers to emulate is unlikely to emerge. They will therefore have to experiment and choose.

A readiness to be different characterizes most of the outstanding new captains of industry. Being different, however, does not represent a strength for the large East Asian conglomerates or for the smaller, family-owned firms. Rather, firms in the region excel at adroit imitation, producing at lower cost than rival producers, with at best some incremental innovation and, as in Japan, with close attention to operational effectiveness. As a result companies can lose sight of the longer-term need to regularly transform the nature of a company by being alert to a wide range of possibilities and selecting the most promising from among them. Oracle, for instance, has sought to define its choices by asking its major customers what they want and then attempting to respond in a comprehensive and innovative way, for instance, it has integrated business systems through the E-business Suite III, thereby providing its customers with comprehensive, Internet-based services.[5]

Among the reorganization strategies brought to the fore, the following seven are uppermost:

- Use the scale, scope, and advantages ICT offers to consolidate and enlarge market share.
- Join forces to create vertical or horizontal B2B exchanges tailored to the characteristics of the firm's products and to maintain competition at healthy levels.
- Focus on a niche, whether a final product or a component. This can be achieved by meeting specific client needs or by achieving control over a proprietary technology or process.[6]
- Build a brand image to differentiate the firm's products from those of its rivals. Few laptop owners ever see the Intel chips inside, but a carefully placed label on most laptops provides a permanent reminder of their presence.
- Tie in suppliers. Collaborating with suppliers and encouraging them to improve their components helps align their incentives with those of their customers. Toyota has done this to outstanding effect. Given the recent surge in outsourcing, collaboration reminds suppliers that forward-looking parts and components purchasers care more about technology and satisfying their customers than they do about price, although sustaining price competitiveness remains a crucial objective (Spear and Brown 1999).
- Seek to mass customize certain kinds of products or services using the Internet and flexible manufacturing systems to individualize products. Dell Computer provides an example. Made to order, mass market products that allow customers their choice from among a fixed range of options drastically reduce waste and inventory costs. According to one estimate, such a step would be worth US$80 billion per year to automobile producers alone (A Long March 2001).
- Add services. The idea here is to sell high-quality services along with a product, allowing the customer to differentiate the bundle of goods and services from that of rival suppliers.

ICT opens several doors to firms seeking to refine their organizations using these seven strategies. A company's primary goal, even for a fledgling dot-com, is to generate enough profits to grow. Such are the exigencies of financing and market competition that size is an advantage. In many industries this dynamic favors the rapid growth of the leading firms through mergers and consolidations. Just five or six years ago the United States had six online services. The number has now shrunk to one. The number of workstation producers has dropped from three dozen in the mid-1980s to a handful today, only four disk drive makers selling directly to producers of computers survive from the 75 that existed in the late 1980s, and most of the online booksellers that appeared in the mid-1990s are no longer in business. Although where services and technology are based on human inputs and intangibles, the significance of scale is by no means obvious (How Seagate 2002).

By reducing the costs of intercompany transactions, ICT encourages the use of external B2B exchanges in certain standardized products, resulting in greater specialization. Earlier fears of rampant outsourcing, commoditization of products, and cutthroat competition appear somewhat unfounded, however.[7] Current trends point to the emergence of B2B exchanges formed by large market incumbents that can generate sufficient volume. U.S. automobile manufacturers, for example, have come together to create Covisint, which manages automobile parts transactions with the major suppliers such as Delphi and Visteon (companies that were spun off as independent operations by the automobile makers themselves and retain close links with them), a marketplace worth US$250 billion (Lucking-Reilly and Spulber 2001). Aerospace companies, energy producers, grocery companies, and others have set up other exchanges. Some of what they trade are standardized items, the so-called indirect goods (for example, pencils or computers) used in many industries where suppliers are many and competition is fierce. However, 80 percent of the products traded in East Asia that feed the manufacturing sector are direct goods, generally customized for users to some degree. Online trading of these goods, using technology provided by Commerce One, Ariba, and i2, is likely to be of a different stripe. Because of the need for joint development of products; customization; and long-term, trust-based relationships, electronic transactions will most probably supplement more traditional forms of interaction (Dhawan and others 2000). The Web will facilitate supply chain management and reduce ordering, fulfillment, and payment costs, but it will not inevitably lead to generalized arm's-length transactions and intense competition between atomistic producers except in certain standardized commodities. We can thus envisage both a greater degree of integrated production structures as well as more cooperative interaction between buyers and suppliers using ICT to enhance efficiency and cut costs.

Large multinationals such as Ericsson, Cisco, and IBM contract out a sizable share of their hardware production to specialized suppliers while concentrating on upstream activities and services. This opens niches for specialized contract manufacturers of electronic equipment such as Flextronics and Solectron, which in turn buy up producers in East Asia and organize regional supply networks so as to encourage competition between suppliers to original equipment manufacturers.[8] Again, in theory, these developments can minimize governance and contracting costs, although it is too early to gauge the magnitude of gains likely to be realized, or even to assume that such forms of disintegrated subcontracting and reintegrating will persist. (For a novel analysis of the effects of globalization on vertical structure, see McLaren 2000.)

In the coming years the effects of ICT on production networking will be influenced by the phasing out of local content requirements. This in turn will also profoundly affect FDI, component manufacturing, and the geographic distribution of assembly operations, especially in the ASEAN countries.[9] In the Japanese automobile industry, for example, much scope exists for rationalizing assembly in fewer locations to take advantage of scale economies. In addition, component manufacturers, many of which are subsidiaries of Japanese firms and are increasingly independent of the automobile manufacturers, will be under pressure to restructure their operations.[10] The growing presence of American and European producers in the region could intensify competition and the search for locations offering the largest mix of advantages. Taken together, these forces have the capacity to transform business structures in East Asia. These changes will occur as firms continue to "slice up the value chain," often with the intention of moving labor-intensive production stages to labor-abundant locations that also offer low-cost transportation and communication infrastructures.

By facilitating the development of networks of firms, ICT supports alternative business models to the large industrial groupings that have dominated the Northeast Asian commercial landscape. In the aftermath of the 1997–98 crisis, the weaknesses of diversified, and often family-controlled, conglomerates—such as the *chaebol* and *keiretsu* arrangements—have become more evident, encouraging efforts at restructuring, disposing of peripheral activities, and reducing overcapacity (see Claessens and others 1999 for a discussion of the extent of family control over major businesses in many East Asian countries and how this may slow legal, regulatory, and corporate governance reform). The inefficiency and unwieldiness of state-owned enterprises, as in China, has been apparent for a couple of decades. In many industries the advantage appears to lie with specialized firms, big and small, that might be assemblers or suppliers of components or services. The typical focused Taiwanese firm seems better placed to reap the gains from ICT and new multiplant, flexible production technologies than does its larger, diversified Korean counterpart. The size of a Korean *chaebol* does, nonetheless, confer advantages mostly for the mature and slower-expanding company, enabling it to raise resources quickly to establish large-scale production facilities, conduct R&D, market on a global scale, and create an internationally recognized brand name (Claessens, Fan, and Lang 2002).

ICT offers firms the means to refine other business strategies by reducing the cost of collecting, analyzing, and communicating information. Although media reports on the new economy have tended to focus on falling communication costs, the ease with which they can collect and mine data is critically important to firms. Firms now have available to them the extremely detailed information on consumer tastes and spending patterns stored in relational databases and compiled, for example, through surveys and bar code readers in supermarkets and elsewhere. The computing power to analyze these vast datasets now exists, allowing firms who retain staff or consultants with the requisite analytical skills to increase sales, improve margins, and identify niches of consumers willing to pay more for specialized or better-quality products (How Data Mining 2001). In the past such niches may have gone undiscovered or the decisions to supply them would be made on hunches—the infamous business intuition.

One hurdle that is likely to remain for the smaller producer and the subcomponent manufacturer is developing a brand name and market reputation, a task likely to take on further significance as e-business becomes commonplace not only for manufacturers but also, and to a greater extent, for service providers (Shapiro and Varian 1999). The intensity and cost of marketing on the Internet is one indicator of how critical the brand name might become. Moreover, advertisers are discovering that as the tempo of Web advertising grows, so does the difficulty of attracting the attention of potential customers. This might call for much greater attention to targeting customers and to using word of mouth before undertaking expensive saturation advertising.[11]

ICT will also expand the scope for mass customization of production. Most manufacturing is not conducted on a built to order basis. Instead firms must estimate future consumer demand and tailor current production schedules accordingly. When firms misjudge, demand shortages emerge, leading to consumer dissatisfaction or the buildup of inventories of unsold goods. Neither situation is good for the firm's long-term viability. Thus firms have every incentive to better match production output to demand. Clearly this incentive predates the introduction of ICT, and indeed, automobile companies have long operated using buffer stocks of vehicles to cope with an unplanned expansion of demand. Internet technologies, however, add a new dimension to mass customization. Purchasers can now place orders for products that better meet their needs and consult with suppliers about potential modifications and varieties. Perhaps the best known example of this is the purchase of personal computers over the Internet from companies such as Dell Computers and Gateway. These companies pre-assemble modules that, when tailored to a customer's given specifications, can be quickly assembled into a final product. In this way the number of parts can be reduced, and yet economies of scale in the pre-assembly of modules can be retained (A Long March 2001).

By expanding the ways in which services can be delivered, ICT has the potential to transform certain services sectors. In the past, for example, many customers had to travel to a bank or similar office to receive financial services. Through ICT they now pay bills and perform other banking transactions online. These technologies have helped banks economize on the number of branches, reducing fixed costs and staffing levels. These financial services developments represent only the tip of the iceberg of potential future innovations in service delivery. The entire communications industry—from telephone companies through moviemakers—sees these new information technologies as a way to sell a wider variety of services directly to customers' homes. Amazon.com, Ebay, and Priceline.com are already expanding aggressively in East Asian markets (Spending Spree 2002). Furthermore, firms and state bodies are experimenting with telemedicine and tele-education. The former offers an alternative to face-to-face consultations between doctors and patients and between doctors themselves, and recent trials in Hong Kong (China) suggest that this approach could be widely applied, especially for the routine care of aged or relatively immobile patients.

That new services often follow in the wake of ICT diffusion speaks to the importance of co-invention. Indeed, some observers have argued that these second-round service innovations make possible the realization of the full benefits of the primary invention: the Internet (Bresnahan 2001). Such observers would argue as well, however, that many factors determine the pace of co-invention (including some of those discussed in chapter 3), not least the magnitude of any switching costs; the ease with which advances can be shared among users; and the network effects, through which the value of a service to any one purchaser depends on the number of other purchasers already using that service.

The greater emphasis on innovation forces companies to pay much more heed to new possibilities arising within their own organizations, to technology available on the market for purchase or licensing, and to technology nurtured by start-ups that could be acquired.[12] One of the more remarkable recent developments, one that the nimbler companies are scrambling to use, is Web-based technology markets. A technology exchange called yet2.com has allowed companies to shop for innovation for a modest membership fee and a 10 percent share of any completed transactions to a maximum of US$50,000. This exchange, and others like it, create more efficient markets for technology and help to monetize intellectual property. With bright new ideas and technologies being invented the world over, yet2.com reinforces the factors discussed in chapter 3 that unify the global market for ideas. Beyond that, Web-based knowledge and markets enable large, highly diversified companies such as General Electric and Procter & Gamble to identify and exploit the technologies already at hand within their own organizations that can be commercialized or licensed (New Rules 2001).

As the potential and current limitations of the Internet become better perceived, companies are beginning to see advantages in marrying the new approaches with the old in many different ways. For East Asian companies with a competitive edge mainly in the old-style industries, the road to success may lie in using ICT to leverage existing strengths deriving from, for example, proprietary content, physical location, product characteristics, and the use of catalogs (see Porter [2001], who endorses the exploiting of complementarities between Internet use and more traditional corporate strategies). Similarly, combining "bricks with some clicks," that is, effectively harnessing the Internet to enhance traditional marketing practices (see Willcocks and Plant 2001), might be the best way for most producers to enter the domain of electronic marketing. The pace can then pick up. Even so, for most firms self-reinvention as Internet-based entities may not be desirable, even if it were feasible.

Gateway offers an example of a new-style computer supplier that found it profitable to use a combination of the telephone, physical stores, and the Internet to reach customers. It speaks to the enduring value created by physical stores that 25 percent of Gateway's sales are through its stores. Moreover, the stores are effective in building the brand, receiving feedback, and satisfying the large group of customers who wish to see a product before buying it (Bricks and Clicks 2000; How PC Makers 2000). ICT's deep penetration into old-line industries can be seen in the oil drilling industry's reliance on computerized seismic modeling, which has radically transformed drilling techniques and the productivity of oil extraction (Rauch 2001).

Companies that take the steps outlined earlier to differentiate themselves from their rivals reduce, but rarely eliminate, competitive pressures. For this reason the rapid shrinkage in the number of firms in some industries need not be a sign of diminishing contestability. On the contrary, even established firms, such as CISCO, EMC, and Intel, must continuously be on their guard against competitors with better products or superior ways of meeting customers' wants, apparent or latent. In the space of two years, for example, Juniper was able to eat into CISCO's apparently impregnable hold on the market for "core" routers. It reduced CISCO's market share by 11 percentage points in 2000 alone. Since then other challengers have emerged, such as Caspian Networks and Hyperchip, and CISCO has fought back with its own "super routers" (A Central Theme 2002). Similarly, Hitachi Data Systems is nibbling into EMC's share of the market for storage devices. All the big storage system producers are being challenged by start-ups offering huge 230-tetrabyte devices with greater capability, and new technological possibilities will continue to spawn others (Hitachi Is Now 2001; Storage Titans 2001).

Examples of ICT penetration into a wide range of activities and its implications for business abound. From an East Asian perspective, two points are noteworthy. First, Internet access is rising throughout the East Asian region, most rapidly in the northeast. ICT-based products constitute a large proportion of total manufacturing output, especially in the Southeast Asian countries. So far the effects of e-business and e-commerce on productivity appear to be minimal, although online transactions in Southeast Asia alone ranged between US$20 billion and US$25 billion in 2000. Research in this area is still sparse, but casual empiricism suggests that e-business and e-commerce are still in the early stages.

Second, and more important, the Western experience to date shows that even though the Web can greatly facilitate market networking, sales, and eventually business efficiency, retailing is still tied to the quality of logistics,[13] and manufacturing is tied to the cost and quality of the product. The power of the Internet is likely to grow, and its full potential gradually realized as many other complementary physical facilities, skills, and organizational capabilities fall into place. Companies and markets will need to be restructured, new business models assimilated, and the advantages of extraordinary amounts of information and computing power used to generate useful services. The next-generation Internet now taking shape under the initiative, once again, of the scientific community will create a global computer grid akin to the electrical grid and will provide instant access to a huge amount of computing power (IBM Joins Push 2001).

Looking ahead—and probably well beyond this decade—the full impact of ICT on productivity and growth will be felt through a number of services that together will account for the lion's share of national output (box 5.1). These include finance, entertainment, health care, education, and government. In finance and entertainment the potential is already apparent, although a long way from being realized. In the other three areas, a few countries have made a start, including countries in East Asia, but technology, standards, regulation, and content will take time to come together. In each case start-up costs will be heavy, and receptivity to electronic delivery of

Box 5.1 Impacts of the Internet

WHERE THE INTERNET MAY BE REVOLUTIONARY

These information-intensive industries are good candidates for transformation by the Web:

- *Financial services.* Most financial services can potentially be handled electronically. Banks are struggling to find convenient ways to let people pay bills online with some success, although initial efforts, such as e-citi by Citicorp, have had to be scaled back.
- *Entertainment.* Much entertainment can easily be digitized, but little of what is available is profitable, and the technological options are still evolving, as are business models that might sustain successful ventures.
- *Health care.* The benefits of shifting health care transactions to the Web could be enormous, but so are the institutional barriers relating to, for instance, certification, standards, privacy, and so on.
- *Education.* E-learning could cut the costs of education, but only at the price of making education more impersonal, and with little guarantee that the end results would improve on traditional approaches.
- *Government.* Delivering information to citizens electronically and processing transactions, for example, tax applications, has enormous appeal, but requires massive investments.

WHERE THE IMPACT MAY BE INCREMENTAL

For these industries, information plays a relatively small role:

- *Retailing.* Although Web sites and advertising have absorbed a lot of funding and attention, dot-com success turned more on the efficiency of logistics and warehousing and on pricing and marketing.
- *Manufacturing.* Web-enabled supply chains and intranets are important, but ultimately a manufacturer's competitiveness depends on the uniqueness, pricing, and quality of its goods, as well as on associated services.
- *Travel.* Online travel sites are popular, but the real constraints on travel are the physical capacity of the air and road systems and the crowding of resort areas.
- *Power.* Online energy exchanges attract publicity, but power generation and transmission capabilities will have the bigger economic impact.

Source: Adapted from *Business Week*, "Rethinking the Internet," March 26, 2001; see also *Business Week*, "How E-Biz Rose, Fell, and Will Rise Anew," May 13, 2002.

content, interaction, or transactions may be slow to materialize. Much will depend on how quickly businesses and other users assimilate Internet-based technology. Much also rests on how regulatory policies shape the growth of the Internet and of the supporting telecommunications infrastructure.

MAKING THE MOST OF THE INTERNET: THE STATE'S ROLE

The growth of the Internet and the extent of its penetration into the business and household sectors in little more than a decade indicates how an environment with few entry barriers and regulatory impediments can lead to rapid change. The attractions of e-mail, the development of browsers, the free sharing of software, and the readiness of private companies to capitalize on opportunities created by prior government-sponsored research and investment have brought into existence not just a new mode of communication, but what is almost a new lifestyle in middle- and higher-income countries. And this is only the beginning, because as the digital divide is closed, the Internet will multiply the sinews of globalization and come to embrace a majority of the world's population.

As the scale, diversity, and value of Internet-based activities climbs, however, laissez-faire development is no longer either feasible or desirable. A framework of rules to regulate aspects of the Internet will be needed so that online transactions become as secure, orderly, and rule-bound as transactions made through other channels. Only through accepted rules can the opportunities that brought the Internet to its current level be preserved and its coexistence with different interpretations of state discretion and prerogatives be assured, but because the Internet is a new, rapidly evolving, and technologically protean phenomenon, much debate has arisen about what rules are desirable and how they can be harmonized among countries. Table 5.5, for example, indicates the level of disagreement within the U.S. population over the merits of state regulation of the Internet. Cross-country differences regarding the appropriate regulation of the Internet are likely to be even sharper. Uncertainty also prevails on how rules would be enforced and on whether the legal systems in place would be equal to the task, especially in the middle- and low-income

Table 5.5 U.S. Public Attitudes toward Government Regulation of the Internet

	Percentage who think this issue is a problem and the			
Issue	**Government should do something**	**Government should not be involved**	**Percentage who think this issue is not a problem**	**Percentage who don't know**
Dangerous strangers making contact with children	79	15	3	1
Availability of pornography to children	75	20	4	1
Availability of information about how to build bombs and other weapons	75	15	8	1
False advertising	62	20	12	4
Pornography and adult entertainment	61	26	10	3
Ability to purchase guns	61	14	18	3
Loss of privacy	54	29	14	2
Hate speech, information that attacks people based on their race, religion, or ethnicity	53	27	15	5
Violent games	51	31	15	3

Source: Blendon and others (2001).

countries. As indicated earlier, regulators and users share a desire to preserve many of the freedoms that have permitted and financed the extraordinary upsurge in innovation. On balance, the Internet's redefinition of business activities and the social environment are viewed in a positive light, but in a number of areas consensus is emerging that a combination of public and private regulation would ensure better outcomes for the Internet's users.

Any views regarding regulation of the Internet must remain highly tentative, not least because the scope of regulation and its feasibility are being constantly modified by technological advances occurring on a regular basis. Judging from the past decade's experience and from current concerns, six broad areas are likely to require some degree of regulation or legal rules. The need for such measures is likely to be universal, and it will become increasingly urgent in East Asia as countries increase their Internet use. These broad areas are the following:

- *Rules governing the development of an ICT infrastructure that would support rapid growth through multiple channels.* These encompass ownership of physical telecommunications infrastructures, which in many countries are still in the public sector. Where they have been privatized, this has most often been done piecemeal, leaving those systems too in need of reorganization. The needed rules would also cover the assignment of bandwidth to providers, the licensing of providers, and the setting of standards permitting broad interoperability conducive to future advances. Finally, these rules would regulate the access to telecommunications services, the cost of placing calls, and the fees levied by Internet service providers (ISPs). This last is likely to be a function of an augmented competition policy that takes into account the special characteristics of the ICT industry, including the contestability of its various segments, based on start-up costs and the significance of scope and network economies.
- *Range and volume of information.* The Internet is remarkable for the range of information available through Web sites and for the volume of communications now conducted there. Inevitably a proportion of this traffic is repugnant to many, and some is considered deeply reprehensible by individual states (Hachigan 2001).[14] Thus

the regulation of access to certain information or messages communicated via the Internet is a matter of concern to policymakers anxious to control the purveyance of pornographic material, for example. To forestall more intrusive state intervention, some firms respond to these concerns with self-policing mechanisms and technology that permits content screening. Responsibility sharing remains fluid, however, with some states adopting a much stronger stance on content and the aggressive use of monitoring, filtering, and firewall and geolocation techniques. For instance, the Singapore government has an expansive set of regulations in place to manage the Internet and to screen content (Singapore: Internet Control 2001). Beyond a point, such control can inhibit Internet use, and the authorities in some countries walk a fine line in both promoting and inhibiting Web-based activity.[15]

- *Upsurge of fraud, cybercrime, and hacking.*[16] This problem underlies the urgency felt about monitoring Internet traffic and Internet use. The terrorist attacks on the United States on September 11, 2001, sharpened concerns that the Web was becoming a tool used by terrorists to coordinate their activities and launder funds. If left unchecked, regulators fear, such clandestine use would inhibit Internet use for legitimate economic purposes; it could also substantially increase transaction costs. Major credit card companies in the United States already admit to worries about fraud. Hackers who invaded computer networks in Southeast Asia and spread computer viruses such as the infamous Love Bug were responsible for losses equal to more than US$500 million in lost production and theft during 2000, an amount that does not even include the announcement effects on current or prospective users of Web-based services.[17] According to some estimates, unauthorized entry into computer systems doubles every 12 to 18 months (Southeast Asia: Cyber Threats 2001). Numerous technological fixes are being developed, such as better encryption techniques and special servers that sit beside routers and keep watch for traffic surges (One to Watch 2001), but regulators are also seeking to win agreement on rules that would require each computer to have a traceable identification, diminishing the degree of anonymity available to Internet users. Countries such as Malaysia and the Philippines are introducing laws making hacking a punishable crime, but the real test will lie in the enforcement of laws and the kinds of punishment meted out to offenders. A survey conducted in the United States indicated that online credit card fraud was equal to 1.13 percent of transactions, 18 times the level on all other credit card transactions. This may be an underestimate, because credit card companies do not want to scare off customers (The Truth 2001). A survey by the Confederation of British Industry revealed that two-thirds of respondents had experienced a serious hacking, virus attack, or fraud, with only one-third of the companies surveyed believing that business to consumer transactions are safe (Cybercrime Threat 2001). Regulators confront a dilemma, namely, too much privacy, and the sanctioning of rules and of associated technologies would open the door to more cybercrime, which the authorities would be powerless to tackle; too little privacy, and some of the users now contributing to the economic gains associated with the Internet will be driven away.

- *Privacy.* The previous point leads to the issue of privacy, arguably the single biggest worry of Internet users (Litan 2001). Continued rapid growth in Internet financial transactions and exchanges of sensitive information will depend on the assurance of privacy. Individuals and companies must feel that information transmitted over the Internet is secure and only accessible to the parties for whom it is intended. If technology and government regulations permit eavesdropping, the Internet is less likely to thrive as a cyber marketplace. In other words, if divulging information over the Internet increases the chances of fraud, theft, susceptibility to industrial espionage, or unwelcome attention from the authorities, fewer transactors will be attracted to the Web, and its utility as a fount for new business ideas will diminish. The U.S. Federal Bureau of Investigation already uses the Internet surveillance DCS 1000 system Carnivore, and the U.S. National Security Agency deploys Echelon to monitor e-mail traffic. Since the September 11, 2001, terrorist attacks, such surveillance is likely to have risen.
- *Intellectual property and copyrights.* Another privacy issue of concern to businesses is the protection of intellectual property and copyright (Litan 2001). The entertainment and software industries are most immediately affected by piracy, copying, and compression programs that make the sharing of music and videos possible. The eventual degree of regulatory oversight will depend on a combination of factors.

First, technological development will to some extent reduce the ease of copying or transmission or facilitate claims from producers for patent fees and copyright dues. Second, evidence is accumulating on the effects on sales of music and video copying. If, on balance, the effect is positive, the case for regulation or encryption would carry little force. Third, developments in software might shift the main flow of earnings to customization and add-on services, which again would minimize the losses from piracy of packaged software. Fourth, legal action taken against Napster in the United States,[18] and international disputes being initiated under the Trade-Related Agreement on Intellectual Property Rights in countries where piracy of software, music, and video is pervasive, demonstrates the relative power of legal remedies. In the process it is helping to map out the regulatory domain, given the capacities of courts and enforcement agencies and the scope for international coordination of efforts to define and protect intellectual property rights.

- *Taxation of services.* The taxation of services traded by way of the Internet presents yet another reason for regulating Internet traffic. With services growing in volume, and with the possibility that using the Internet to transact services will become even easier, governments are beginning to worry about the loss of tax revenue. According to Tanzi (2001), in the United States, states stand to lose 4 percent of their sales tax revenues by 2004. The government's willingness to take unilateral action has been inhibited by the fear that attempts to monitor and tax business transactions would result in a flight of human and physical capital to other countries. Loss of revenue is a mounting concern, however, and some form of concerted action is in the cards over the medium run, especially with the increasing availability of technologies that can identify the city from which a user is accessing the Internet.

In sum, the phenomenal growth of the Internet since 1995 argues against heavy-handed regulation. Moreover, the experience of other networked industries in industrial and middle-income countries underscores the limits of regulation. In the United States, the advantages from increased entry following the deregulation of telecommunications and transport sectors altered choices for producers and strengthened incentives to innovate (Meyer and Menzies 2000).

While markets often do need guidance, regulation is never a panacea. The dangers of corruption and stifled development are ever present, as is regulatory capture by the industry, which can lead to forbearance when trouble starts. As with the financial services industry, a judicious mix of market-based oversight and government regulation would seem desirable for the ICT sector, especially given the centrality of innovation and the uncertainty regarding its future evolution.

Some of the technological advances aimed at enhancing Internet access will likely also address these concerns adequately.[19] Developing the software standards and equipment needed to provide transaction security and safety against hackers is in the industry's interests, but it is also becoming apparent that self-regulation and technology alone cannot allay the mix of concerns evinced by governments, producers, and users—again, concerns exacerbated by the September 11, 2001, terrorist attacks on the United States. In addition, the international harmonization of policies and standards will require sustained intergovernmental negotiation.

The provisional and tentative lessons after just a decade of experience are that governments should articulate a clear agenda of policy objectives. Rather than rushing in with poorly conceived, difficult to implement regulations, they must work with industry and users to find solutions that require the minimum of regulatory oversight and intervention. The situation is so fluid, the useful theory and empirical evidence so sparse, and the cost of undermining ICT development so substantial that countries will need to proceed cautiously. The ship of Internet regulation will have to be constructed on the high seas one plank at a time, with need and utility carefully weighed against the risk of a redundant superstructure that only adds to transaction costs. The least desirable approach for the East Asian countries—or, for that matter, for the industrial countries—to take would be to introduce broad and sweeping rules on the basis of limited information. These could become the source of numerous roadblocks in the future. Equally disadvantageous would be rules introduced under pressure from powerful, new, ICT-based industries looking to minimize competitive pressures.

FROM FIXED-LINE TO WIRELESS INTERNET ACCESS

The last section discussed many of the policy questions that arise when individuals and firms access the Internet. Other areas of concern exist, however, of which the most central include the following:

- The demand for Internet-based services, which in turn will determine the scale and structure of a sustainable telecommunications infrastructure
- The cost of Internet access, including not only the fees ISPs charge, but also local telephone rates
- The financing and operation of the so-called Internet backbone, which connects networks of ISPs to one another
- The financing and development of the last mile of distribution of high-speed, broadband services to households
- The widespread use of different wireless technologies, the so-called second- and third-generation technologies (2G, 2.5G, and 3G), and within the decade, 4G.[20]

Before turning to each of these five issues in turn, recall that both private and state-owned firms have participated in running the Internet since it was commercialized in 1995, and that Internet use and access vary considerably across nations. By the end of 2001 the Internet had 500 million users (How E-Biz Rose 2002), with nearly 34 million in China alone, a 50 percent increase over the end of 2000 (Chronicle and Documentation 2002, p. 124). In East Asia, Korea and Singapore had Internet penetration rates exceeding 30 percent in January 2001, placing them 6th and 10th, respectively, in terms of national Internet connectivity (Iceland tops the list with a 60 percent penetration rate, followed by Norway and Sweden). In addition, active use of the Internet by East Asian individuals and firms ensured that 4 of the top 10 ISPs in 2000 were located in the region (Nifty in Japan and Chollian, Hitel, and Unitel in Korea). Worldwide, international Internet capacity exceeded international telephone capacity for the first time in 2000. The former now stands at close to 300 gigabits per second, a fivefold increase over 1999, and yet another testament to the extensive investments in capacity that have occurred in recent years (ITU 2001b).

Demand for Telecommunications Services

The Internet was initially seen as a means of sustaining communications in the event of a nuclear attack, and later as a channel for communication among members of the scientific community (Naughton 2000). Its widespread appeal and use springs from the attractions and convenience of e-mail. This "killer app" produced a surge in demand for connectivity and for the associated telecommunications facilities. This prompted huge investments by telecommunications operators in fiber-optic transmission lines, wireless and satellite technology, and purchase of the spectrum, all in anticipation of increasing demand for Internet access and for use of content. In the United States alone, 39 million miles of fiber-optic strand had been laid by 2001. However, demand, while rising, is not rising fast enough to absorb these investments, and only 3 percent of the fiber was lit by 2001. Moreover, while digital subscriber line (DSL) and 2.5G wireless use is on the rise, barring the appearance of another killer app, the demand for broadband access and the utilization of capacity, both in the telecommunications sector and in the telecommunications manufacturing industry, will continue to lag behind what now appear to have been greatly inflated market expectations. All this has had dire consequences for the profitability of surviving telecommunications and equipment suppliers. This is worrisome on four counts.

First, to provide either broadband wireless or fixed-line service, a great deal of additional investment will be required above and beyond the hundreds of billions of dollars already poured into the telecommunications business. Broadband wireless transmission and handsets and last-mile connections to the fiber-optic backbone will entail much additional spending. Whether these resources will be raised is unclear given the recent history of stock market losses of companies such as Qwest and Vodaphone and the collapse of WorldCom.

Second, the likely contribution of broadband access to GDP growth or to productivity has yet to be discerned, let alone demonstrated, and until this is done convincing markets to provide additional billions in cheap capital will be difficult.

Third, user surveys do not indicate that consumers have as yet revealed an inclination to surf the Internet using mobile phones. Moreover, a survey of 2,400 users showed that only 4 percent thought that they would ever use phones to spend money online, and only 2 percent had attempted to do so with their 2.5G phones (The Telecos Work 2001).

Fourth, although NTT DoCoMo i-mode suggests that a demand exists for short messaging and the exchange of cartoons, news clips, and financial information, such traffic is scarcely the kind of killer app that will generate large profits. The current hope (and this changes on a monthly basis) is that voice-over DSL will give the telecommunications companies the demand they want, because most of their business is from voice services. Data, particularly financial data, provide the bulk of traffic, but voice services are where the money is. Voice-over DSL would give small businesses multiple voice channels and Internet access all on a single line (FT Telecoms 2001). If telecommunications companies could combine a variety of attractive voice and data services with sophisticated billing technology that permits providers to charge optimally for type of service and customer, then, observers argue, the current squeeze on earnings would give way to an era of sustained growth (FT Telecoms' Billing Systems 2001).

Costs of Internet Access

The costs to consumers, firms, and governments of using the Internet to send and receive data messages—whether text, diagrams, or moving graphics—will be an important determinant of the competitiveness of clusters and the efficiency of logistics. The success of Singapore as a transport hub and core of the fastest growing cluster in Southeast Asia, for example, has much to do with the creation of a state-of-the-art telecommunications infrastructure (Arun and Yap 2000).[21] Internet access costs, including both the price of access and the costs of forgone time when downloading information, are themselves in part determined by the quality and extent of a nation's communications infrastructure.

Initially, fixed-line telephony was the principal infrastructure for accessing the Internet. Consequently, those East Asian nations with either little such infrastructure or highly regulated and inefficient telecommunications service providers saw slower diffusion of ICT. In addition, the emergence of the Internet has strengthened the case for moving away from state-owned telecommunications providers that face no competition, especially in the provision of local telephone services. The worldwide trend toward deregulation and privatization in telecommunications began in the 1980s and accelerated in the 1990s; however, East Asia still has much catching up to do.[22] In 2000 only half of the telecommunications operators in the Asia-Pacific region were privately owned, compared with 63 percent in Europe and 74 percent in the Americas (ITU 2000). Furthermore, just under 40 percent of local telephone service providers in the region experience competition. Finally, of the 96 new independent regulators created throughout the world in the 1990s, only 13 percent were in the Asia-Pacific region (for recent analyses of the Chinese and Korean telecommunications markets, see Lu 2000 and Jung 2000, respectively). This record is disappointing in light of cross-country empirical research suggesting that, even though the region could significantly increase telecommunications and Internet use by introducing competition, privatization, or independent regulators, the biggest improvements occur after all three reforms are in place (Fink, Mattoo, and Rathindran 2001).[23]

Lowering the price of local telephone calls is perhaps the most important step to reducing the cost of Internet access. Typically this requires allowing competition for local telephone services, with more than one firm using the telecommunications infrastructure to meet customers' needs. Setting the correct prices for access to this infrastructure is critical, as it also determines the funds available for further investments in infrastructure. Furthermore, without constraints on the pricing of access, a firm that both owns the telecommunications infrastructure and offers local telephone service has a strong incentive to charge high interconnection fees, thereby raising its rivals' costs. These rival firms will be further disadvantaged in the marketplace if they pass their higher costs on to their customers. Not surprisingly then, pricing access to telecommunications infrastructure has tended to be placed in the hands of independent regulators.

The specifics of pricing access—or of "interconnection" as the literature refers to it—are extremely technical and involve several thorny issues. Only a sample of the tradeoffs involved can be conveyed here. Like most economic assets, access to telecommunications infrastructure ought to be priced at the cost to society of the resources used at the margin. What constitutes this marginal societal cost is the source of some debate. Should it be based primarily on the nature of the infrastructure technology being employed, which is relatively easy to calculate, or should it also take into account the cost of the marginal increase in congestion created by the call? Policymakers appear to favor pricing access based on congestion (OECD 1999). One advantage of doing so is that the infrastructure operator recoups some, maybe all, of its investment outlays. An alternative might be to adopt the former noncongestion-based calculation for pricing access and to charge consumers a lump sum fee. Unfortunately, empirical evidence suggests that lump sum fees discourage telephone use among the poorest, and for the better-off, reduces demand for multiple household lines. However, pricing above technologically determined marginal costs, as in the congestion-based schemes, is likely to become less feasible over time (for an accessible account of pricing issues, see Wiseman 2000).

The Internet Backbone

As we noted earlier, global capacity to transmit information over the Internet has expanded rapidly. By and large, this investment has been conducted by profit-driven firms rather than state-owned corporations. In addition to establishing ISPs, many firms have invested in the Internet backbone that connects networks of ISPs and enables the seamless transmission of data around the globe.

To recover their investment outlays, backbone providers have moved away from so-called peering arrangements, in which the entity sending messages across the backbone kept any revenues (such as monthly access fees to ISPs) derived from individuals or firms for transmission of their messages (for an account of the decisions of U.S. backbone providers in this regard, see Jew, Nicholls, and Floro 2000). This "sender keeps all" arrangement provided no compensation to those providing the backbone infrastructure over which the messages were sent, and explains why access to the Internet backbone was said to be free.[24] In the absence of any direct payments for access to the backbone, firms have little incentive to upgrade its quality. This has not yet become a critical issue; however, because recent investment created a huge amount of unlit fiber-optic capacity, complete with optical circuits that, with suitable incremental investment in wavelength division multiplexing, could easily meet demand over the foreseeable future.

The difficulty arises in deciding what alternative to the "sender keeps all" model should be adopted. A natural alternative would be for backbone providers to charge ISPs based on their use of a segment of the backbone, with some adjustment for the quality of the backbone service. Thus, in principle, payment for backbone services could remain a matter for contracting between private firms. Furthermore, competition among backbone providers might create the impetus for upgrading the backbone and keeping access charges low.

Unfortunately, private sector contracts alone may not lead to optimal outcomes. By moving away from sender keeps all toward charging for backbone access, the cost of Internet access to individuals and firms will inevitably rise. Whether the charges are lump sum or per unit, Internet use will be affected.[25] Essentially, however, this is the price to be paid for maintaining and upgrading the backbone. The central public policy question to be answered is what factors will determine access price. First, without intense competition between backbone providers—and recent consolidations among U.S. and European firms indicate that the market will be less than perfectly competitive—prices are likely to rise above socially optimal levels (however, see Kende 2000, who argues that anticompetitive behavior is unlikely to emerge).

Second, backbone providers that also operate ISPs may offer lower access charges to their own ISPs, perhaps enabling the latter to charge their subscribers lower prices than their competitors. Alternatively, backbone providers may charge much higher access prices to rival ISPs, again effectively undermining the rival's competitiveness. Given subscribers' sensitivity to ISP charges, these backbone providers can effectively tilt the playing field toward their own ISPs.

Third, backbone providers may refuse access (or interconnection) to other backbone providers, hoping that subscribers will flock to their related ISPs (see Kende 2000 for a detailed discussion of these issues). (This actually happened in 1997 and 1998, when an Australian incumbent backbone provider refused to provide interconnection to a new entrant.) The effect could be particularly powerful if—as is often claimed—the demand for an ISP's services is a function of the existing subscriber base. Such network economies provide a strong incentive for incumbents to resist new entrants, whose attempts to lure away subscribers might quickly spiral into a substantial collapse in demand for the incumbent's services.

Each of these three potential problems can be treated under standard competition and regulatory policies. Oversight of mergers and acquisitions can tackle the first problem. Pricing access and refusals to deal are standard fare for regulators in network industries. In a sense, the provision of the Internet backbone raises new issues for policymakers, but solutions lie in the well-established policies and best practices that have evolved since deregulation began in the late 1970s.

The Last Mile

The last-mile challenge is to bring the full potential of broadband Internet access to every home user. To clarify what this means, we should start with what might be referred to as the first generation of Internet access: the telephone. The original means of Internet access for residential customers was to dial up an ISP over the telephone. However, the speed of such data transmission was extremely slow, around 9.6 kilobits per second, and as individuals sought to send ever more text, images, videos, and voice messages over the Internet, demand for faster connections grew. Initially integrated services digital network lines were introduced to meet this demand. This technology worked over conventional telephone lines and improved dial-up speeds to a maximum of 64 kilobits per second. Subsequently, asynchronous DSL and cable modems were introduced toward the end of 1999 in the United States, but take-up has been limited to 12 percent of ISP subscribers, a total of 8.1 million in 2001 (Broadband Internet Access 2001; ITU 2001a), rising to 10 million by early 2002.

The last-mile challenge to bring the full potential of broadband to the home has a number of solutions, primarily wireless, cable, or fiber-optic lines. These technologies must be brought further into neighborhoods and combined with content-reducing or content-compressing technologies, especially for wireless devices (Chasing the Bottleneck 2001). The closer the fiber nodes are to the home, the easier it will be to provide service of 2 to 3 megabits per second, well above the 600 kilobits per second speed of current broadband modems.

The U.S. experience with last-mile delivery of broadband service highlights the nature of the problems facing providers: the strength of demand and of business models, not of technology. In 1996 the United States created a class of competitive local exchange carriers to provide DSL service using the local networks of the Bell telephone companies. Because of low consumer uptake, poor business models, and resistance from the Bells, most of the competitive local exchange carriers have either been taken over or have gone bankrupt. The survivors and the Bells have been left to struggle with the deployment of a mix of services at prices that will yield decent earnings. A good deal of market consolidation appears to be inevitable, with a small number of companies providing a mix of twisted copper wire, fiber-optics, cable, and satellite-based services over the last mile. Currently, the cable companies have the largest number of broadband subscribers and are best placed to offer concurrent video, voice, and data services (The Cable Guys 2001). Even though the number of subscribers is rising, the level of use and current basic rates do not generate sufficient earnings. For that to happen, people must be induced to substantially expand usage: companies must provide content and services of a different order. In addition, pricing techniques and billing technology have to evolve to generate incentives and to permit full exploitation of the capacity to target content closely and to discriminate pricing (as achieved by NTT DoCoMo in Japan).

The physical aspects of the last-mile problem can be solved if the capital is forthcoming, whether by digging up streets or through wireless means. The spread of broadband use, however, will depend on its perceived utility and on access pricing. For many East Asian countries, wireless technology might offer the easier mode of advance.

Wireless Access

Means of voice communication and the basic method of Internet access both changed substantially during the 1990s. Technological advances throughout the 1990s expanded the use of cellular phones and allowed the use of mobile telephones, television cable modems, satellite-based systems, and asynchronous DSLs to access the Internet. In 2000 about 3 percent of all voice traffic for new phone subscribers in the United States was wireless only, and this is expected to rise to 10 percent by the end of the decade (Yen and Chou 2001). In Japan, by December 2000 two-thirds of Internet users employed mobile phones to access the Internet, compared with 30.7 percent for the older dial-up technology (ITU 2000). In mid-2001 China had 165 million fixed-line accounts and 120 million wireless subscribers (China Braces 2001). Almost 70 percent of Koreans had acquired mobile phones by the end of 2001, and of these more than 7 million were using them to access the Internet (Quantum Leap 2002; South Korea 2002). As figure 5.2 makes clear, even a relatively poor nation such as Indonesia has seen cellular phone subscriptions take off in recent years. Soon Indonesia will join the 40 other economies that had more mobile than fixed-line phones in use as of December 2000 (ITU 2001a). The International Telecommunications Union estimates that in 2002 there will be 1.11 billion land lines and 1.4 billion mobile phone subscribers worldwide (ITU 2002).

Between 1990 and early 2001 the number of mobile telephone subscribers worldwide increased 75-fold to 725 million people. These subscribers used 2G phones, based on either one of the competing global system for mobile telephony, time division multiple access, or code division multiple access (CDMA) standards, which allowed for much faster access to the Internet. An especially popular application of 2G phones is the short message service, which sends text from one

Figure 5.2 Comparison of Number of Cellular Subscriptions with Fixed-Line Telephones, Indonesia, 1996–2001

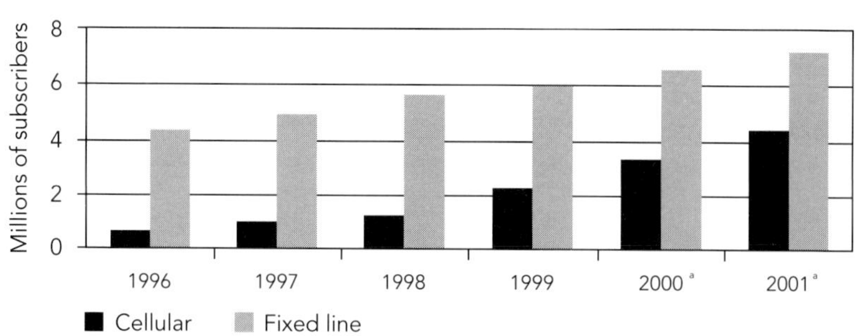

a. Projected.

Source: Business Asia, "Lifestyle in a Phone," May 29, 2000.

mobile phone to another. In January 2001 alone, approximately 15 billion messages of this sort were sent around the world (ITU 2001a).

The use of mobile phones to browse the Internet was the next important development. Some Web sites were adapted to fit on the small screens of mobile phones. In 2000 firms began using the Wireless Application Protocol (WAP) and General Packet Radio Service to launch such browsing services, and by the end of the year 100 mobile operators were doing so. Take-up of WAP-enabled services was slow, however, with only 5 million subscribers by December 2000. This poor take-up rate arose from the shortcomings of the compression technology, the pricing methods, the relatively slow speed of Internet connections to the World Wide Web, the small amount of content that was WAP accessible, and a shortage of handsets.[26]

The poor performance of WAP and General Packet Radio Service can be contrasted with the success of the i-mode service launched in Japan in February 2000. Adapting Hypertext Markup Language (HTML)-based Web sites for i-mode has been easier than doing so for WAP, and by opening its platform to third parties, NTT DoCoMo has encouraged the entry of content providers, including both registrants and informal users. By 2001 more than 40,000 i-mode-compatible sites were offering a wide range of content. An additional appealing feature of the i-mode service is that users pay only for information received rather than for time online.

Downloading streaming audio messages, still images, and videos still takes considerable time on 2G or 2.5G phones, and this has prompted the design of 3G services.[27] While 3G services have a common standard, International Mobile Telecommunications-2000 (ITU 2000), 3G mobile networks embrace three incompatible modes all based on the code division multiple access (CDMA) technology developed during World War II: Universal Mobile Telecommunications in Europe, CDMA-2000 in the United States, and wideband (W)–CDMA in Japan. These networks will support packet-switched, broadband Internet access and, with higher bandwidth, will provide downloading speeds of at least 144 kilobits per second and up to 2 megabits per second.

Such services require the use of a higher-quality spectrum, which many nations (but not the United States) auctioned to potential 3G service suppliers in 2000. In light of the subsequent economic downturn and the considerable technical difficulties in launching 3G services, the winners of these auctions appear to have vastly overestimated the commercial potential of 3G services, at least in the short run. In late 2001 NTT DoCoMo launched its Freedom of Multimedia Access 3G service based on W-CDMA, with Korea following with its so-called IXRTT using CDMA-2000. Both have struggled to overcome teething difficulties and to deliver on their promises (3G by Any 2002). Providers in Europe and North America have faced similar obstacles. This delay reflects both technical difficulties and concerns about funding the deployment of 3G technologies, especially since the lucrative mobile phone market has attracted several new firms and profit margins have narrowed. Signs show that the Korean government, which had previously encouraged competition among mobile phone providers to build a sizable domestic market, now favors consolidation through mergers and acquisitions into a small number of large firms. The government is defending this change in policy on the grounds that only larger firms can afford to invest in 3G technologies; however, it risks sending the wrong signals, dampening the entry of new firms and encouraging bigger firms to believe that the government will effectively underwrite their large investments in technology and service development. As with the Internet, state-sponsored, if not state-led, telecommunications development could easily deter technological change and drain initiative from the industry. This is important, because the 4G technology currently being developed might, once deployed, save on investment outlays while delivering far superior services.

WIRELESS INFRASTRUCTURE, COMPETITION, AND POLICY

The question, however, remains: Can a highly competitive market for telecommunications services attract the considerable funds needed to develop and maintain the infrastructures that competing suppliers need? Figure 5.3 illustrates the magnitude of these expenditures throughout the late 1990s. Part of the answer may lie in the successful bundling of Internet access with other services that would add to revenues. Furthermore, suppliers may be able to offer premium services that effectively enable them to price discriminate among their customers more effectively (see Greenstein and Spiller 1996 for evidence that U.S. households are willing to pay more for improved Internet access). The speed of data retrieval is likely to be the principal determinant of uptake, as those individuals and firms with high time opportunity costs will choose faster services. Another will be the quality and range of content that can be accessed, especially on mobile phones.[28]

A source of future funds and expertise for the East Asian market could be overseas telecommunications operators, once these have regained their financial strength. Concerns about national security—usually the stumbling block to allowing foreign investment—might be assuaged by creating joint ventures, including separate subsidiaries, or other collaborative measures not involving takeovers by or mergers between foreign and domestic firms. One constraint on both domestic and foreign investments is legal restrictions that prevent private firms from owning telecommunications infrastructure assets. Providers of mobile phone services in Thailand, for example, can only set up networks for a fixed period of time, during which they

Figure 5.3 Investment in Telecommunications as a Share of GDP, Selected East Asian Economies, 1990–99

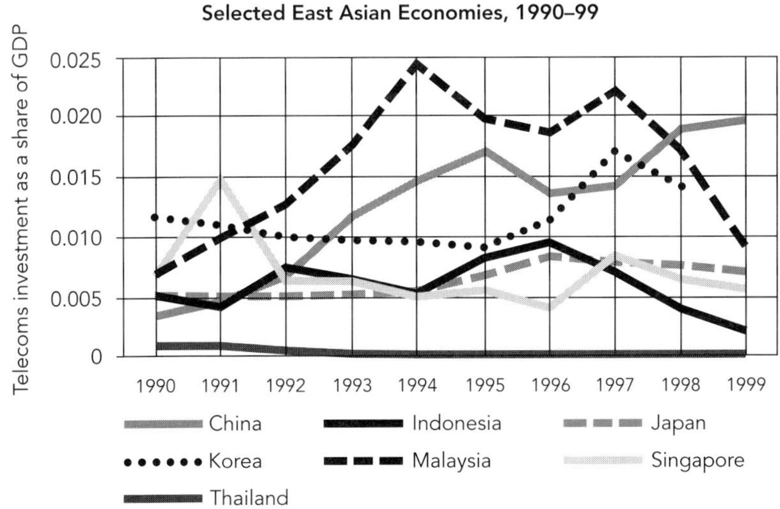

Note: GDP = gross domestic product.

Source: International Telecommunications Union database.

have to pay one of the two state telecommunications agencies, the Telephone Organization of Thailand or the Communications Authority of Thailand, 22 percent of their revenues. Furthermore, when the fixed period expires, the state agencies have the right to take over the private firm's network. Not surprisingly, this results in high monthly charges to Thai mobile phone users and reduced diffusion of the technologies, and has led to a reluctance to invest in marginally lucrative areas. As a consequence, e-commerce still accounts for just 0.04 percent of Thailand's GDP (E-commerce Emasculated 2000).

The intensification of competition among telecommunications and other providers of ICT services will also call into question the future of unfunded mandates imposed on firms by regulators. The imposition of universal service requirements, for example, will further raise the need for public outlays, as telecommunications firms are unlikely to be able to continue to cross-subsidize loss-making services when competition in previously sheltered—and typically profitable—services intensifies. The funding of universal service requirements, effectively hidden before competition was admitted, would then become more transparent, in turn provoking a debate about whether other technologies can attain universal access more cheaply than fixed-line telephony.[29]

We turn now to the consequences for regulatory policy of the growing convergence in the services offered by telecommunications operators, other data transmission firms, broadcasters, and entertainment and publishing firms. Typically telecommunications and broadcasting firms have their own industry regulators and publishers do not. To the extent that the cost of supplying the same service differs across firms located in industries with different regulatory burdens, a degree of regulatory competition may emerge. Firms will prefer to supply the service in the industry with the least regulatory burden, and industry regulators will probably find themselves under pressure to respond by lowering regulatory standards. Such regulatory competition raises the question of whether devising common regulatory and competition policy principles for these three industries would be desirable.

The implications of regulatory competition for the pricing of interconnections are more stark. Reconciling the profitability of those firms that use a given network infrastructure (that are encountering considerable competition from sellers of similar services in other industries) with interconnection charges high enough to provide a market return on the investments made by the owners of that infrastructure may become increasingly difficult. As the latter's revenues depend on the extent to which the network is used and the firms using the network can easily exit, the only viable option is to cut interconnection fees until enough firms supplying services over the network are profitable. If the final demand for services does not eventually rise enough so that interconnection fees provide the infrastructure owners with an adequate rate of return, then perhaps policymakers should be prepared to let some network providers decline.

The unpredictability of innovations in these industries—and their effects on the fortunes of firms—implies that plenty of shakeouts could occur in the digital transmission industries.[30] Having adequate legal and financial institutions to facilitate exit (for example, bankruptcy laws) and entry (for instance, venture capital funds) will be an important prerequisite for benefiting from this technological convergence. A role for policymakers will be to ensure that the shakeout is not accelerated by the pricing and exclusionary practices of dominant firms, thus antitrust policymakers and enforcers will have to be vigilant. Even so, the end result may well be that a small number of firms—and possibly even one—will emerge as the dominant supplier of digital transmission services. Such an outcome could strengthen pressures to regulate dominant suppliers, but prior experience of the capture of similar regulators by corporate interests—resulting in an increased likelihood of frustrated entry by new competitors—should caution against taking this step. Instead, retaining vigorous competition policy oversight of these dominant firms while ensuring that other firms can introduce new technologies probably offers the best chance for sustaining competitive pressures over the longer term. Looking ahead, an interesting area for research and policy debate will be the degree to which industry-specific regulatory structures can be replaced by cross-industry competition policies based on the experience of leading OECD countries.

INTERNET-BASED GROWTH IN EAST ASIA

Computerization and the Internet, together with the development of telecommunications, are at the core of the ICT revolution. Investment in computers and the telecommunications infrastructure has already begun to contribute to GDP growth in East Asia; however, the real breakthrough in productivity is likely to come from the expansion of e-business; e-commerce; and Internet use for finance, health care, entertainment, education, and governance. Transnational production networks and the initiatives of governments in countries such as Singapore have accelerated the adoption of the Internet for these purposes, helped by investment in physical facilities, but as in the United States, business organizations and market institutions must adapt greatly before they can realize the full effects on cost reduction and productivity. The trends are promising. Whether they will be sustained, however, depends on how these new developments surmount the slackening of economic growth in the medium term. For East Asia, regulatory action by individual governments will also determine how much is invested in telecommunications hardware, how widely the Internet is integrated into the business world, and how the standards and rules of the various economies will be harmonized across the region.

NOTES

1. Taylor (2001) makes the general point that ICT is likely to take much longer than five years (the length of the boom years) to work itself through the US$10 trillion plus U.S. economy.
2. Electronic transactions amounted to US$336 billion out of the total of US$11.5 trillion in the U.S. economy at the end of 2000. B2B transactions reached US$90 billion in 1999 (Lucking-Reilly and Spulber 2001; *Business Week*, "Lessons of the Cyber Survivors," April 22, 2002). Worldwide B2B transactions reached nearly US$500 billion in 2001 and retail transactions climbed to US$112 billion (*Business Week*, "How E-Biz Rose, Fell, and Will Rise Anew," May 13, 2002).
3. Some of the adjustments are questioned by Kay (2001), who doubts their validity.
4. According to the Bank of Korea, 40 percent of the growth in Korea in the late 1990s was traceable to ICT (OECD 2000).
5. Rather than selling bits of software, Oracle now sees itself as providing Internet-based technology. Oracle's Chairman and Chief Executive Officer Larry Ellison claims that "what we are selling is cars. We have a marketing system that talks to the sales system, that talks to the service system that talks to the accounting system. All the pieces fit together. Our critics say 'But you haven't got the best windshield in the world.' That may be true, but our windshield fits in our car. That's the reason there's no air blowing on your face when you are driving" (*Business Week*, "The Oracle Speaks," February 26, 2001, p. 99).

6. The unhappy experience and demise of Webvan.com, the online grocery business, highlighted the tentative nature of new business models. Webvan collapsed because it built up a huge infrastructure well ahead of demand and was not vigorously frugal in managing inventory (*Business Week*, "Webvan Left the Basics on the Shelf," July 23, 2001).
7. Leamer and Storper (2001) maintain that because most transactions require long-term relationships, B2B exchanges will have to struggle to survive.
8. More and more of the first-tier electronic component manufacturing and assembly is becoming the preserve of six large electronic manufacturing service providers, which actually make hardware for the likes of Sun, Intel, and IBM and now also for NEC and Canon. These are Celestica, Flextronics, Jabil Circuit, Sanmina, SCI Systems, and Solectron (*Red Herring*, "Outsourcing Companies Benefit When Their Customers Are Under Stress," April 1, 2001).
9. For a selection of excellent papers on the effects of FDI in the region, see Ito and Krueger (1999); for broader surveys of the latest research on international business networks see Feenstra and Rauch (1999) and Rauch (1999a); and for an extensive case study of one MNC's production network see Peking University, Tsinghua University, and University of South Carolina (2000).
10. For recent analyses of the behavior of Japanese MNCs, see Beechler and Bird (1999) and Mody, Dasgupta, and Sinha (1999).
11. Companies are reevaluating Internet advertising that has consumed a large part of dot-com budgets. Most of the effort is wasted, as click-through visitor rates are extremely low.
12. An extension of this is so-called expertise automation, which assists businesses by brokering connections between people and by delivering specific skills when and where needed (*Red Herring*, "From the Ground Floor," March 6, 2001).
13. For instance, multimodal transport capability and door-to-door delivery are still underdeveloped in the coastal areas of China, and logistics are weak throughout the interior of the country (Shaw and Wang 2002).
14. According to State Council Decree Number 292, issued in October 2000, each Internet content provider in China is to supply to the authorities on demand the content offered on their sites plus records of all those visiting their sites for up to 60 days prior to the date of request. In addition, Internet content providers are required to police their own sites and eliminate subversive material. In early 2001 China had 265,000 Internet content providers. For further details on the evolution of Internet use and its control see Harwit and Clark (2001).
15. Filters and firewalls can be circumvented by dialing out to a foreign ISP, geolocation can be sidestepped by accessing sites using a computer in another country, and public key encryption can defeat eavesdropping (*Economist*, "The Internet's New Borders," August 11, 2001). Moreover, services such as Freenet promise anonymity by distributing files around the world on computers belonging to Freenet members, with the result that no file has a unique Internet address (*New Scientist*, "Out of Control," March 25, 2000). Nevertheless, as *Economist* notes, most users are unable to employ such measures, with the result that where governments desire, a high degree of control is possible. Interestingly, the use of much touted public key encryption software produced by companies

such as Entrust and Baltimore Technologies has been slow to catch on, because of the need for common architectures and new ways of doing business (*Financial Times*, "Information Technology Survey," September 5, 2001).

16. On the threat from hacking and computer viruses such as Code Red, see *Scientific American*, "Code Red for the Web," October 2001. The spreading use of Bluetooth-enabled and Wi-Fi devices will increase the risks of unauthorized use and break-ins.

17. The denial of service attacks on Yahoo.com, Amazon.com, and Buy.com in February 2000, with sites rendered inoperative by as few as 50 unwitting computers acting in concert, provided a foretaste of the vulnerability to attacks by hackers on businesses, public agencies, and key infrastructure nodes (*Oxford Analytica*, "United States: Internet Insurgency," February 14, 2000; see also *Information Security*, "Fighting the Rising Tide," and "Deciphering the Cost of a Computer Crime," November 2000).

18. At its peak, Napster had 90 million users. Having had to pay damages for infringing songwriters' copyrights, Napster's future is uncertain. It also faces competition from new challengers and two industry-backed services: Music Net, backed by Warner Music, and Pressplay, backed by Sony and other companies (*Financial Times*, "Napster Closer to Music Deal," September 25, 2001).

19. Making predictions about technologies that will shape the future of the Internet and its communications infrastructure is risky. Certainly the 3G (and eventually 4G) technology, once it is widely deployed, will lead to a quantum leap in data transmission from today's 10 kilobytes per second to as much as 2 megabits per second, permitting streaming video and audio. But other technologies will critically supplement advances in wireless networking. Voice browsers will make the use and navigation of the Web much easier. Short-range wireless communication between equipment will be simplified by Bluetooth (short-range wireless technology permitting communication between electronic equipment, for example, phones and laptops) and other similar technologies. Peer-to-peer technology is another genie that is set to grow and ramify. More complex e-commerce applications and multitasking will stimulate demand for more powerful computers. Lastly, once they are widely adopted by individual industries as a standard comparable to hypertext markup language (HTML), extensible markup languages (XML), which describe each packet of information as a bar code does, will enormously ease the manipulation, sorting, and organizing of information (see *Economist Intelligence Unit*, "3G in Asia: Outlook and Opportunities," January 10, 2001; *New Scientist*, "Everything Anywhere," October 21, 2000; *Scientific American*, "The Wireless Web," October 2000).

20. The 2G system uses the cellular structure and circuit switching of the first-generation cell phones, but with the added advantage of digital transmission. The 2.5G technology employs packet switching and "always on" phones, but it is constrained by a narrow bandwidth that limits the transmission of graphics and video. The wide bandwidth of 3G phones will overcome this constraint and permit 2 megabit per second transmission of full-motion video.

21. For a recent exposition on the many ways in which telecommunications and transportation infrastructures influence the demand for one another in urban

clusters, and more important, the spatial allocation of economic activity, see Wheeler, Aoyama, and Wolf (2000).

22. The next big step is the break-up of China Telecom into separate companies similar to the Baby Bells in the United States. These would provide a mix of services within regions (*Red Herring*, "China Braces for a Break-Up," September 15, 2001). For a review of the extent and effects of telecommunications reform in developing economies see Noll (1999), and for its international antecedents see Drake (1999). The reform of local telephony is given special attention in Baumol and Sidak (1994). Joskow (1998) reviews the more general experience of reforming infrastructure industries in developing countries, many of which share the network economies feature of telecommunications. Holler (1999) provides a review that is similar to that in Joskow, but focuses entirely on telecommunications markets.
23. Boyland and Nicoletti (2000) provide an econometric account of complementary reforms in the telecommunications sectors of the OECD nations. Wallsten (1999) does likewise for selected Latin American and African countries. Li, Qiang, and Xu (2000) take a different approach and use statistical tools to locate the circumstances under which nations privatize and deregulate their telecommunications sectors.
24. As many of the backbone providers were also ISPs, they earned revenues from the latter activity, effectively cross-subsidizing their backbone investments.
25. Recall that empirical evidence referred to earlier in this chapter suggests that higher lump sum access charges for the Internet reduce take-up among lower-income groups.
26. Aside from the slowness in transferring data, WAP is also hamstrung by the need to connect whenever calling up a new Web page.
27. Early attempts during 2001 to introduce 3G base station and handset technologies by Nokia and NTT DoCoMo, for example, encountered teething difficulties that are being ironed out through software improvements. But the future profitability of providers rests on rapid increases in demand for wireless data and e-mail services, availability of useful content, and advances in compression and transmission technologies facilitating the transmission of huge amounts of data. The latter are more likely to be solved quickly than are the former, with multipath scattering using multiple antennae (each with its unique echo signature) offering a way of increasing long distance transmission of large volumes of data (*Nature*, "Talking Cheap in the City," January 18, 2001). For a detailed account of 3G technologies and their commercial applications see *Financial Times*, "Understanding 3G," June 4, 2001.
28. Korea, whose government has taken aggressive steps to integrate the nation into the knowledge-based economy, has funded relatively more of its investments in ICT from public means than other East Asian economies. It is too early to say whether such public investments have attained a rate of return that more than compensates for the forgone alternative use of these resources.
29. Crandall and Waverman (2000) thoroughly discuss the issues raised here in the context of telecommunications service provision in Canada, the United Kingdom, and the United States. Although these authors do not consider the East

Asian experience, the technological and competitive pressures that they identify are at work on both sides of the Pacific.

30. Although the effect of shakeouts within a sector of the digital transmission industry will tend to raise the monopoly power of the surviving firms in that sector, the technological convergence across these sectors implies that the surviving firms will face greater competition from survivors in other sectors. Therefore, as shakeout and technological convergence have opposing effects on the market power of surviving firms, making strong claims for or against the future role of competition policy in the digital transmission industry is probably inappropriate.

CHAPTER 6

MANAGING THE GLOBAL INTERFACE

The growing importance of services, the more intensive use of ICT, and the emergence of clusters as central poles of national economic geographies all characterize the unfolding growth dynamic in East Asia. Previous chapters showed that this dynamic draws on the outside world by attracting FDI, skilled and highly educated professionals, some venture capital, and data and information exchange. How East Asian nations can redesign their policies toward the world economy—unilaterally and collectively—to take full advantage of this dynamic is the principal focus of this chapter.

To make the most of the new growth dynamic, East Asian countries must adopt a much broader set of market-opening policies. Without downplaying the importance of relatively open regimes for trading goods and investing in manufacturing, reliance on such arrangements is clearly no longer adequate for growth. Services sectors must also be exposed to greater international competition, in particular, the telecommunications sector, which is to international commerce in the 21st century what ports and railways were to commerce in the 19th and 20th centuries. Another important change in mindset for policymakers and business people will be to consider a wider range of sources of value added in an information-intensive and globalizing economy. Many industries in the Group of Seven nations, which have faced considerable import competition (much of it from East Asia), have managed to reorganize themselves successfully, letting go of production stages dominated by lower-skilled workers. Evidence for such successful reorganization is apparent in global industries such as textiles and apparel, electronics, and automobiles. By recognizing the existence of these opportunities and tailoring them to the region's circumstances, East Asia can provide itself with a much needed antidote to the often heard pessimism about the effect of China's continued integration into the world trading system.

REAPING THE BENEFITS OF OPEN TRADE AND INVESTMENT REGIMES

While this chapter focuses on how East Asia can exploit its strong links with the world economy, we should not overlook the long-standing benefits that the region has garnered from its relatively open policies toward overseas trade and investment. The evidence of these benefits continues to pour in.[1] E. Kim (2000), for example, estimated the beneficial effects of trade liberalization on firm productivity in Korea and on reducing the market power of domestic firms as measured by price-cost markups. In addition, Lawrence and Weinstein (2001) revisited the determinants of sectoral productivity growth in Japan during its growth spurt in the 1960s and 1970s, and found that import competition provided an additional stimulus to firms to enhance their productivity. Such findings reinforce the case for trade reform.

Another channel by which openness boosts domestic growth is through the importation of equipment. Mazumdar (2001) presents evidence that nontariff barriers reduce the importation of equipment and that this, in turn, depresses productivity growth in the importing nation. Unlike Lee (1995), a frequently cited study of the effects of equipment on growth in developing countries, Mazumdar adopts an approach that discriminates better between the contribution to productivity growth of domestically produced equipment and of imported equipment. Taking full advantage of cutting-edge equipment typically requires well-educated and scientifically proficient managers and employees. Thus Miller and Upadhyay's (2000) confirmation that, among developing economies, the growth-promoting effect of openness is greater in nations with more human capital is not surprising.

The amount of recent literature on the contribution of trade reform pales compared with the mushrooming literature on the beneficial effects of FDI on East Asia's growth performance.[2] Figure 6.1 indicates the scale of projected FDI inflows in 2001, as well as the stock

Figure 6.1 Projected FDI, Selected East Asian Economies, 2000 and 2001

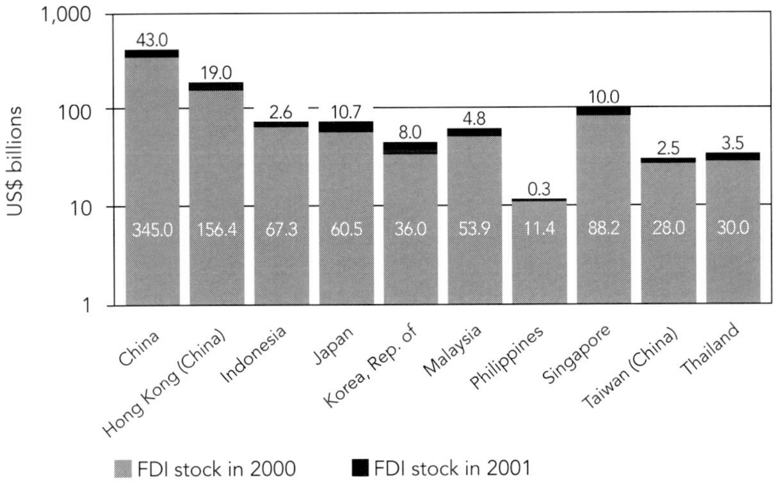

Note: FDI = foreign direct investment.
Source: Business Asia, "Bucking the Trend," March 5, 2001.

of existing FDI in several East Asian economies in 2000. In 2001 the total stock of FDI in mainland China was twice as large as that in any other economy in the region. Even though there has been some amount of "round tripping" of funds from the Chinese mainland through Hong Kong (China) (funds that are then invested back in the mainland and erroneously measured as FDI), the FDI stock in East Asia is now firmly concentrated in the economies of the northeastern part of the region, and this trend seems likely to continue.

This concentration of FDI reflects not only China's opening up to foreign investment throughout the 1990s, but also liberalization in Japan and Korea after 1997. As figure 6.2 makes clear, the biggest changes in FDI inflows since 1995 occurred in Japan and Korea. China's FDI has risen approximately US$5 billion since 1995, while the rest of East Asia saw a slight fall in FDI inflows. This implies that the observed increase in the northeastern economies' share of the region's total FDI inflows does not come at the expense of overseas investment inflows into Taiwan (China) and the ASEAN economies. Nonetheless, some companies such as Seagate and Motorola are

Figure 6.2 Shift of FDI to Northeast Asia, Selected Years

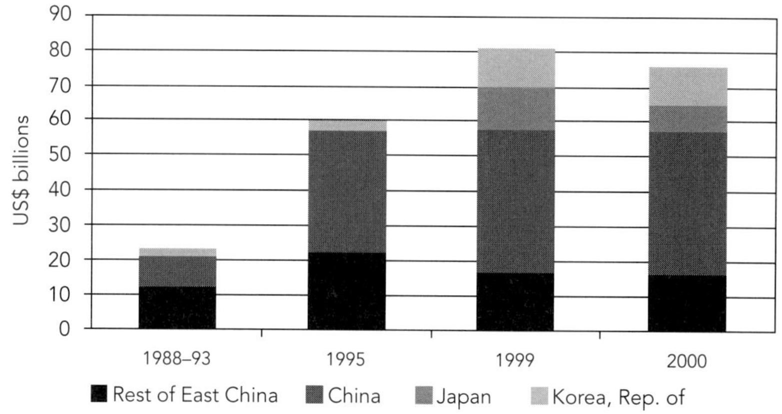

Note: FDI = foreign direct investment. Given the concern that much FDI into Hong Kong (China) has actually come from the Chinese mainland, this figure excludes FDI inflows into the former.
Source: UNCTAD (2000; 2001, appendix B1).

shifting some of their production facilities from Southeast Asia to China (East Asia Manufacturing Questions 2002).

The relative importance of the numerous rationales for FDI differs across the economies in the region. Some foreign investors are motivated by a desire to supply the recipient nations' markets, whereas in many industries in China and in other lower-wage economies, such as Indonesia, FDI is principally directed toward export platforms (Feenstra and Hanson 2001; Hill and Athukorala 1998). Although the latter motivation is a long-standing one (see, for example, Wells 1993), in recent years a new development has emerged. As the examples in the next section will make clear, firms are systematically creating regional production networks that locate each stage of a production process in the economy in which that function is best performed (along some quality or cost consideration). This results in shipments of parts and components across more than one national border before the final product is assembled and delivered to customers, contributing to greater intraregional trade flows.

In Korea FDI is increasingly in the form of mergers and acquisitions, and such investments can be expected to introduce managerial innovations as well as potentially fusing Korean firms into MNCs' networks of activities throughout the world (JETRO 2001; Mody and Negishi 2001; UNCTAD 2000). Likewise, foreign investment in Japan is playing a role in restructuring certain underperforming manufacturing and financial firms. These include GE Capital's acquisition of the Japan Leasing Corporation, Renault's investment in Nissan, and Daimler Chrysler's purchase of a stake in Mitsubishi Motors (JETRO 2001).[3] In both Japan and Korea increasing amounts of FDI are being directed toward the distribution sector, especially retailing, as evidenced by the aggressive investments made by the French supermarket chain Carrefour, its British rival Tesco, and Wal-Mart. (On Wal-Mart's carefully orchestrated entry into the Japanese retail sector, see Wal-Mart Develops 2002.) These firms are bringing greater competition into one of the most inefficient sectors of these economies, much to the benefit of consumers (see, for example, A Hyper Market 2001, which describes the popularity of foreign retailers of everyday products among Asian consumers).

Recent research has shed light on the factors underlying these FDI flows. Urata and Kawai (2000), for example, examined the differences in overseas investment behavior by small, medium, and large Japanese firms. Since the late 1980s smaller Japanese firms have invested abroad in larger numbers, joining the long-standing practice of the large Japanese conglomerates. Urata and Kawai confirm that, irrespective of firm size, such overseas investment decisions are driven by the availability of low-wage labor, the quality of infrastructure in the potential recipient, the presence of good governance, and a sizable local market. They found evidence, however, that smaller Japanese firms were more sensitive to each of these factors than the larger firms. In addition, smaller Japanese firms place a greater premium on investing in areas with existing agglomerations of similar firms, reinforcing the importance of clusters as the emerging paradigm of economic activity in East Asia.[4]

The desire to control costs is an important determinant of overseas FDI by Japanese multinationals, according to evidence presented by Mody, Dasgupta, and Sinha (1999).[5] Given that firms in East Asia frequently invest in each other's economies, this suggests that governments in the region have strong incentives to keep down the costs of raw materials, of intermediate inputs such as business services, and of transportation. This is best achieved by stimulating competition in the markets that supply these goods and services through trade reforms, reassessing the benefits of long-standing domestic regulations, and relaxing restrictions on FDI.

Evidence is also growing that both workers and local firms acting as suppliers gain from FDI. In their study of Indonesian manufacturing firms, Lipsey and Sjöholm (2001) found that, controlling for the different characteristics of manufacturing plants, foreign firms pay somewhat higher wages. Moreover, the competition for talent induces local firms to raise their wages as well. This beneficial finding should not be taken too far, however, as much research has shown that attracting FDI in the first place requires the availability of a large pool of skilled and educated workers (see Noorbakhsh, Paloni, and Youssef 2001). This research reinforces the importance of improving secondary and tertiary education systems, a point discussed in chapter 3.

In sum, even though East Asian nations have reaped considerable benefits from relatively open regimes toward FDI, the magnitude of these benefits depends on the presence of the complementary factors—human capital, competitive factor and service markets, and a focus on excellence in both service and manufacturing innovation—that have been the traditional focus of East Asian firms. These factors will be increasingly important as the region adjusts to China's integration into the world economy, whose export growth parallels that of the rest of the region (figure 6.3).

Even though China's integration into the world economy is unlikely to decimate the manufacturing industries of the rest of East Asia, firms elsewhere in the region will certainly be called on to adjust their industrial structures, to coordinate their commercial activities across borders, and possibly to relocate their labor-intensive production stages to China. Low tariffs and transportation costs, especially via air transport, make shipping parts and components across many borders before they are sent to consumers as finished products a reasonable option. More important, perhaps, is the quality of ICT, which facilitates the coordination and organization of activities over large distances. In the 1990s production networks or global supply chains, formed partly as a result of the development of ICT, allowed Western firms to respond better to rising import competition from every source, including East Asia. Understanding how these Western firms

Figure 6.3 Growth of China's Low- and Medium-Tech Exports, 1990–2000

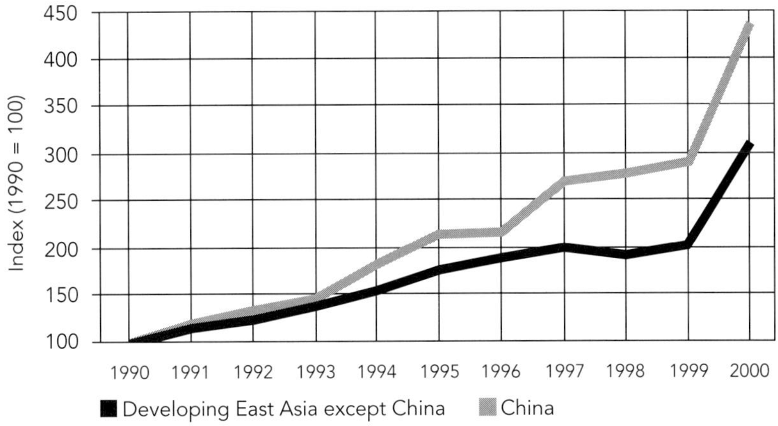

Source: World Bank Systemwide Initiative on Malaria and Agriculture database.

responded to increased import competition may shed light on the opportunities for East Asian firms and governments, but using this information will require that the East Asian firms take a broader view of commercial organization than has typically been the case to date.

The first step in developing this enriched view is to recognize that ICT and efficient transportation systems permit more rapid responses to changes in consumer demand and the customization of products. The U.S. textile industry provides perhaps the best example of the use of these advances to respond to import competition (Abernathy and others 1999, 2001). Producers handle consumers' wide range of tastes by offering a large variety of products, the fashion component of which yields greater profits than basic apparel products. To avoid being saddled with lots of unsold stock, however, which is costly to stores and that must eventually be heavily discounted, thereby lowering profits, retailers and wholesalers are making greater use of ICT advances—principally bar code technology and computer programs that analyze sales data—to better predict demand. This permits making the product in smaller quantities and detecting changes in demand more easily. To meet particularized demand and minimize their inventories, retailers and wholesalers now place a larger number of smaller orders with their suppliers, and they expect fast turnaround. Likewise, suppliers demand rapid responses from the firms supplying them with fabrics, buttons, dyes, and so on, as well as from logistics firms. Thus, for this section of the clothing market, the cost of production is not the only major determinant of a firm's competitiveness. Inventory management, accurate assessment of demand patterns, and rapid delivery (also referred to as rapid replenishment of stocks) are at a premium. Analysts argue that a firm's capacity to integrate all the relevant technologies (information, communications, and production) is critical to competing effectively in this industry (Abernathy and others 1999). For some East Asian firms, acquiring that capacity may initially require partnering with other firms closer to the cutting edge. This entire strategy, however, will be fatally undermined if governments have not provided adequate ICT and transportation infrastructures in the first place.

Thun (2000) provides evidence that the Taiwanese counterparts of U.S. textile and apparel firms have ensured their survival by concentrating value added in commercial activities other than the production process. To be sure, these firms have increasingly relocated production stages to the Chinese mainland to take advantage of the lower wage costs there, but they have also concentrated on earning their profits from what is becoming a large, distinct branch of management practice, namely, supply chain management. That is, they locate suppliers in China, monitor the quality of their work, transmit orders and deal with buyers, organize shipments, and sometimes engage in rudimentary marketing. Their expertise in managing supply chains has grown to such an extent that some such firms have departments that provide technical expertise and computer programs that enable other firms to better manage chains of suppliers and respond to demand shocks. The shoe industry in Taiwan (China) has evolved in a similar way. Hsing (1999) describes how product cycles in casual shoes grew from two to eight per year in the mid-1980s. This forced Taiwanese shoe manufacturers to fulfill smaller orders placed at more frequent intervals. Reinforcing this shift was the deliberate choice of Taiwanese shoe manufacturers to offer a greater variety of shoes, including fashion shoes made with synthetic materials, special orders, and work shoes.[6] These firms responded by creating networks of shoe manufacturers in lower-wage East Asia economies and specialized in coordinating these networks, introducing new production techniques and materials and, where possible, exploiting economies of scope.

The foregoing examples demonstrate what is often called value migration, that is, the process whereby the principal source of value added in a commercial activity shifts from one stage to another. In the examples, value added derives increasingly from organization, coordination, marketing, logistics, and the ability to forecast demand accurately, rather than from the actual production process. Feenstra and Hanson (2001) provide striking evidence of the profitability of being an intermediary in the supply of differentiated products. They calculated, industry by industry, the average percentage increase or markup in unit prices of goods first imported from China by Hong Kong (China) merchants, then processed or marketed, and finally re-exported. From 1988 to 1998 the median markups were relatively stable, ranging from 28 to 34 percent, suggesting that substantial rents exist from coordinating economic activity in and beyond China.

Although many of the same factors are at work in both the textile and automobile industries, one difference is apparent: the ability to integrate an enormous number of different parts and components in a seamless fashion and to continue to do so even when innovations in one part call for changes in others is a critical determinant of a successful automobile company. Dyer and Nobeoka (2000) analyzed how Toyota—a world leader in this respect—has accomplished this by facilitating knowledge sharing among firms in a network. To encourage suppliers to share knowledge about innovations, Toyota invests heavily in supplier start-ups and discourages short-term opportunism by retaining key suppliers over many years. In this case both the network organizer and the suppliers earn profits principally from innovations, and network formation and communication are themselves facilitated by ICT.

The evolution of the East Asian HDD industry affords a compelling example of how firms can compete on dimensions other than cost. As McKendrick, Doner, and Haggard (2000) have documented, during the 1990s suppliers of HDDs also competed on time to market schedules; time-to-volume (the time needed to attain a sufficient scale of production); and reliability (or a reduction in defects). Personal computer manufacturers demanded enhanced performance from HDD producers across all these dimensions. Locations such as

Penang and Singapore—which in the 1980s were the initial recipients of overseas investment in HDD production by American firms—found they could retain this industry even while wages rose as their economies grew. This was facilitated in part by the desire of U.S. HDD firms to maintain a portfolio of different production sites, which acted as insurance against shocks to any one economy or plant, whether caused by exchange rate movements, labor unrest, or interruptions in supply or outbound shipments. This led to the creation of what McKendrick, Doner, and Haggard (2000) call a regional production system throughout East (principally Southeast) Asia.

An important key to the continuing success of the Singaporean HDD industry, however, was the product's increasing technical complexity. McKendrick, Doner, and Haggard (2000, p. 165) argued that

> [N]o other location possessed the depth of engineering resources to make them. Singapore also assumed a more explicit role in developing and managing the regional production network, functioning as a transfer station for the introduction of new product(s). Finally, the country began to diversify into new niches, including media, drive design, and other branches of data storage.

In short, Singapore was where new disk drives were tested, errors were corrected, and initial production runs were executed. Only after development in Singapore would the production of newer versions of disk drives move to different production sites in Southeast Asia, such as Malaysia and Thailand. Even then, some purchasers with specific or technically demanding needs maintained connections with Singaporean firms for their small production runs.[7]

Competition from lower-wage locations is thus neither new nor a specifically China-related phenomenon. Many industries in Western nations have been successfully adjusting to such competition for decades. The dimensions of time, customization, and reliability have proven to be as important to competition as labor costs. Because of ICT, firms are better able to customize products, analyze demand patterns, and organize production and suppliers. Moreover, integrating these different ICT-related functions is increasingly critical to commercial success. Government policy has played a role by keeping borders open, facilitating the creation and flow of ideas within and across borders, and ensuring that low-cost and high-quality logistics and communications facilities are open to firms.

As discussed in chapter 3, efficient international air freight services are extremely important for production networks and supply chains. Without these services, regions effectively remove themselves from contention as potential production locations. In this context, for an East Asian economy to protect its national air carriers from competition in its domestic market is highly disadvantageous. Protection lessens the airlines' motivation to improve its reliability and reduce transit and transshipment times. Developments in ICT have made processing orders and scheduling pickups and deliveries more efficient, as demonstrated by Federal Express's operations throughout East Asia. Indeed, part of the pressure on Federal Express to enhance its services comes from the competition it faces from UPS throughout the region, and now also in China.

The Impetus for Regional Integration

Whether driven by FDI, strategic alliances, or the formation of supply chains or production networks, the forces described in the last section point to a thickening web of commercial ties across the Pacific Ocean and within East Asia. These forces have not exerted themselves in a policy vacuum. On the contrary, throughout the 1990s governments have taken a number of steps toward regional integration. At the turn of the century, however, the taste for grander initiatives has given way to far less ambitious proposals to form bilateral trade agreements. This section accounts for the current state of affairs and evaluates whether bilateral agreements are the best way for governments to take advantage of the commercial dynamics discussed earlier.

Although our focus here is regional initiatives, bear in mind that East Asian nations could pursue trade and investment reforms either unilaterally or through negotiations at the WTO. The latter has traditionally been the more politically palatable, principally because domestic export interests are often willing to support proposed WTO agreements that offer greater market access abroad. This path to trade reform lost considerable appeal, however, after the signing of the Uruguay Round. That round proved to be a monumental accomplishment, bringing in new disciplines for trade and investment in services, intellectual property rights, and agricultural protection rules, in addition to the usual reduced tariffs on manufactured goods. Countries signed this agreement as a single undertaking, which prevented them from cherry picking only those constituent agreements that best suited their interests (Hoekman and Kostecki 2001).

More recently, industrial and developing economies were able to agree on an agenda for a new multilateral round. In November 2001 participants at the WTO Ministerial Meeting in Doha, Qatar, agreed to begin negotiations on traditional market issues, including agriculture; regulatory issues; and matters relating to the implementation of previous agreements, an important item for many developing economies. Whether these negotiations will succeed, and whether the ghost of the failure to launch a trade round in Seattle in 1999 has been exorcised, remains to be seen. Furthermore, the lukewarm reception many observers gave to the Doha Ministerial Declaration no doubt reflects the growing dissatisfaction with the WTO as a source of trade reforms, dissatisfaction that continues in the run-up to the 2003 WTO Ministerial Meeting in Mexico.

Unfortunately, neither ASEAN's nor the Asia-Pacific Economic Cooperation's (APEC) trade initiatives have lived up to prior expectations. ASEAN was formed in 1967 with five founding members: Indonesia, Malaysia, the Philippines, Singapore, and Thailand. The initial objective was to foster regional stability and promote political and economic cooperation. Throughout the 1990s, the latter goal came to dominate, and the original ASEAN members agreed in 1993 to form an ASEAN Free Trade Area (AFTA). Trade reform at first focused on tariff reductions on manufactured goods. In 1995, however, ASEAN members agreed to expand AFTA to include services, intellectual property rights, investment negotiations, and nontariff barriers. Furthermore, ASEAN members agreed in 1998 to accelerate the rate at which tariffs were reduced to between zero and 5 percent, with the overall target for zero tariffs on manufactured goods set for the early part of this decade (around 2003).

ASEAN's membership expanded throughout the 1990s to include Vietnam in 1995, the Lao People's Democratic Republic and Myanmar in 1997, and Cambodia in 1999. (Brunei Darussalam joined in 1984 after gaining independence from the United Kingdom.) These new members are not expected to phase out tariffs and other trade barriers as quickly as the original members, generating fears that a two-speed ASEAN has emerged (Problematic Newcomers 2001). Vietnam has until 2006, while Cambodia, the Lao People's Democratic Republic, and Myanmar have until 2008 to reduce their tariffs below 5 percent. Another wrinkle has been the use of exclusion lists and similar methods to avoid phasing out tariffs on sensitive agricultural and manufacturing items.

This ambitious program of trade reform has, however, been called into question in recent years. In January 2000 Malaysia stepped back from its commitments to reduce tariffs on automobile parts. Even though in May 2000 ASEAN ministers had agreed to allow Malaysia to retain these tariffs until 2005, confidence in the movement toward freer intraregional trade was shaken. Other members, notably Thailand, have subsequently announced that they too are reconsidering their commitments to liberalizing their automobile industries in light of Malaysia's move. This backsliding effectively undermines plans to allow automobile parts to move across ASEAN's borders tariff-free, a scheme known as the ASEAN Industrial Cooperation Scheme that has attracted applications from 50 foreign investors, including Volvo, Honda, and Toyota (Free Trade Retreat 2000).

Malaysia's move was blamed, in part, on the aftereffects of the East Asian financial crisis, which analysts claimed undermined the viability of its automobile industry. Given the severe downturn in Southeast Asian exports in 2001 and the slowdown in the world economy in 2001 and 2002, pressures for protecting national firms in the ASEAN regions are likely to intensify, further postponing AFTA's likely completion date. This gloomy outlook may explain why one of AFTA's most vocal supporters, Singapore, has turned to negotiating its own bilateral trade agreements.

Looking beyond Southeast Asia, ASEAN's attempts to forge closer economic and political ties with three of its northeastern neighbors (China, Japan, and Korea) are still in their infancy. At the meeting of finance ministers of these so-called "ASEAN Plus Three" in Chiang Mai, Thailand, in May 2000, the ministers agreed to expand regional currency swaps and—despite the lack of progress in completing AFTA—to explore the possibility of a free trade area encompassing all their economies. To date, progress on the former has been greater than on the latter, and several currency swaps were signed at a meeting of finance ministers of the ASEAN Plus Three group in Honolulu in

May 2001. These included a US$2 billion dollar–won arrangement between Japan and Korea, a US$1 billion dollar–ringgit arrangement between Japan and Malaysia, and a US$3 billion dollar–baht arrangement between Japan and Thailand. These arrangements are in addition to a previously agreed on US$1 billion intra-ASEAN swap arrangement, an existing US$5 billion dollar–won arrangement between Japan and Korea, and a US$2.5 billion agreement between Japan and Malaysia. Thus in total, the East Asian nations have created a US$14.5 billion web of commitments to help stabilize their currencies and to ward off speculative attacks. More such arrangements are expected in the near term, especially between Japan and the Philippines (Currency Swaps 2001).

While these arrangements sound impressive, for several reasons they represent only tentative steps toward regional monetary cooperation. First, their scale (US$14.5 billion) is tiny compared with the daily turnover in East Asian currency markets, thus whether these arrangements could prevent a stampede out of any one East Asian currency is an open question. Second, the US$6 billion of arrangements agreed on in Honolulu require International Monetary Fund conditionality before funds can be mobilized. This effectively renders these intraregional arrangements hostage to a Washington-based agency, circumscribing a regional response to potential future crises. Third, these arrangements do not require countries to cede any sovereign policy-setting rights, a concession that has been central to Europe's success with intraregional exchange rate management.

Diplomatic and strategic concerns seem to overwhelm trade and investment priorities in ASEAN and its related forums, as evidenced by the cautious reception given to China's proposal for a free trade area with the ASEAN economies. Concerns that this potential free trade area might become a vehicle for greater Chinese influence in Southeast Asia prompted suggestions that it be expanded to include Korea and Japan. In sum, ASEAN Plus Three appears to be going through a teething stage, and the scope of any durable regional free trade initiative is unclear in terms of both membership and of sectors covered.

The forum that advanced intraregional cooperation and liberalization the most in the Pacific region during the 1990s was APEC. It was founded in 1989, when representatives of 12 nations, meeting in Canberra, prepared a work program for future economic cooperation across the Asia-Pacific region.[8] At subsequent meetings the group made progress on trade facilitation. China, Hong Kong (China), and Taiwan (China) joined APEC in 1991, and APEC's profile was further raised when the United States invited the heads of state of APEC economies to a summit in 1993, which marked a turning point in U.S. attitudes toward APEC. Afterwards the United States issued a "vision statement" that recognized the growing economic interdependence across the Pacific and within East Asia. Cooperation flourished on a range of trade, investment, and other issues, and commitments were fleshed out in greater detail at the subsequent 1994 and 1995 summits held in Bogor, Indonesia, and Osaka, Japan, respectively.

Recognizing deeper historic divisions and rivalries within the region, APEC has been founded on three core principles: consensus, voluntarism, and unilateralism. APEC members tend to move together, by consensus, or not at all. Reforms agreed to in this forum are not codified in explicit regional agreements with rules, enforcement mechanisms, or formal ex post monitoring. Nations implement reforms unilaterally, principally through published individual action plans of measures taken in 15 regularly updated policy areas, but they frequently extend those benefits to nonmembers as well. This formula has been useful in encouraging nations to reform their economies and to shore up domestic support for their reforms. At the Bogor summit APEC leaders declared that their reforms are meant to move APEC members toward regional free trade: by 2010 for industrial nations and by 2020 for developing nations.

Even those sympathetic to APEC's vision, goals, and methods, however, have become increasingly concerned about the organization's lack of progress toward its stated goals. Central among these concerns are the slow adoption of APEC's reform agenda, the member nations' failures to set specific and observable goals beyond their Uruguay Round commitments, and the weak mechanisms for evaluating members' actions and the lack of incentives for encouraging members to align their actions with collectively agreed on goals. In its first policy report the APEC International Assessment Network argued that APEC had developed a form of "soft institutionalism" where "[d]uring its first decade, APEC has created a set of norms, procedures and structures that define its essence" (APIAN 2000, p. 4). Their argument ran as follows:

> [W]e believe that this soft institutionalism served APEC well during its infancy. Many of those who criticize APEC for not accomplishing more fail to understand the nature of soft institutionalism and why the region's realities allowed no other choice. We also believe that as APEC enters its second decade, it must constantly engage in self-examination. It must consider whether its soft institutionalism is facilitating decision making, whether the vision and mandates of the leaders are being transformed into tangible actions, and whether APEC officials are receiving the critical feedback integral to sound governance.

They also argued (pp. 4–5): "What may have been realistic at the outset may have become an avoidable obstacle to further achievement. What may have seen hopelessly idealistic at the beginning may have become more feasible as members gain confidence in APEC and in each other. What seemed dangerous may now appear comfortable and desirable."

The Trade Policy Forum of the Pacific Economic Cooperation Council expressed concern about APEC's lack of progress. It found that "[g]enerally, the Individual Action Plans lack detail, or do not shed sufficient light on the medium and longer term policy developments. Progress is more significant in areas where APEC has focused on collective actions" (Pacific Economic Cooperation Council 1999). This analysis revealed that the individual action plans contained only moderate coverage of nontariff barriers and few unambiguous commitments to liberalize services. In contrast, it found, by and large, clear commitments and programs in relation to reducing tariffs, liberalizing investment, removing impediments to the movement of business people, and implementing Uruguay Round reforms.

Where APEC has sought to liberalize a particular sector, however, it has quickly accomplished concrete reforms. The first WTO agreement on trade in information technology products, which reduced barriers to trade in this critical component of the knowledge-based economy, was originally negotiated among APEC members in 1996 before being quickly extended to include all WTO members at the Singapore WTO Ministerial Meeting. This agreement provided for the elimination of tariffs on all ICT-related goods by January 2000. Signatories to this agreement now represent more than 90 percent of the US$500 billion plus global ICT trade (Wilson 1998). A central question, however, is whether this liberalization of a leading sector of the East Asian economy provides a model for future negotiations within APEC.

In sum, while APEC reform initiatives have accomplished tangible improvements in selected aspects of the trans-Pacific business environment, given its current schedule, future reforms are likely to fall short of the organization's potential. A greater prioritization of reform initiatives, a willingness to codify commitments and to back them up with strengthened evaluation and enforcement mechanisms, and, perhaps most important of all, a move toward collective rather than unilateral commitment to implementation will be needed to turn APEC's long-term goals into reality.

In what is perhaps a testament to current difficulties in stimulating regional and multilateral trade reform, several nations on both sides of the Pacific have turned to a third option: negotiating bilateral reductions in trade barriers (for an economic analysis of some proposed and potential bilateral and subregional initiatives, see Scollay and Gilbert 2001). Even Japan and Korea, those longtime skeptics of the benefits of preferential trade reform, have begun exploring potential bilateral arrangements with other East Asia partners (see, for example, details of Japan's change in trade strategy in Japan Ponders Free Trade Alliances 2001).

From a regionwide perspective, the most optimistic scenario is that these bilateral agreements will grow in size, eventually yielding an East Asian or pan-Pacific arrangement. Without recounting the now familiar, but still relevant, debate about whether such preferential deals are stumbling blocks or building blocks to the completion of multilateral trade deals, a few points ought to be made (for contributions to this debate, see Bhagwati and Panagariya 1996; Panagariya 1999; Winters 1999; World Bank 2000). First, the recent enthusiasm for signing codified agreements with bilateral trading partners is difficult to square with the frequently heard reluctance to sign such agreements in APEC forums.

Second, the amount of trade reform involved in some of the completed deals is actually quite small, suggesting that bilateral arrangements will have a limited impact. The Closer Economic Partnership signed by New Zealand and Singapore in November 2000, for example, will eliminate tariffs on trade in goods. In reality, this means that Singapore must remove its one remaining tariff on New Zealand's imports (on beer), and the only significant tariff barriers that New Zealand must eliminate are on textiles, clothing, and footwear, which account for a trivial share of their bilateral trade (New Zealand 2000). In contrast, freer trade in services is to be phased in over 10 years, with loopholes built in to delay implementation. In other bilateral negotiations, notably between Japan and its trading partners, agricultural trade tends to be excluded. The bilateral trade agreement negotiated between Japan and Singapore, for example, focuses on liberalizing investment regulations and services sectors, and not on freeing trade in goods.[9]

Third, given the limited scope of some of the proposed arrangements, the estimated gains for the nations signing them are small. In an assessment of many potential bilateral agreements, Scollay and Gilbert (2001) estimated that the gains of tariff elimination to bilateral signatories are almost always worth less than 0.5 percent of their GDP. As these findings include the effects of eliminating tariffs on agricultural goods, which few nations appear willing to countenance, the actual gains are likely to be much smaller. Meanwhile, the effects on countries not party to such arrangements are typically adverse: their exports suffer as a result of preferential liberalization by the signatories. Thus such agreements tend to have a deleterious "beggar thy neighbor" aspect to them.

Fourth, bilateral arrangements may well spread only to those nations with sizable markets, and hence the greatest potential for export growth from such arrangements. Remarkably, certain members of the Japanese business community are unenthusiastic about the prospects of a free trade agreement with Korea because of the relatively small size of the latter's markets for certain products (Japan/South Korea 2000). Furthermore, the inevitable exclusion of some sensitive sectors from bilateral arrangements suggests that the size of a nation's tradable sector is a poor indicator of the size of the markets that might be opened up to competition.

These points imply that the web of bilateral arrangements that might eventually develop may link only a small number of economies on both sides of the Pacific, creating opposing sets of "insiders" (who have signed bilateral deals) and of "outsiders" (who have not). Such a development would represent a step back from the goals and vision underlying the APEC initiative.

By the end of the 1990s, clear differences were apparent between business-led and policy-led economic integration in East Asia. Businesses across the region were expanding their activities across borders, investing proportionally less in export-oriented manufacturing and more in services. Moreover, to the extent that they were engaged in manufacturing, they were increasingly fragmenting production across national borders, with labor-intensive activities concentrating in China. Firms increasingly built links with foreign counterparts through strategic alliances, joint ventures, and in some cases outright mergers and acquisitions. This proliferation of international commercial contacts contrasts with policymakers' stalled attempts to liberalize trade and investment flows across the region, and as we have seen, whether the recent interest in bilateral arrangements will eventually lead to tangible regional reform is at best unclear. Faced with this dichotomy, a reassessment of the priorities underlying regional integration initiatives is in order.

Toward a New Regional Commercial Initiative

The slow progress in accomplishing reforms through APEC's individual action plans in recent years can be attributed in part to their overly ambitious scope, both in terms of sectors covered and of membership. The bilateral response has been to narrow the scope along one dimension—membership—while preserving a fairly broad sectoral coverage. An alternative response could be to narrow the scope of sectoral coverage, that is, to focus the sectoral coverage on those policies that directly affect the dynamic elements of the business landscape outlined in this study. In essence, this proposal would involve replicating APEC's successful formula with the Information Technology Agreement on a larger scale. Such a proposal would not only concentrate negotiating effort, but it would present an opportunity to tailor regional initiatives to the likely growth poles of the 21st century. Such an approach does not imply leaving tariffs on manufactured goods unaltered; as argued earlier, lower tariffs on parts and components underpin the profitability of production networks throughout the region.

A new regional commercial initiative should give more prominence to services than has been the case in the past. As we have seen in previous chapters, the economic role of educational, health, logistical, and transportation services will likely grow in importance in the near future. These services should therefore be considered in all negotiations on services, not just the routinely considered communications and financial services, though the benefits of reforming the latter are sizable. Mattoo, Rathindran, and Subramanian (2001) found that economies with fully liberalized telecommunications and financial services sectors can grow up to 1.5 percent per year faster than those with more restrictive policies. As well as reducing the costs to firms of purchasing these services, a reduction that in turn bolsters their competitiveness also leads to an increase in direct exports of services.

Considerable scope exists for reducing barriers to trade and FDI in services in East Asia (Ito and Krueger 2000). Recent econometric analysis reveals the restrictiveness of national nontariff barriers in several services sectors (see Findlay and Warren 2001 for details). Table 6.1 estimates these barriers on a 100-point scale for several East Asian economies, and shows just how far Korea, the Philippines, and Thailand are behind world best practices. In the case of telecommunications, figure 6.4 shows that Japan is the only economy in the region whose communications sector comes close to approaching the efficiency of its U.K. and U.S. counterparts.

Chapter 4 emphasized the importance of a competitive national financial system in underpinning this new growth dynamic. Also of considerable interest is the role, if any, played by external reforms. Figure 6.5 summarizes the findings of one recent study of the effects on the margins charged by domestic banks of restrictions on overseas trade in banking services and on investments in banks (Kalirajan and others 2001). These border barriers can be expected to ease the competitive pressures on domestic banks, enabling them to charge higher margins and earn supranormal profits. Figure 6.5 shows just how distorting those barriers can be, for instance, Malaysian domestic banks charge interest margins 60 percent higher than would be the case in the absence of such barriers. The flip side to these higher margins is reduced loans to firms, some of which may be in dynamic industries.

The objective of negotiations pertaining to the regional commercial initiative should be to devise horizontal disciplines that apply across all the services sectors. This avoids the tendency for service

Table 6.1 Indexes of the Restrictive Effect of Policies toward FDI, Selected East Asian Economies and the United States (no restrictions = 0, maximum value = 100)

Economy	Business services	Communications	Distribution	Financial services	Transportation services
China	36	82	28	45	46
Hong Kong (China)	2	35	5	23	9
Indonesia	56	64	53	55	53
Japan	6	35	5	36	11
Korea, Rep. of	57	69	63	88	57
Malaysia	32	42	8	61	12
Philippines	48	76	48	95	98
Singapore	26	52	25	38	25
Thailand	78	84	78	88	78
United States	1	35	0	20	3

Note: FDI = foreign direct investment. The economies are ranked by the simple mean of the sectoral indexes of FDI restrictiveness. Hence, for East Asia, mean restrictiveness is the lowest in Hong Kong (China) and the highest in Thailand.
Source: Hardin and Holmes (1997).

Figure 6.4 Degree of Protection in the Telecommunications Sector, Selected Economies

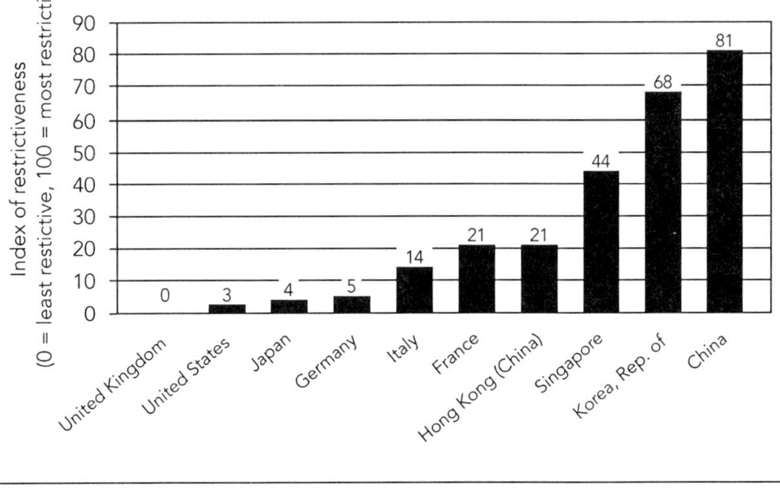

Source: Warren (2001).

Figure 6.5 Effect on Net Interest Margins of Trade and FDI Barriers to Banking Services, Selected Economies

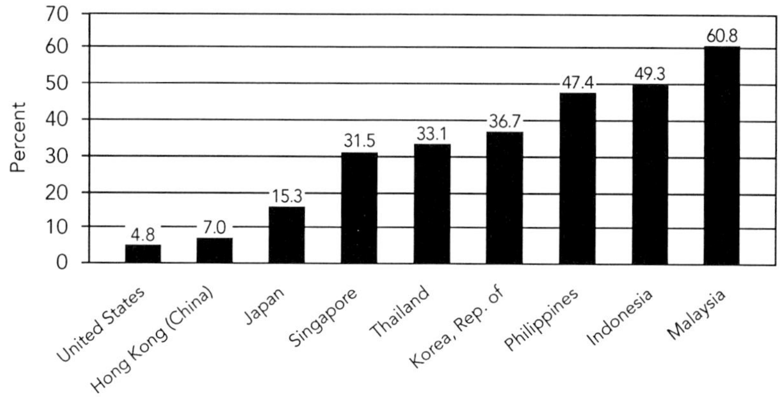

Note: FDI = foreign direct investment.
Source: Kalirajan and others (2001).

negotiations to fragment along sectoral lines, with the risk that inconsistent disciplines will be adopted. Those horizontal disciplines should be geared first toward attaining the most efficient allocation of resources, and second toward improving market and investment access. Unlike many goods markets, where maximizing access to overseas firms and goods typically results in improved resource allocation, the natural monopoly nature of the technologies underlying much service provision implies that some restrictions on entry, both domestic and foreign, may be needed to best allocate societal resources. This suggests that nations should be able to suspend the traditional disciplines of most favored nation status and national treatment only if a proposed measure enhances efficiency. No other feasible measure is available that plausibly enhances efficiency to the same extent, yet restricts foreign market access less. The nature of the measures will vary across services sectors, and with a growing body of experience with deregulation and the implementation of the General Agreement on Trade in Services, a set of best practices is beginning to emerge (see Hoekman 2000; Mattoo 2001).

Ensuring that market access commitments and domestic regulatory structures are such that telecommunications and other services providers set prices close to, or ideally equal to, incremental costs may not, however, be enough. Competition from rivals (see Nickell 1996 for a detailed study of the beneficial effects on firm productivity growth) may have to be supplemented by competition in the market for corporate control. Allowing mergers and acquisitions, from domestic sources as well as from abroad, will also provide incumbents with strong incentives to keep their costs down and to innovate. Profit-maximizing bidders for domestic firms may be motivated by acquiring market power, however, not just by implementing cost reductions, and society benefits little from the replacement of one incumbent by another that has no more constructive goal than raising prices.[10] Furthermore, European experience with the single market program suggests that such merger and acquisition activity peaks during bouts of market integration, especially in services sectors (Sleuwaegan 1998), suggesting that implementation of the new commercial initiatives outlined earlier must be complemented by more vigorous review of mergers and acquisitions.[11]

By the 1990s more than 70 economies had enacted competition laws (Palim 1998). A growing body of academic research supports this growing emphasis on competition policies to enhance resource allocation in an era of integrating markets. Dutz and Hayri (1999) have shown that, even after controlling for the height of national trade barriers, countries with more active policies toward fighting monopoly power tend to see their economies grow more rapidly. In a study of Eastern European and other transition economies, Dutz and Vagliasindi (2000) found that enhanced enforcement, not merely enactment, of competition policies facilitates the growth of higher-productivity firms in an industry, that is, inefficient firms cannot be cushioned by the profits acquired through the exercise of market power. Symeonidis (2000) offers evidence directly relevant to East Asia, especially given the previous reluctance of nations in the region to enforce competition laws, showing that greater competition (leading to lower prices) and a shakeout in U.K. industries followed a decision by the British authorities to stop condoning restrictive practices. This evidence, plus the history of competition policy enforcement by the European Commission (see Gerber 1998 for an excellent historical account), reinforces the case for bolstering competition enforcement even during periods of falling trade and investment barriers and integrating markets.

To minimize the likelihood that enhanced enforcement of national competition policy results in conflicting decisions on, for example, the desirability of a merger of firms with operations in many jurisdictions, bilateral, and preferably regional, mechanisms for information sharing, and even joint decisionmaking, should be developed. Given differences in legal regimes and traditions, this process of enhanced cooperation will inevitably take some time, and initially cooperation will probably be limited to clear-cut violations of competition laws, such as cartel investigations. Any such collaboration in East Asia could build on the lessons obtained from a growing body of comparable experience between certain Latin American nations, between the United States and Canada, and between the United States and the EU.[12]

The next stage of policy-led regional integration in East Asia will also require a shift away from soft institutionalism toward codified and enforceable agreements monitored and, if necessary, enforced by an independent secretariat. Hard institutionalism, if one might call it that, will reduce the probability of backsliding by signatories, which in turn will increase confidence that firms, both domestic and foreign, will not see their plans interrupted. On this point Winters (1997) has argued that one of the important roles the European Commission has played during recessions has been to act as a counterbalance to national governments that were inclined to renege on their liberalizing commitments to provide short-run help to their own firms. Moreover, the narrowed scope of this proposed commercial initiative, compared with APEC's current trajectory, will go some way toward reassuring those concerned about the potential dilution of national sovereignty.

"Less is more" should guide the creation of this new regional commercial initiative: "less" because "more" appears, in the face of APEC's experience, to be a recipe for diffusing negotiating effort and a lack of progress. "Less" does not mean a smaller impact, however. This regional commercial initiative would be targeted toward the growth poles of the global economy in the coming decade.

CONCLUSION

By and large, East Asian nations have viewed the principal benefits of openness to be export-led growth in manufacturing industries. These enabled the East Asian nations to grow rapidly and helped to speed up their recovery from the financial crisis. The supply-side dynamics outlined in this chapter and elsewhere in this study suggest that policies toward openness need to be revisited, with implications for the nature and pace of national and regional trade reform. Innovations in ICT, as well as falling international transportation costs, have transformed the strategies of local and multinational firms. Competition has intensified, leading to a narrowing of margins in manufacturing and traded services. Firms have responded by combining higher value added services with goods; expanding outsourcing; concentrating on supplying demanding consumers prepared to pay premiums for timeliness, reliability, and innovations; and attempting to raise profits by setting up and enhancing the efficiency of supply chains. These changes enhance the importance of services—business logistics, telecommunications, and transportation—as the drivers of corporate strategy and competitiveness.

The important remaining policy and research question is whether these dynamics fundamentally alter how nations maximize the gains from openness. In addition to bolstering competition in the key services and providing an environment conducive for the sizable infrastructure investments that will lay the foundation for East Asian competitiveness, greater attention will almost surely be given to maintaining exchange rate stability, initially through national means, and in the future possibly through more formal regional mechanisms. Indeed, the deepening of interdependence along so many commercial and financial dimensions calls into question whether the region is best served by the growing patchwork of ad hoc initiatives between nations, or whether, over the longer term, a move toward a more rules-based, supranational system of regional governance might better serve the people of East Asia.

NOTES

1. For a useful overview of the benefits of lowering barriers to trade and investment in East Asia, see Lloyd and MacLaren (2000). This paper also highlights the benefits from future services sector liberalization. For more broad-ranging surveys on the consequences of trade and investment openness for growth, see Bhagwati and Srinivasan (1999) and World Bank (1999), and for skeptical views, see Rodriguez and Rodrik (1999) and Rodrik (1999).

2. For recent overviews of the effects of FDI on developing economies see Graham (2000) and Moran (1998, 2001). Ito and Kreuger (1999) offer analyses specific to East Asia. Hill and Athukorala (1998) provide an overview of the region's recent experience with FDI, although they only report FDI data through 1996. JETRO (2001) and UNCTAD (2000, 2001) provide more up-to-date FDI inflow and outflow data.
3. See Blomström, Konan, and Lipsey (2000) for an analysis of the role of both inward and outward FDI in restructuring Japanese manufacturing and service activities.
4. Kreinin, Abe, and Plummer (1999) report on a large survey of Japanese overseas investors. While they confirm most of Urata and Kawai's findings, some differences emerge, for instance, Kreinin, Abe, and Plummer report that smaller firms see the availability of cheap labor as less of an advantage than the larger firms.
5. See also the evidence in Basu and Miroshnik (2000). Chen and Ku (2000) found that controlling costs is an important motive for Taiwanese overseas investors.
6. In contrast, in the 1970s and 1980s rivals located in other countries tended to concentrate on supplying a narrower range of goods. At that time, for example, Korea produced primarily athletic shoes and Brazil focused on fashion shoes made with genuine leather.
7. Singapore's success in retaining HDD production underlines the importance of the policy recommendations made in earlier chapters. The deep pools of engineering talent came from somewhere, as did the state-of-the-art logistical infrastructure. Government policy played a deliberate role in these areas, as well as in supporting the development of top-notch (both domestic and foreign) suppliers to the HDD firms and encouraging corporate as well as university R&D. This approach to fostering industrial development differed considerably from the much maligned industrial policy of old, which was founded on explicit discrimination against foreign firms, directed lending, and a retreat behind national borders. In this case Singapore did not secure local markets for domestic producers through tariffs and restrictive government procurement policies. Rather, it took advantage of the fact that picky purchasers, whose needs change frequently, would provide enough demand for the industry. Policy was directed to ensuring that all the building blocks needed to meet that demand were in place.
8. The 12 nations were Australia, Brunei Darussalam, Canada, Indonesia, Japan, Korea, Malaysia, New Zealand, the Philippines, Singapore, Thailand, and the United States.
9. For a discussion of the negotiations between Japan and Singapore on their "free trade agreement," see *Financial Times*, "Japan Ponders Free Trade Alliances," June 6, 2001. Korea's negotiations with Chile are said to be foundering because of Korea's reluctance to open up its agriculture sector.
10. The classic analysis of these two motives for mergers and acquisitions, which of course have direct implications for assessing the desirability of merger enforcement policies, is Farrell and Shapiro (1991). Viscusi, Vernon, and Harrington (2000) review the economics of mergers, monopoly, and the exercise of market power and discuss the implications for competition or antitrust policies.

11. In sectors where goods and services can cross national borders, but must pass through distribution outlets before reaching consumers, European experience suggests that policymakers must keep an eye open for exclusive dealing agreements between manufacturers and distributors that effectively restrict competition in national markets or that prevent (or make more costly) arbitrage between markets (Goyder 1998). Similar concerns about blocked distribution systems have been raised in conjunction with Japan's imports (Scherer 1999).
12. Lloyd and Associates (2001) describe the extent of bilateral cooperation on competition policy enforcement between the countries of the North American Free Trade Agreement, between Australia and New Zealand, and within the EU. Evenett, Lehmann, and Steil (2000) offer a detailed account of cooperation between the EU and the United States on merger enforcement and the difficulties experienced in trans-Atlantic cooperation on investigations into vertical restraints and international cartels. De Leon (2001) analyzes recent experience with national and regional initiatives on competition policy in Latin America.

CHAPTER 7

INNOVATING TO WIN

When the developing regions of the world are compared, East Asia is conspicuous on a number of counts. On average, East Asian economies are the most highly industrialized, and manufactures comprise the bulk of their generally high ratio of exports to GDP. Moreover, five East Asian economies are among the world's top 20 trading economies, and until recently, the region has strongly supported the cause of multilateral trade liberalization.

For close to 30 years, East Asian economies have grown faster, largely as a consequence of their relative political stability, better macroeconomic management, and associated high rates of savings and investment. Because of their consistent performance, several have attracted large flows of FDI that contribute to growth by augmenting domestic resource mobilization and by transferring technology. Other regions contain countries that have grown rapidly for several years at a stretch, or for even longer periods, such as Botswana and Mauritius (Acemoglu, Johnson, and Robinson 2002; Rodrik 2000), but no other region has a core group of sizable economies that have sustained a steady pace of growth, and so generated mutually reinforcing neighborhood effects.

These facts are well known and are woven deep into the discourse on development. However, East Asia's performance is remarkable in several other respects that deserve more attention, because they have a large bearing on the individual economies' future development in an integrating world, a world that differs increasingly in crucial respects from that of the 1970s and 1980s. The 1990s provided a foretaste of this new environment, revealing both globalization's benefits and pitfalls for open economies. The 1990s also underscored the mounting penetration of innovation, particularly that led by ICT, into almost every sphere of economic activity and its potential for reshaping social and governance institutions. ICT is changing the rules of international competition. It is beginning to relegate manufacturing expertise and efficiency to a secondary place, behind the capacity to create and use knowledge to achieve competitiveness. In this environment, ceaseless innovation closely attuned to global market opportunities determines the tempo of growth.

Innovation has long been central to industrial prowess, and the high achievers have generally been those economies that excel at product or process innovation. However, innovation in the early 21st century is a more complex, knowledge-intensive activity than ever before, one requiring a many-stranded enabling environment. Whether East Asia retains its lead among the developing regions of the world will depend on how the region's nations reorient their learning processes and capitalize on their established international reputations in manufacturing that they have built over the past three decades, but arguably, the consolidation of a knowledge system that routinizes innovation and leverages it to sustain competitiveness will be of greater significance in the long run.

Why has innovation acquired such prominence? What factors are linked with innovativeness and its translation into commercially viable outcomes? To what extent have East Asian economies already assembled some of the building blocks required for competing in markets where continuous innovation determines not just the growth, but also the survival of certain economic activities? What mix of policies could revive confidence in the future of the East Asian economies that have struggled to regain their stride after the 1997–98 crisis?

WHY INNOVATION MATTERS

The salience of innovation is rooted in a number of facts and perceptions as follows:

- The pace of patenting has increased sharply since the late 1980s, especially in electronics, biotechnology, and the information sciences.

This acceleration is apparent in most industrial and emerging economies.

- The product cycles for a wide range of goods and services are becoming much shorter, and businesses must now plan on unflagging product improvement and on introducing new and better varieties into the marketplace.
- A revolution has occurred in the use of computers and in computing capacity; the emergence and spread of telecommunications technologies; and the use of the Internet for business purposes, knowledge sharing, and a constantly expanding host of other applications, many of which are novel and give rise to entirely new wants, thereby raising the demand for innovative capacity.
- The computerization allied with the Web has altered the dynamics of knowledge sharing in the sciences, engineering, and finance, to name just a few areas. This enhances the productivity of research; facilitates the introduction of financial instruments; and permits the launch of a variety of new services, which in turn have begun transforming business practices.
- The efficiency of production is being heightened by ICT-enabled production networking, which squeezes the most out of distributed manufacturing through specialization and scale economies in assembly, automation of supply chain management, and advances in logistics.
- The combined effects of all these factors were visible in the performance of the U.S. economy during the second half of the 1990s. Even after adjusting for cyclical elements, productivity was growing at a rate of 2.5 percent per year, approaching levels last seen in the 1960s, the golden age of postwar growth. The U.S. achievement is directly associated with higher spending on research and development, investment in ICT, and large gains in the productivity of high-tech manufacturing industries. Although European and East Asian growth rates were not based on comparable advances in productivity, the factors responsible for U.S. performance have begun to impinge on businesses in these regions, promising similar long-run improvements in productive efficiency.
- The research carried out on the technological epochs ushered in by railways, electricity, the automobile, and the telephone and telegraph

> suggest that the full productivity and technological benefits of innovations are realized over three to four decades, during which time financial manias can lead to the overbuilding of infrastructure and much ebb and flow of business activity. In other words, the general purpose technologies introduced by ICT will have profound consequences for innovation, for growth, and for the severity of business cycles.

What conditions promote innovation? The findings presented and discussed in chapters 3–6 point to a few key conclusions with repeatedly demonstrated relevance for East Asia. The kind of creative thinking that leads to innovation demands openness to ideas and the movement of knowledge workers. Social ideology and institutions must tacitly or actively support freedom of thought, expression, debate, experimentation, and association through participation in learned societies. This must be across the board, and not just in a few selected scientific disciplines. With globalization, such openness and its underlying political, social, legal, and economic institutions are becoming ever more widespread, but in many parts of the world they are still resisted, treated with suspicion, and viewed as subversive of a desirable established order. Barring entirely unforeseen developments, greater mobility, the Internet, and urbanization are all likely to accelerate a worldwide trend toward the kind of openness that is hospitable to creativity within and across disciplinary boundaries.

Openness is permissive, but good ideas spring from prepared minds, sometimes working independently, but more often in fruitful interaction in groups that attain a critical mass. This requires training an adequate number of skilled researchers with mastery of their own specialties and the capacity to advance the frontiers of knowledge. It also depends on the emergence of a well-equipped infrastructure of research universities and institutes that bring together researchers and the business community. Both are predicated on a certain level of expenditure on tertiary education and on research.

The direction taken by innovation is increasingly in the hands of individuals, companies, and universities. In most countries the government and public research institutes have a diminishing role in setting an agenda, but public funding and national strategic directives are likely to remain significant drivers, especially in lower- and middle-income countries. The trend in the industrial countries is away from large laboratories and toward a decentralization of research,[1] helped along by ICT that permits knowledge sharing and easy interaction among smaller groups of researchers. The increased frequency of scholarly meetings also allows for more face-to-face contact. These conditions foster the financing of smaller-scale research activities and the commercialization of new findings. New kinds of finance, especially venture capital, permit highly productive specialized research, frequently of an applied nature, that complements broader investigations and basic research.

As the role of defense-related research and public financing has receded, individual businesses and universities are becoming centers of research activities and conduits for its launch on the market. Fueling this decentralized research, based on individual or corporate initiative, is the possibility of reaping rewards through commercialization. This depends on the force of incentives. First, market competition and stock market valuation must demand continuous innovation, and by the same token the stock market must handsomely reward success. Second, if the research takes place within firms, the corporate environment must provide avenues to subject promising findings to a commercial test. New so-called intrapreneurial mechanisms can be helpful in this regard, but, as argued in chapter 3, much depends on organizational structure, that is, the interaction among different parts of a company, the management's strategy, and the resources available for trying out new ideas. The pharmaceutical companies are particularly aggressive in this regard, especially the smaller biotech firms, not least because only a small proportion of plausible research leads result in a profitable product, and those that hold promise typically take 10 to 15 years to bring to market (Champion 2001; O'Keefe 2001).

When innovation depends on individuals or groups, the ease of obtaining seed money to set up trial ventures strongly influences the supply of innovation. In this connection, regulatory barriers and the costs of registration and licensing compose one set of hurdles that governments have begun to scale down. Market liberalization has also contributed to this. Until recently, financing for new businesses was primarily a function of government and informal social networks, but as discussed in chapter 4, institutional credit policies will leave a greater footprint in the future. In the 1990s venture capital began to spread throughout East Asia, setting in motion other financial developments that widen the options for potential start-ups.

This brings us to the larger issue of overall financial development affecting growth, and as international financial integration increases, this is closely related to macroeconomic stability. The 1997–98 crisis started in the financial sector before widening to affect the foreign exchange market and the real economy. The financial sector distortions that precipitated the crisis, while contained by bank closures, mergers, restructuring, recapitalization, and more stringent regulation, remain a source of concern for most East Asian economies. Creating the economic environment in which innovation can thrive and new financial instruments can nourish start-ups, as well as the growth of existing firms with good products and business models, will require a complete overhaul of the financial sector and much stricter adherence to sound institutional practices.

The fate of innovation rests with the coming together of skills and services. Successful commercialization depends on a mix of management and technical skills. It also requires a number of handmaidens other than financiers, including lawyers, accountants, marketing strategists, advertisers, software providers, and logistics experts. The spark of innovation has a future only when it can be fanned by a number of crucial service providers. Hence the location of invention matters.

Chapter 3 noted that most innovations occur in relatively few clusters, that is, in practice, innovative activity tends to be highly localized. Clusters can be seedbeds of innovation, because of the potential inherent in intellectual spillovers and agglomeration economies. Empirical observation, aside from delineating the geography of innovation, also elucidates the characteristics of dynamic clusters. Frequently a university or a major research-oriented firm and the presence of a skilled work force can provide the basis of innovation and entrepreneurship.[2] The successful cluster only begins to take shape, however, when firms multiply to form mutually supporting networks. Once a source of ideas and the availability of skills are established, a virtuous spiral derives from the coming together of the many supporting services, noted earlier, that help bring innovative ideas to commercial fruition. Silicon Valley, with its prime location, favorable history of scientific development dating back to the early postwar period, and thick labor market is the emblematic cluster. However, several high-tech clusters have congealed in East Asia, including around Tokyo, in Kyoto, adjacent to Beijing and Taipei, and in Singapore. These and others are fertile sources of innovation. It is the continued productivity of these clusters and the appearance of new ones that is likely to provide the driving force behind growth in East Asia over the coming decades.

While localized clusters are a key element of the innovative system of the early 21st century, the globalization of knowledge development means that clusters must establish links that permit the exchange of knowledge and the optimal distribution of production facilities. This is the local-global dimension of innovative activity that, by way of openness, boosts innovation and its spillover effects.

Local-global links derive their strength from the twining of three separate strands. One major strand is the telecommunications network, the major channel for knowledge sharing and dissemination within and between clusters. Thus the quality of the telecommunications system and of information technology and their continuous upgrading matters will matter increasingly over time, as noted in chapter 5. The second strand is that the circulation of ideas must be paralleled by the easy movement of professional and technical people. Indeed, face-to-face contact is a vital complement to electronic exchange. This form of openness calls for a world-class transport infrastructure, which means, in practice, that innovative clusters must have first-rate airport facilities with dense international connections. The final strand is participation in international scientific collaboration. This brings us back to the criterion of openness with which we started. People must be able to move among countries with the minimum of hindrance, thereby cementing the international relationships now brought ever closer by ICT. Innovative economies must be open in every sense of the term, with the effective institutions, not just the physical facilities, needed to secure that openness, a point we noted at the outset.

CAN EAST ASIA RETAIN ITS LEAD?

To what extent do East Asian countries meet the necessary conditions for innovativeness? Before attempting to answer this question, we note that the region is heterogeneous, with countries at different levels of development and with widely differing innovative capabilities. If generalizing and comparing East Asia with other developing regions is possible, however, we can make some observations. First, the leading East Asian economies give much greater priority to technology, recognizing that it will become the dominant source of growth, eventually superseding factor accumulation. Hence R&D spending, already relatively high, is rising. The scale of patenting in economies such as China, Korea, and Taiwan (China) points to the efficacy of such outlays.

Second, compared with other developing regions, and even with many of the industrial countries, the leading East Asian economies have large stocks of skilled and professional workers as a share of their total work forces. The annual additions to the ranks of such workers are also higher than in most other parts of the world. Thus East Asia is attempting to meet the challenges posed by the knowledge economy more speedily than its competitors.

Third, the per capita availability of computers in East Asia is high, and the region is well ahead of other developing areas with respect to indicators such as Internet access, telephone lines per capita, and the use of wireless equipment. Connectivity and Internet use in several East Asian countries approach or exceed those in the industrial countries, and are significantly higher than in Eastern Europe and Latin America. Furthermore, East Asia has taken an early lead in introducing broadband and wireless access, which permit viewing graphics-heavy Web pages, streaming video, and accessing audio content.

Fourth, with the exception of the São Paulo region in Brazil, the border areas of Mexico, and Bangalore and Mumbai in India, other industrializing countries cannot match the high-tech cluster development now under way in China, Korea, Malaysia, the Philippines, Singapore, Thailand, and Taiwan (China) (although in most instances these are not creative high-tech clusters comparable to those in the advanced OECD economies that are pushing the frontiers of technology outward). East Asian countries have succeeded in building a diverse group of clusters that draw on spillovers from universities (China and Taiwan [China]), major MNCs (Penang and Singapore), state enterprises (China and Korea), and transport hubs (Singapore). In addition, East Asian hubs, like those in Mexico and Bangalore, are linked with those in the United States and Europe through capital and labor flows, as well as through production networking arrangements. The local-global links integrating East Asia with the world economy run deeper than they do in most other parts of the world.

Fifth, other regions of the world, notably Latin America and South Asia, have large diasporas of skilled and professional workers who constitute a source of capital, technology, market intelligence, contacts, and entrepreneurship. The pool of East Asian expatriate professionals in the industrial countries, however, is larger, commands greater wealth, and is far more deeply engaged in high-tech business activities. The human capital bridges linking East Asia and the industrial countries are wider and of longer standing than those between the West and other developing regions.

Sixth, industrialized clustering and the commercialization of innovative activity in East Asia is reinforced by the expansion of financial markets. Again, compared with other developing regions stock market capitalizations in several East Asian economies are higher, both in absolute terms and as a share of GDP. Although much financial restructuring and deepening remains to be done, East Asia leads the rest of the developing world with respect to key financial ratios, and when combined with high savings rates, the region is better positioned to support the growth of the knowledge economy.

Seventh, East Asian economies are also distinguished from other industrial countries by their level of corporate maturity in two respects. A number of non-Japanese companies have graduated from the role of original equipment manufacturing to that of fully fledged transnational corporations, with a recognized brand name and international standing. Samsung, Hyundai, ACER, and Quanta spring quickly to mind, with Haier, Huawei Technologies, and Kolon close behind. Others in China, such as Legend and the Great Wall, are moving up the ranks. Moreover, a large number of East Asian companies have entered into production, subcontracting, technology sharing, and research alliances with Western firms. These arrangements appreciably improve their capacity to innovate, penetrate markets, and eventually carve out niches for themselves marked with their own brand names.

These recently acquired strengths complement the other factors noted earlier and are responsible for East Asia's performance between 1970 and 1997. Together they amount to a formidable set of entrenched advantages. Whether they are sufficient to sustain the region's growth momentum well into this century, after the experience of the recent crisis period, cannot be ensured. The 1997 to 2001 period has drawn attention to systemic problems that must be addressed before East Asia can fully capitalize on its many favorable attributes. In this light, we must now consider some policy imperatives for the coming decades.

WHAT SHOULD EAST ASIA DO?

As we have argued, East Asian economies are at different stages of development, but to preserve—and to increase—their competitiveness through innovation and the opportunities presented by ICT, they need to move quickly to frame and implement policies in five areas.

Reform and restructuring of the banking system are matters of priority for several reasons. A weak banking system can trigger a crisis; stores up fiscal burdens for the future; slows growth; diverts capital to less competitive firms; and cannot satisfy the needs of new, dynamic, high-tech entrants. Recent research clearly shows that causality runs from financial development to growth.

Corporate governance in East Asia has lagged where management skills have fallen behind, and the pressure on managements to pursue strategies aimed at maximizing shareholder value are often weak. Policies to build institutions, both legal and financial, that shore up shareholders' rights and sharpen the market for corporate control would significantly augment management capabilities.

In an increasingly knowledge-based economy, the supply of workers with the requisite skills and penchant for creativity will determine how much innovation takes place and how it is used to enlarge market shares. Many East Asian economies are increasing the availability of skills, but quality remains deficient. The situation requires continuing attention to the several dimensions of secondary and tertiary education that influence analytical skills and the aptitude to innovate.

Although computer use in East Asia is spreading and telecommunications facilities are improving by the day, e-business and e-commerce are greatly hampered by the inadequacy of supporting services. These include secure credit card transactions, fulfillment, logistics, and legal services. Until these and other business services are strengthened through policies promoting competition, as discussed in chapters 5 and 6, many of the gains from the ICT revolution will not be realized.

The early willingness to embrace openness was responsible for East Asia's success in trade and is one of the factors responsible for the large inflows of FDI. The need for openness has risen in a world where innovation is the touchstone of competitiveness and innovation itself is influenced by flows of trade, human capital, and ideas. After the financial crisis, the backlash against globalization has dampened the pace of trade liberalization in East Asia and raised doubts about the merits of capital account liberalization. The direct and indirect advantages of trade liberalization are significant. Trade liberalization, preferably multilateral trade reform, deserves to be actively pursued. As we argued in chapter 5, a regional initiative focused on reform of the services sector would provide a further shot in the arm. Similarly, if East Asia can reform its banking sectors and regulatory frameworks, then freeing the capital account would, over the longer term, aid national financial market development. Innovation also rests on the circulation of ideas and knowledge workers. Much of East Asia has become more open to such flows. Persisting with this trend would be good economics, and possibly good politics as well.

We would like to end by sounding a few notes of caution. Greater innovativeness can certainly contribute to East Asia's productivity and competitiveness, but as the experiences of Japan, the European countries, and the United States show, measures that enhance supply do not necessarily translate into higher growth. Instead the economy can become awash in capacity for which no demand materializes. For gains in productivity and innovation to lead to growth, demand—both domestic and external—must also expand. During the years of high growth East Asian households saved mightily, and the East Asian economies relied heavily on exports to generate the requisite levels of demand. As the growth in this external demand has weakened and become more volatile, the need for domestic demand to serve as the principal driver of growth has increased. This is a matter of immediate concern in Japan, where high household savings have constrained economic activity (Yusuf, Lee, and Kuchiki 2002). In sum, supply-side measures must be backed up by demand management that balances the need to mobilize domestic resources with the need to maintain demand levels. Even though East Asian economies must devise supply-side policies equal to the task ahead, demand management will require continuing and sensitive attention.

The second note of caution is that an innovative economy rests on a willingness to engage in trial and error, with the full knowledge that not every new idea will be commercially viable. This requires societies to become more tolerant of failure. If they do not, fewer entrepreneurs will come forward with ideas in the first place, and those that do may well cling to unprofitable ideas well beyond what is prudent. Establishing the right economic incentives for innovation will be difficult enough without social pressures further conditioning choices. Initially, returning expatriates will embrace most of the new opportunities, but this pattern need not persist over time, especially as more dynamic members of the local population see the benefits of successful innovation and invest in and move closer to the technological frontier, becoming the catalysts for the next phase of East Asia's development.

A final note of caution relates to the future role of China in the regional economic balance of power and the competitiveness sweepstakes. Many countries fear that given its vast labor force of unskilled and technical workers, China will forge an overwhelming absolute advantage in a wide range of products, in the process draining other nations' hard-won economic achievements. This is unlikely to be the case. A more plausible scenario is that a new geographic distribution of industry will emerge based on evolving comparative advantage, and that East Asian economies will see that—like their counterparts in the industrial economies—they can enjoy sustained improvements in living standards when faced with growing competition from imports and for investment.

NOTES

1. Although corporate R&D by companies such as Intel and IBM has continued to grow, many of the larger companies in the United States and, for instance, in Korea, prefer to rely more on smaller start-ups and universities (*Fortune*, "Look Who's Doing R&D," November 27, 2000).
2. Bresnahan and others (2001) have pointed out that the development of high-tech clusters also depends on the availability of many traditional inputs, such as skilled workers and infrastructure.

REFERENCES

The word "processed" described informally produced works that may not be commonly available through libraries.

Abernathy, Frederick H., John T. Dunlop, Janice H. Hammond, and David Weil. 1999. *A Stitch in Time*. New York: Oxford University Press.

———. 2001. "Globalization in the Apparel and Textile Industries: What Is New and What Is Not?" Harvard Center for Textile and Apparel Research, Cambridge, Mass.

Acemoglu, Daron K., Simon Johnson, and James Robinson. 2002. "An African Success Story: Botswana." In Dani Rodrik, ed., *Analytical Development Narratives*. Princeton, N.J.: Princeton University Press.

Adams, Gerard F., and Byron Gangnes. 2001. "Will Japan's Current Account Turn to Deficity?" In Magnus Blomström, Byron Gangnes, and Sumner LaCroix, eds., *Japan's New Economy: Continuity and Change in the Twenty-First Century*. New York: Oxford University Press.

Adams, James D. 2001. "Comparative Localization of Academic and Industrial Spillovers." Working Paper 8292. National Bureau of Economic Research, Cambridge, Mass.

"All Wired Up." 2000. *Far Eastern Economic Review*, July 6.

APIAN (APEC International Assessment Network). 2000. "Learning from Experience." Singapore.

"Are the Foreign Born a Source of Strength for U.S.?" 1999. *Science*, August 20.

Arun, Mahizhnan, and Mui Teng Yap. 2000. "Singapore: The Development of an Intelligent Island and Social Dividends of Information Technology." *Urban Studies* 37(10):1749–56.

"Asian Capitalism: The End of Tycoons." 2000. *Economist*, April 29.

"Asia's High Tech Future: Beyond the Lab." 2000. *Business Week*, November 27.

Aswicahyono, Haryo, M. Chatib Basri, and Hal Hill. 2000. "How Not to Industrialise? Indonesia's Automotive Industry." *Bulletin of Indonesian Economic Studies* 36(1):209–41.

Audretsch, David, and Paula Stephan. 1996. "Company-Scientist Locational Links: The Case of Biotechnology." *American Economic Review* 86(3):641–52.

Aw, Bee Y., X. Chen, and M. J. Roberts. 1997. "Firm Level Evidence on Productivity Differentials, Turnover and Exports in Taiwanese Manufacturing." Working Paper 6235. National Bureau of Economic Research, Cambridge, Mass.

Backman, Michael. 1999. *Asian Eclipse: Exposing the Dark Side of Business in Asia*. Singapore: John Wiley (Asia).

Baily, Martin Neil. 2001. "Macroeconomic Implications of the New Economy." Institute for International Economics, Washington, D.C. Processed.

Baily, Martin N., and Eric Zitzewitz. 1998. *The East Asian Miracle and Crisis: Microeconomic Evidence from Korea*. Washington, D.C.: McKinsey and Company.

Bartelsman, Eric J., and Mark Doms. 2000. "Understanding Productivity: Lessons from Longitudinal Microdata." *Journal of Economic Literature* 38(3):569–94.

Barthelemy, Jerome. 2001. "The Hidden Costs of IT Outsourcing." *MIT Sloan Management Review* 42(3):60–69.

Basu, Dipak R., and Victoria Miroshnik. 2000. *Japanese Foreign Investments 1970–1998, Perspectives and Analyses*. New York: M. E. Sharpe.

Basu, Susanto, John G. Fernald, and Matthew D. Shapiro. 2001. "Productivity Growth in the1990s: Technology, Utilization, or Adjustment?" Working Paper 8395. National Bureau of Economic Research, Cambridge, Mass.

Baumol, William J., and J. Gregory Sidak. 1994. *Toward Competition in Local Telephony*. Cambridge, Mass.: MIT Press.

Bayoumi, Tamim. 2001. "The Morning After: Explaining the Slowdown in Japanese Growth in the 1990s." *Journal of International Economics* 53(2):241–59.

Beaudry, Paul, and David A. Green. 2001. "Population Growth, Technological Adoption and Economic Outcomes: A Theory of Cross-Country Differences for the Information Era." Working Paper 8149. National Bureau of Economic Research, Cambridge, Mass.

Becker, Jasper. 2000. *The Chinese*. New York: Free Press.

Beechler, Schon L., and Allan Bird. 1999. *Japanese Multinationals Abroad*. New York: Oxford University Press.

Behrman, Jere R., Nancy Birdsall, and Miguel Szekely. 2001. "Economic Policy and Wage Differentials in Latin America." Washington, D.C.: Inter-American Development Bank. Processed.

Bekaert, Gaeert. 1999. "Emerging Equity Markets and Market Integration." *National Bureau of Economic Research Reporter* (Winter 1999/2000).

Bekaert, Gaeert, Campbell R. Harvey, and Christian Lundblad. 2001. "Does Liberalization Spur Growth?" Working Paper 8245. National Bureau of Economic Research, Cambridge, Mass.

Berger, Suzanne, and Ronald Dore, eds. 1996. *National Diversity and Global Capitalism*. Ithaca, N.Y.: Cornell University Press.

Berger, Suzanne, and Richard K. Lester, eds. 1997. *Made by Hong Kong*. Hong Kong, China: Oxford University Press.

Bhagwati, Jagdish, and Arvind Panagariya, eds. 1996. *The Economics of Preferential Trade Agreements*. Washington, D.C.: American Economics Institute Press.

Bhagwati, Jagdish, and T. N. Srinivasan. 1999. "Outward Orientation: Are the Revisionists Right?" Economic Growth Center Working Paper 806. Yale University, New Haven, Conn.

Bils, Mark, and Peter J. Klenow. 2000. "Does Schooling Cause Growth?" *American Economic Review* 90(5):1160–79.

Black, Duncan, and J. Vernon Henderson. 1999. "A Theory of Urban Growth." *Journal of Political Economy* 107(2):252–84.

Blair, Margaret M., and Steven M. H. Wallman. 2001. *Unseen Wealth: Report of the Brookings Task Force on Intangibles.* Washington, D.C.: The Brookings Institution.

Blendon, Robert J., John M. Benson, Mollyann Brodie, Drew E. Altman, Marcus D. Rosenbaum, Rebecca Flournoy, and Minah Kim. 2001. "Whom to Protect—and How?" *Brookings Review* 19(1):44–48.

Blomström, Magnus, Denise Konan, and Robert E. Lipsey. 2000. "FDI in the Restructuring of the Japanese Economy." Working Paper 7693. National Bureau of Economic Research, Cambridge, Mass.

Bloom, David E. M., and Jeffrey G. Williamson. 1999. "Demographic Transitions and Economic Miracles in Emerging Asia." Working Paper 6268. National Bureau of Economic Research, Cambridge, Mass.

Boersch-Supan, Axel. 2001. "Labor Market Effects of Population Aging." Working Paper 8640. National Bureau of Economic Research, Cambridge, Mass.

Bordo, Michael D., and Antu Panini Murshid. 2000. "Are Financial Crises Becoming Increasingly More Contagious? What Is the Historical Evidence on Contagion?" Working Paper 7900. National Bureau of Economic Research, Cambridge, Mass.

Bordo, Michael D., Barry Eichengreen, and Douglas A. Irwin. 1999. "Is Globalization Today Really Different from Globalization a Hundred Years Ago?" In Susan M. Collins and Robert Z. Lawrence, eds., *Brookings Trade Forum 1999.* Washington, D.C.: Brookings Institution Press.

Bordo, Michael, Barry Eichengreen, Daniela Klingebiel, and Maria Soledad Martinez-Peria. 2001. "Financial Crises: Lessons from the Last 120 Years." *Economic Policy* (April).

Boyland, Oliver, and Giuseppe Nicoletti. 2000. "Regulation, Market Structure, and Performance in Telecommunications." Economics Department Working Paper 237. Organisation for Economic Co-operation and Development, Paris.

"The Box that Launched a Thousand Ships." 2000. *The New Yorker,* December 11.

Branscomb, Lewis M., Fumio Kodama, and Richard Florida. 1999. *Industrializing Knowledge: University-Industry Linkages in Japan and the United States.* Cambridge, Mass.: MIT Press.

Branstetter, Lee, and Yoshiaki Nakamura. 2002. "Has Japan's Innovative Capacity Declined?" In Magnus Blomström, Jeniffer Corbett, Fumio Hayashi, and Anil Kashyap, eds., *Structural Impediments to Growth in Japan.* Chicago: University of Chicago Press.

Bresnahan, Timothy. 2001. "Prospects for an Information Technology-Led Productivity Surge." Available on http://www.stanford.edu/~tbres/.

Bresnahan, Timothy, Alfonso Gambardella, AnnaLee Saxenian, and Scott Wallsten. 2001. "'Old Economy' Inputs for 'New Economy' Outcomes: Cluster Formation in the New Silicon Valley." Stanford Institute for Economic Policy Research Policy Paper 00-43. Stanford, Calif.

"Bricks and Clicks." 2000. *Far Eastern Economic Review,* July 6.

"Broadband Internet Access." 2001. *Red Herring,* October 1.

Brownbridge, Martin, and Colin Kirkpatrick. 2000. "Financial Regulation in Developing Countries." *Journal of Development Studies* 37(1):1–24.

Burkart, Mike, Fausto Panunzi, and Andrei Shleifer. 2002. "Family Firms." Working Paper w8776. National Bureau of Economic Research, Cambridge, Mass.

"The Cable Guys." 2001. *Red Herring*, October 15.

Callen, Tim, and Warwick J. McKibbin. 2001. "Policies and Prospects in Japan and the Implications for the Asia-Pacific Region." Working Paper 01/131. International Monetary Fund, Washington, D.C.

Calomiris, Charles W., and Joseph R. Mason. 2001. "How to Restructure Failed Banking Systems: Lessons from the U.S. in the 1930s and Japan in the 1990s." Paper read at the 12th Annual East Asian Seminar on the Economies, June 28–30, Hong Kong (China).

"Can Compaq Escape from Hardware Hell?" 2001. *Business Week*, July 9.

Castells, Manuel, and Peter Hall. 1994. *Technopoles of the World.* London: Routledge.

"A Central Theme of the Next Build-Out." 2002. *Red Herring*, April.

Champion, David. 2001. "Mastering the Value Chain." *Harvard Business Review* (June):109–15.

"Chasing the Bottleneck." 2001. *Red Herring*, October 15.

Chen, Tain-Jy, and Ying-Hua Ku. 2000. "The Effect of Foreign Direct Investment on Firm Growth: The Case of Taiwan's Manufacturers." *Japan and the World Economy* 12(2):153–72.

"China Braces for a Break-Up." 2001. *Red Herring*, September 15.

"China Moves to Encourage Growth of Private Schools." 2001. *Financial Times*, May 28.

"China's Leader Commits to Basic Research, Global Science." 2000. *Science*, July 16.

Choe, Chongwoo, and Imad A. Moosa. 1999. "Financial System and Economic Growth: The Korean Experience." *World Development* 27(6):1069–82.

Choudhri, Ehsan U., and Dalia S. Hakura. 2000. "International Trade and Productivity Growth: Exploring the Sectoral Effects for Developing Countries." *IMF Staff Papers* 47(1):30–53.

"Chronicle and Documentation." 2002. *China Quarterly*, June.

Ciccone, A., and R. Hall. 1996. "Productivity and the Density of Economic Activity." *American Economic Review* 86(1):54–70.

Claessens, Stijn, Joseph P. H. Fan, and Larry Lang. 2002. "The Benefits and Costs of Group Affiliation: Evidence from East Asia." Center for Economic Policy Research Discussion Paper 3364. London.

Claessens, Stijn, Simeon Djankov, Joseph Fan, and Larry Lang. 1999. "Expropriation of Minority Shareholders in East Asia." Working Paper. World Bank, Washington, D.C. Processed.

Coe, David, Alexander Hoffmaister, and Elhanan Helpman. 1997. "North-South R&D Spillovers." *Economic Journal* 107(440):134–49.

Cohen, Stephen S., and Gary Fields. 1999. "Social Capital and Capital Gains in Silicon Valley." *California Management Review* 41(2):108–30.

"The Contender." 2000. *Business China*, October 23.

Cooke, Philip. 2000. "Business Processes in Regional Innovation Systems in the European Union." In Zoltan J. Acs, ed., *Regional Innovation, Knowledge, and Global Change*. London: Pinter.

Cooke, Philip, and Kevin Morgan. 1998. *The Associational Economy: Firms, Regions, and Innovation*. New York: Oxford University Press.

Cortright, Joseph, and Heike Mayer. 2001. "High Tech Specialization: A Comparison of High Technology Centers." Survey Series 1. Washington, D.C.: The Brookings Institution.

Crafts, Nicholas. 1998. "East Asian Growth before and after the Crisis." *IMF Staff Papers* 46(2):139–66.

Crandall, Robert, and Leonard Waverman. 2000. *Who Pays for Universal Service?* Washington, D.C.: Brookings Institution Press.

Culliname, Kevin, and Mahim Khanna. 2001. "Economies of Scale in Large Container Ships." *Journal of Transport Economics and Policy* 33(2):185–208.

"Currency Swaps." 2001. *Oxford Analytica*, June 5.

"Cybercrime Threat to E-business." 2001. *Financial Times*, August 29.

Deckle, Robert, and Kenneth Kletzer. 2001. "Domestic Bank Regulation and Financial Crises: Theory and Empirical Evidence from East Asia." World Bank, Washington, D.C. Processed.

de la Potterie, Bruno van Pottelsberghe, and Frank Lichtenberg. 2001. "Does Foreign Direct Investment Transfer Technology across Borders?" *The Review of Economics and Statistics* 83(3):490–98.

De Leon, Ignacio. 2001. *Latin America Competition Law and Policy: A Policy in Search of Identity*. New York: Kluwer Law International.

Department of Trade and Industry. 2001. *Business Clusters in the UK—A First Assessment*. Available on http://www.dti.gov.uk/publications.

De Swaan, Tom. 2000. "The Changing Role of Banking Supervision." Keynote address, *Economic Policy Review* 6(4), Federal Reserve Bank of New York.

Devan, Janamitra, and Parth S. Tewari. 2001. "Brains Abroad." *The McKinsey Quarterly* 4.

Dhawan, Rajat K., Ramesh Mangaleswaran, Asutosh Padhi, Shirish Sankhe, Karsten Schween, and Paresh Vaish. 2000. "The Asian Difference in B2B." *The McKinsey Quarterly* 4.

Djankov, Simeon, Rafael La Porta, Florencio Lopez-de-Silanes, and Andrei Schleifer. 2000. "The Regulation of Entry." Working Paper 7892. National Bureau of Economic Research, Cambridge, Mass.

———. 2002. "Courts: The Lex Mundi Project." Discussion Paper 3344. Center for Economic Policy Research, London.

Dowling, Malcolm, and David Ray. 2000. "The Structure and Composition of International Trade in Asia: Historical Trends and Future Prospects." *Journal of Asian Economics* 11(3):301–18.

Drake, William J. 1999. "Toward Sustainable Competition in Global Telecommunications: From Principal to Practice." Washington, D.C.: Aspen Institute.

"Driving the Info Highway." 2001. *Scientific American*, October.

Dumais, Guy, Glenn Ellison, and Edward L. Glaeser. 1997. "Geographic Concentration as a Dynamic Process." Working Paper 6270. National Bureau of Economic Research, Cambridge, Mass.

Dutta, Soumitra, and Beatrix Biren. 2001. "Business Transformation on the Internet: Results from the 2000 Study." *European Management Journal* 19(5):449–62.

Dutz, Mark, and Adam Hayri. 1999. "Does More Intense Competition Lead to Higher Growth?" Working Paper 2249. Center for Economic Policy Research, London.

Dutz, Mark, and Maria Vagliasindi. 2000. "Competition Policy Implementation in Transition Economies: An Empirical Assessment." *European Economic Review* 44(4-6):762–72.

Dyer, Jeffrey H., and Kentaro Nobeoka. 2000. "Creating and Managing a High-Performance Knowledge-Sharing Network: The Toyota Case." *Strategic Management Journal* 21(3):345–67.

Dyer, Jeffrey H., Prashant Kale, and Harbir Singh. 2001. "How to Make Strategic Alliances Work." *MIT Sloan Management Review* 42(4):37–43.

"E-commerce Emasculated." 2000. *Far Eastern Economic Review*, September 21.

"East Asia: Free Trade Frustrated." 2001. *Oxford Analytica Daily Brief*, April 5.

"East Asia Manufacturing Questions." 2002. *Oxford Analytica*, January 14.

Easterly, William. 2001. *The Elusive Quest for Growth*. Cambridge, Mass.: MIT Press.

Easterly, William, and Ross Levine. 2001. "It's Not Factor Accumulation: Stylized Facts and Growth Models." *World Bank Economic Review* 15(2):177–219.

Easterly, William, Roumeen Islam, and Joseph E. Stiglitz. 2000. "Shaken and Stirred: Explaining Growth Volatility." World Bank, Washington, D.C. Processed.

Easterly, William, Michael Kremer, Lant Pritchett, and Lawrence H. Summers. 1993. "Good Policy or Good Luck? Country Growth Performance and Temporary Shocks." Working Paper w4474. National Bureau of Economic Research, Cambridge, Mass.

"Economic Bust, Patent Boom." 2002. *Technology Review*, May.

"Enough for Everyone." 2002. *Far Eastern Economic Review*, June 13.

Enright, Michael J., Edith E. Scott, and David Dodwell. 1997. *The Hong Kong Advantage*. New York: Oxford University Press.

"Entrepreneurial Fresh Air." 2001. *Economist*, January 13.

"EU Financial Regulation." 2001. *Economist*, March 3.

Evans, Peter. 1995. *Embedded Autonomy*. Princeton, N.J.: Princeton University Press.

———. 1998. "Transferable Lessons? Re-examining the Institutional Prerequisites of East Asian Economic Policies." *Journal of Development Studies* 34(6):66–89.

Evenett, Simon J., Alexander Lehmann, and Benn Steil, eds. 2000. *Antitrust Goes Global: What Future for Transatlantic Cooperation?* Washington, D.C.: Brookings Institution Press.

Fagerberg, Jan. 1994. "Technology and International Differences in Growth Rates." *Journal of Economic Literature* 32(3):1147–75.

Farrell, J., and C. Shapiro. 1991. "Horizontal Mergers: An Equilibrium Analysis." *American Economic Review* 80(1):107–25.

Feenstra, Robert, and Gordon Hanson. 2001. "Intermediaries in Entrepot Trade: Hong Kong Re-Exports of Chinese Goods." Working Paper 8088. National Bureau of Economic Research, Cambridge, Mass.

Feenstra, Robert C., and James Rauch. 1999. "Introduction to Symposium on 'Business and Social Networks in International Trade.'" *Journal of International Economics* 48(1):3–6.

Feldman, Maryann P., and Frank R. Lichtenberg. 1997. "The Impact and Organization of Publicly-Funded Research and Development in the European Community." Working Paper 6040. National Bureau of Economic Research, Cambridge, Mass.

Felipe, Jesus. 1999. "Total Factor Productivity Growth in East Asia: A Critical Survey." *Journal of Development Studies* 35(4):1–41.

Findlay, C., and T. Warren, eds. 2001. *Impediments to Trade in Services: Measurements and Policy Implications*. London: Routledge.

Fink, Carsten, Aaditya Mattoo, and Randeep Rathindran. 2001. "Liberalizing Basic Telecommunications: The Asian Experience." World Bank, Washington, D.C. Processed.

Forbes, Naushad, and David Wield. 2000. "Managing R&D in Technology-Followers." *Research Policy* 29(9):1095–1109.

"Free Trade Retreat." 2000. *Oxford Analytica*, May 4.

"FT Telecoms: Reinventing DSL for the Internet Age." 2001. *Financial Times*, March 21.

"FT Telecoms' Billing Systems." 2001. *Financial Times*, September 19.

Garrett, Geoffrey. 1998. *Partisan Politics in the Global Economy*. Cambridge, U.K.: Cambridge University Press.

Gerber, David. 1998. *Law and Competition in Twentieth Century Europe: Protecting Prometheus*. Oxford: Claredon Press.

"Getting the Most Out of Infotech." 2001. *Business Week*, July 9.

Glaeser, Edward. 1997. "Learning in Cities." Working Paper w6271. National Bureau of Economic Research, Cambridge, Mass.

Glaeser, Edward, H. Kallal, J. Scheinkman, and A. Shleifer. 1992. "Growth in Cities." *Journal of Political Economy* 100:1126–52.

Globerman, Steven. 2000. "Trade Liberalisation and the Migration of Skilled Professionals and Managers: The North American Experience." *The World Economy* 23(7):901–22.

Goldstein, Morris, Graciela Kaminsky, and Carmen Reinhart. 2000. *Assessing Financial Vulnerability: An Early Warning System for Financial Markets*. Washington, D.C.: Institute for International Economics.

Gordon, Robert. 2002. "Technology and Economic Performance in the American Economy." Working Paper 8771. National Bureau of Economic Research, Cambridge, Mass.

Goto, Akira, and Hiroyuki Odagiri. 1997. *Innovation in Japan.* Oxford: Claredon Press.

Gourevitch, Peter, Roger Bohn, and David McKendrick. 2000. "Globalisation of Production: Insights from the Hard Disk Drive Industry." *World Development* 28(2):301–17.

Goyder, D. G. 1998. *E.C. Competition Law.* New York: Oxford University Press.

Graham, Edward M. 2000. *Fighting the Wrong Enemy: Antiglobal Activities and Multinational Enterprises.* Washington, D.C.: Institute for International Economics.

Graham, Margaret B. W., and Alec T. Shuldiner. 2001. *Corning and the Craft of Innovation.* New York: Oxford University Press.

Greenstein, Shane, and Pablo T. Spiller. 1996. "Estimating the Welfare Effects of Digital Infrastructure." Working Paper 5770. National Bureau of Economic Research, Cambridge, Mass.

Griliches, Zvi. 1992. "The Search for R&D Spillovers." *Scandinavian Journal of Economics* 94(0)(Supplement 1992):S29–47.

"Grooming a Science Elite." 2001. *Far Eastern Economic Review,* August 2.

Hachigan, Nina. 2001. "China's Cyber Strategy." *Foreign Affairs* 80(2):118–33.

Haggard, Stephen. 2000. *The Political Economy of the Asian Financial Crisis.* Washington, D.C.: Institute for International Economics.

Hall, Peter. 2000. "Creative Cities and Economic Development." *Urban Studies* 37(4):639–49.

Hanson, Gordon H., and Robert C. Feenstra. 2001. "Intermediaries in Entrepot Trade: Hong Kong Re-exports of Chinese Goods." Working Paper 8088. National Bureau of Economic Research, Cambridge, Mass.

Hanushek, Eric A., and Dennis P. Kimko. 2000. "Schooling, Labor Force Quality, and the Growth of Nations." *American Economic Review* 90(5):1184–1206.

Hardin, A., and L. Holmes. 1997. "Services Trade and Direct Foreign Investment." Staff Research Paper. Industry Commission, Canberra.

Harhoff, Dietmar. 1999. "Firm Formation and Regional Spillovers." *Economics of Innovation and New Technology* 8:27–55.

Harwit, Eric, and Duncan Clark. 2001. "Shaping the Internet in China: Evolution of Political Control over Network Infrastructure and Content." *Asian Survey* 41(3):377–408.

Hellmann, Thomas. 2000. "Venture Capitalists: The Coaches of Silicon Valley." Stanford University, Department of Economics, Stanford, Calif. Processed.

Henderson, J. Vernon. 1999. "Marshall's Scale Economies." Working Paper 7358. National Bureau of Economic Research, Cambridge, Mass.

Henderson, J. Vernon, Zmarak Shalizi, and Anthony J. Venables. 2000. "Geography and Development." World Bank, Washington, D.C. Processed.

Hill, Hall, and Prema-Chandra Athukorala. 1998. "Foreign Investment in East Asia: A Survey." *Asian-Pacific Economic Literature* 12(2):23–50.

"Hitachi Is Now a Big Thorn in EMC's Side." 2001. *Red Herring,* September 15.

Hobday, Michael. 1995. *Innovation in East Asia: The Challenge to Japan.* Aldershot, Hants, U.K.: Edward Elgar.

Hoekman, Bernard. 2000. "The Next Round of Service Negotiations: Identifying Priorities and Options." *Federal Reserve Bank of St. Louis Review* 82(4):31–37.

Hoekman, Bernard, and Michel M. Kostecki. 2001. *The Political Economy of the World Trading System: The WTO and Beyond.* New York: Oxford University Press.

Holler, Manfred J. 1999. "On the Regulation of Telecommunications Markets." Working Paper 163. World Institute for Development Economics Research, United Nations University, Helsinki, Finland.

"How Data Mining Makes Businesses Smarter." 2001. *Red Herring*, October 1.

"How E-biz Rose, Fell, and Will Rise Anew." 2002. *Business Week*, May 13.

"How PC Makers Are Re-programming Themselves." 2000. *Business Week*, October 30.

"How Seagate Got Its Groove Back." 2002. *Business Week*, June 24.

"How to Produce Better Math and Science Teachers." 2000. *Science*, September 1.

Howe, Michael J. A. 1999. *Genius Explained.* Cambridge, U.K.: Cambridge University Press.

Hsing, You-Tien. 1999. "Trading Companies in Taiwan's Fashion Shoe Networks." *Journal of International Economics* 48(1):101–20.

Hummels, David. 2001. "Time as a Trade Barrier." Purdue University, Department of Economics, West Lafayette, Ind. Processed.

Humphrey, John, and Hubert Schmitz. 2000. "Governance and Upgrading: Linking Industrial Cluster and Global Value Chain Research." Brighton, Sussex, U.K.: Institute of Development Studies.

Hung, Shih-Chang. 2000. "Institutions and Systems of Innovation: An Empirical Analysis of Taiwan's Personal Computer Competitiveness." *Technology in Society* 22(2):175–87.

Hussain, Qaizar, and Clas Wihlborg. 1999. "Corporate Insolvency Procedures and Bank Behavior: A Study of Selected Asian Economies." Working Paper 135. International Monetary Fund, Washington, D.C.

Hutchcroft, Paul D. 1999. *Booty Capitalism.* Ithaca, N.Y.: Cornell University Press.

"A Hyper Market." 2001. *Economist*, April 7.

Ianchovichina, Elena, Will Martin, and Emiko Fukase. 2000. "Assessing the Implications of Merchandise Trade Liberalization in China's Accession to WTO." Available on http://www1.worldbank.org/wbiep/trade/China_WTO.html.

"IBM Joins Push to Construct Next-Generation Internet." 2001. *Financial Times*, August 2.

"Is the University-Industrial Complex Out of Control?" 2001. *Nature*, January 11.

Ito, Takatoshi. 2001. "Growth, Crisis, and the Future of Economic Recovery in East Asia." In Joseph E. Stiglitz and Shahid Yusuf, eds., *Rethinking the East Asian Miracle.* New York: Oxford University Press.

Ito, Takatoshi, and Anne O. Krueger, eds. 1999. *The Role of Foreign Direct Investment in East Asian Economic Development.* National Bureau of Economic Research. Chicago: University of Chicago Press.

———, eds. 2000. *Services Trade in the Asia-Pacific Region: East Asia Seminar on Economics 11.* Chicago: University of Chicago Press.

ITU (International Telecommunications Union). 2000. *Asia-Pacific Telecommunications Indicators 2000*. Geneva.

———. 2001a. "Mobile on the Eve of 3G." *ITU Telecommunications Indicators Update* (April–June).

———. 2001b. "Numbering Cyberspace." *ITU Telecommunications Indicators Update* (January–March).

———. 2002. "Draft Report on the Telecommunications Environment Analysis." Document: SUBTDAG-7/7-E. Seventh meeting of the Telecommunications Development Advisory Subgroup Dealing with Private Sector Issues, January 14–15, Geneva.

Iversen, Torben, and Thomas R. Cusack. 2000. "The Causes of Welfare State Expansion: Deindustrialization or Globalization." *World Politics* 52(3):313–49.

Jaffee, Adam B. 1989. "Real Effects of Academic Research." *American Economic Review* 79(5):957–70.

Jaffee, Adam B., Manuel Trajtenberg, and Rebecca Henderson. 1993. "Geographic Localization of Knowledge Spillovers as Evidenced by Patent Citations." *Quarterly Journal of Economics* 108(3):577–98.

"Japan Acts to Speed Technology Transfer from Universities." 1999. *Nature*, September 2.

"Japan Ponders Free Trade Alliances." 2001. *Financial Times*, June 6.

"Japan/South Korea: Regional Free-Traders?" 2000. *Oxford Analytica*, December 29.

Jeremy, David J. 1981. *Transatlantic Industrial Revolution: The Diffusion of Textile Technologies between Britain and America, 1790–1830s*. Oxford: Blackwell.

JETRO (Japan External Trade Organization). 2001. "Accelerated Corporate Realignment through Mergers and Acquisitions." In *JETRO White Paper on Foreign Direct Investment, 2001*.

Jew, Bernadette, Rob Nicholls, and Andrew Floro. 2000. "New Issues for Internet Interconnection." *Telecommunications Online* (February). Available on www.telecom magazine.com.

Jorgenson, Dale W., and Kevin J. Stiroh. 2000. "Raising the Speed Limit: U.S. Economic Growth in the Information Age." *Brookings Papers on Economic Activity* 0(1):125–211.

Joskow, Paul L. 1998. "Regulatory Priorities for Reforming Infrastructure Sectors in Developing Countries." World Bank, Washington, D.C. Processed.

Jung, H. S. 2000. "Program on Information Resources Policy." Harvard University, Center for Information Policy Research, Cambridge, Mass.

Kalirajan, K., G. McGuire, D. Nguyen-Hong, and M. Schuele. 2001. "The Price Impact of Restrictions on Banking Services." In C. Findlay and T. Warren, eds., *Impediments to Trade in Services: Measurements and Policy Implications*. Sydney: Routledge.

Kamarck, Elaine Ciulla, and Joseph S. Nye, Jr., eds. 2002. *Governance.com: Democracy in the Information Age*. Washington, D.C.: The Brookings Institution.

Kaminsky, Graciela, and Carmen Reinhart. 1999. "The Twin Crises: The Causes of Banking and Balance of Payments Problems." *American Economic Review* 89(3): 473–500.

Kato, Takao. 2001. "The End of 'Lifetime Employment' in Japan? Evidence from National Surveys and Field Research." *Journal of Japanese and International Economics* 5(4):489–514.

Kaufmann, Daniel, Aart Kraay, and Pablo Zoido-Lobaton. 1999. "Governance Matters." Policy Research Working Paper 2196. World Bank, Washington, D.C.

Kay, John. 2001. "What Became of the New Economy?" *National Institute Economic Review* 177:56–69.

Keefer, Philip. 2001. "When Do Special Interests Run Rampant? Disentangling the Role of Elections, Incomplete Information, and Checks and Balances in Banking Crises." World Bank, Washington, D.C. Processed.

Kende, Michael. 2000. "The Digital Handshake: Connecting Internet Backbones." OPP Working Paper 32. Federal Communications Commission, Washington, D.C.

Kenney, Martin, and Richard Florida. 2000. *Venture Capital in Silicon Valley: Fueling New Firm Formation.* Stanford, Calif.: Stanford University Press.

———. 2001. "Venture Capital." In *International Encyclopedia of the Social and Behavioral Sciences.* Oxford and New York: Pergamon Press.

Kiley, Michael T. 1999. "Computers and Growth with Costs Adjustment: Will the Future Look Like the Past?" Finance and Economics Discussion Series 1999-36. Federal Reserve Board, Washington, D.C.

Kim, Euysung. 2000. "Trade Liberalization and Productivity Growth in Korean Manufacturing Industries: Price Protection, Market Power, and Scale Efficiency." *Journal of Development Economics* 62:55–83.

Kim, Linsu. 1997. "The Dynamics of Samsung's Technological Learning in Semiconductors." *California Management Review* 39(3):86–100.

———. 2000. "The Dynamics of Public Policy, Corporate Strategy, and Technological Learning: Lessons from the Korea Experience." Korea University, College of Business Administration, Seoul.

Kirby, Julia. 2001. "Reinvention with Respect." *Harvard Business Review* (November):117–23.

Konstadakopulos, Dimitrios. 2000. "Learning Behavior and Cooperation of Small High Technology Firms in the ASEAN Region." *ASEAN Economic Bulletin* 17(1): 48–59.

Kotler, Philip, Michael Alan Hamlin, Irving Rein, and Donald H. Haider. 2002. *Marketing Asian Places.* Singapore: John Wiley.

Kreinin, Mordechai E., Shigeyuki Abe, and Michael G. Plummer. 1999. "Motives for Japanese FDI: Survey, Analysis, and Implications in Light of the Asian Crisis." *Journal of Asian Economics* 10(3):385–94.

Krueger, Anne O., and Jung Ro Yoo. 2001. "Chaebol Capitalism and the Currency-Financial Crisis in Korea." Paper presented at the National Bureau of Economic Research Conference, Cambridge, Mass.

Kueh, Yak-Yeow. 2001. "The Greater China Growth Triangle in the Asian Financial Crisis." In Shahid Yusuf, Simon Evenett, and Weiping Wu, eds., *Facets of Globalization: International and Local Dimensions of Development.* Washington, D.C.: World Bank.

Lakshmanian, T. R. 2001. "Rotterdam: A Strategic Hub in the Global Trade-Transport Chain." In T. R. Lakshmanian, Uma Subramanian, William R. Anderson, and Frannie A. Leautier, eds., *Integration of Transport and Trade Facilitation*. Washington, D.C.: World Bank.

Lan, Ping. 1996. "Role of IJVs in Transferring Technology to China." In Roger Baran, Yigang Pan, and Erdener Kaynak, eds., *International Joint Ventures in East Asia*. New York: International Business Press.

Landefeld, Steven J., and Barbara M. Fraumeni. 2001. "Measuring the New Economy." *Survey of Current Business* 81(3):23–39.

Landes, David S. 1980. "The Creation of Knowledge and Technique: Today's Task and Yesterday's Experience." *Daedalus* 109:111.

———. 1998. "The Wealth and Poverty of Nations." New York: W. W. Norton.

La Porta, Rafael, Florencio Lopez-de-Silanes, and Andrei Schleifer. 2000. "Government Ownership of Banks." Working Paper 7622. National Bureau of Economic Research, Cambridge, Mass.

La Porta, Rafael, Florencio Lopez-de-Silanes, Andrei Schleifer, and Robert Vishny. 1998. "Law and Finance." *Journal of Political Economy* 106(6):1113–55.

———. 1999. "Investor Protection: Origins, Consequences, Reform." Working Paper 7428. National Bureau of Economic Research, Cambridge, Mass.

Lardy, Nicholas R. 1999. "The Challenge of Bank Restructuring in China." In Bank for International Settlements, ed., *Strengthening the Banking System in China: Issues and Experience*. Basel.

———. 2001. "Foreign Financial Firms in Asia." Washington, D.C.: The Brookings Institution.

———. 2002. *Integrating China into the Global Economy*. Washington, D.C.: The Brookings Institution.

Lau, Sim Yee, and Yoichiro J. Higuchi. 1999. "Technology Transfer in East Asia Six: A Multivariate Analytical Inquiry." *Asia-Pacific Development Journal* 6(1):19–34.

Lawrence, Robert Z., and David E. Weinstein. 2001. "Trade and Growth: Import Led or Export Led? Evidence from Japan and Korea." In Joseph E. Stiglitz and Shahid Yusuf, eds., *Rethinking the East Asian Miracle*. New York: Oxford University Press.

Leamer, Edward E., and Michael Storper. 2001. "The Economic Geography of the Internet Age." Working Paper 8450. National Bureau of Economic Research, Cambridge, Mass.

Lecuyer, Christophe. 1998. "Academic Science and Technology in the Service Sector of Industry: MIT Creates a 'Permeable' Engineering School." *AEA Papers and Proceedings* 88(2):28–33.

Lee, Jisoon. 2001. "Education Policy in the Republic of Korea." Departmental Working Paper 22648. World Bank Institute, Washington, D.C.

Lee, Jong-Wha. 1995. "Capital Goods Imports and Long-Run Growth." *Journal of Development Economics* 48(1):91–110.

Levine, Ross. 1997. "Financial Development and Economic Growth: Views and Agenda." *Journal of Economic Literature* 35(2):688–726.

Levine, Ross, and Sara Zervos. 1998. "Stock Markets, Banks, and Economic Growth." *American Economic Review* 88(3):537–54.

Levine, Ross, Norman Loayza, and Thorsten Beck. 2000. "Financial Intermediation and Growth: Causality and Causes." *Journal of Monetary Economics* 46(1):31–77.

Li, Wei, Christine Zhen-Wei Qiang, and Lixin Colin Xu. 2000. "The Political Economy of Telecommunications Reforms." World Bank, Washington, D.C. Processed.

Lim, Youngil. 1999. *Technology and Productivity*. Cambridge, Mass.: MIT Press.

Lin, Justin Yifu, and Yang Yao. 2001. "Chinese Rural Industrialization in the Context of the East Asian Miracle." In Joseph E. Stiglitz and Shahid Yusuf, eds., *Rethinking the East Asian Miracle*. New York: Oxford University Press.

Lindblad, J. Thomas. 2000. "Korean Investment in Indonesia: Survey and Appraisal." *Bulletin of Indonesian Economic Studies* 36(1):167–84.

Lindert, Peter H., and Jeffrey G. Williamson. 2001. "Does Globalization Make the World More Unequal?" Working Paper 8228. National Bureau of Economic Research, Cambridge, Mass.

Lipsey, Robert E., and Fredrik Sjöholm. 2001. "Foreign Direct Investment and Wages in Indonesian Manufacturing." Working Paper W8299. National Bureau of Economic Research, Cambridge, Mass.

Litan, Robert E. 2001. "Law and Policy in the Age of the Internet." Working Paper 01-04. American Economics Institute and Brookings Joint Center on Regulatory Policy, Washington, D.C.

Liu, Tung, and Kui-Wai Li. 2001. "Impact of Liberalization of Financial Resources in China's Economic Growth: Evidence from Provinces." *Journal of Asian Economics* 12(2):245–62.

Lloyd, P. J., and Donald MacLaren. 2000. "Openness and Growth in East Asia after the Asian Crisis." *Journal of Asian Economics* 11(1):89–105.

Lloyd, Peter J., and Associates. 2001. "Harmonizing Competition Policies in the East Asian Region." World Bank, Washington, D.C. Processed.

"A Long March." 2001. *Economist*, July 14.

Lu, Ding. 2000. "China's Telecommunications Infrastructure: On Its Own Way." In Takatoshi Ito and Anne Krueger, eds., *Deregulation and Interdependence in the Asian Pacific Region*. Chicago: University of Chicago Press.

Lucking-Reiley, Daniel, and Daniel Spulber. 2001. "Business-to-Business Electronic Commerce." *Journal of Economic Perspectives* 15(1):55–68.

Lucky, Robert. 2000. "The Quickening of Science Communication." *Science* 289(July): 14.

Maddison, Angus. 2001. *The World Economy: A Millennial Perspective*. Paris: Organisation for Economic Co-operation and Development.

Magretta, Joan. 1998. "Fast, Global, and Entrepreneurial: Supply Chain Management, Hong Kong Style." *Harvard Business Review* (September/October):103–14.

Mako, William P. 2001. "Corporate Restructuring Strategies: Recent Lessons." Paper presented at the Asian Regional Seminar on Financial Reform and Stability, March 29, Hyderabad, India.

Mansfield, Edwin, and Jeoug-Yeon Lee. 1996. "The Modern University: Contributor to Industrial Innovation and Recipient of Industrial Support." *Research Policy* 25:1047–58.

Markusen, Ann. 1996. "Sticky Places in Slippery Space: A Typology of Industrial Districts." *Economic Geography* 72(2):293–314.

Markusen, Ann, Karen Chapple, Greg Schrock, Daisaku Yamamoto, and Pingkang Yu. 2001. "High-Tech and I-Tech: How Metros Rank and Specialize." University of Minnesota, Hubert H. Humphrey Institute of Public Affairs, Minneapolis.

Mason, Andrew, and Naohiro Ogawa. 2001. "Population, Labor Force, Saving, and Japan's Future." In Magnus Blomström, Byron Gangnes, and Sumner LaCroix, eds., *Japan's New Economy: Continuity and Change in the Twenty-First Century.* New York: Oxford University Press.

Mathews, John A. 1997. "A Silicon Valley of the East: Creating Taiwan's Semiconductor Industry." *California Management Review* 39(4).

———. 1999. " A Silicon Island of the East: Creating a Semiconductor Industry in Singapore." *California Management Review* 41(2):55–78.

Mathews, John A., and Dong-Sung Cho. 2000. *Tiger Technology.* Cambridge, U.K.: Cambridge University Press.

Mattoo, Aaditya. 2001. "Shaping Future GATS Rules for Trade in Services." Policy Research Working Paper 2596. World Bank, Washington, D.C.

Mattoo, Aaditya, Randeep Rathindran, and Arvind Subramanian. 2001. "Measuring Services Trade Liberalization and Its Impact on Economic Growth: An Illustration." Working Paper 2655. World Bank, Washington, D.C.

Mauro, Paolo. 1995. "Corruption and Growth." *Quarterly Journal of Economics* 110(3):681–713.

Mazumdar, Joy. 2001. "Imported Machinery and Growth in LDCs." *Journal of Development Economics* 65(1):209–24.

McKendrik, David G., Richard F. Doner, and Stephen Haggard. 2000. *From Silicon Valley to Singapore: Location and Competitive Advantage in the Hard Disk Drive Industry.* Stanford, Calif.: Stanford University Press.

McKinsey and Company. 2001. *Why the Japanese Economy Is Not Growing: Micro Barriers to Productivity Growth.* Washington, D.C.: McKinsey Global Institute.

McLaren, John. 2000. "Globalization and Vertical Structure." *American Economic Review* 90(5):1239–54.

Meinel, Carolyn. 2001. "Code Red for the Web." *Scientific American* (October): 42–51.

Meyer, John R., and Thomas R. Menzies. 2000. "The Continuing Vigil: Maintaining Competition in Deregulated Airline Markets." *Journal of Transport Economics and Policy* 34(1):1–20.

Miller, Stephen M., and Mukti Upadhyay. 2000. "The Effects of Openness, Trade Orientation, and Human Capital on Total Factor Productivity." *Journal of Development Economics* 63:399–423.

"A Miracle Revised." 2001. *Financial Times,* August 10.

Mishkin, Frederic S. 1996. "Bank Consolidation: A Central Banker's Perspective." Working Paper 5489. National Bureau of Economic Research, Cambridge, Mass.

———. 2000. "Financial Policies and the Prevention of Financial Crises in Emerging Market Countries." Paper presented at the National Bureau of Economic Research Conference, October.

Mishkin, Frederic S., and Philip E. Strahan. 1999. "What Will Technology Do to Financial Structure?" Working Paper 6892. National Bureau of Economic Research, Cambridge, Mass.

Mody, Ashoka, and Shoko Negishi. 2001. "Cross-Border Mergers and Acquisitions in East Asia: Trends and Implications." *Finance and Development* 38(1):6–9.

Mody, Ashoka, Susmita Dasgupta, and Sarbajit Sinha. 1999. "Japanese Multinationals in Asia: Drivers and Attractors." *Oxford Development Studies* 27(2):149–64.

Moran, Theodore H. 1998. *Foreign Direct Investment and Development: The New Policy Agenda for Developing Countries and Economies in Transition.* Available on http://www.iie.com/publications/publication.cfm?pub_id=53.

———. 2001. *Parental Supervision: The New Paradigm for Foreign Direct Investment and Development.* Washington, D.C.: Institute for International Economics.

National Science Foundation. 2000. *Science and Engineering Indicators 2000.* Washington, D.C.

Naughton, John. 2000. *A Brief History of the Future: From Radio Days to Internet Years in a Lifetime.* Overlook, N.Y.: Overlook Press.

"A New Front in the Free Trade Wars." 2002. *Business Week*, June 3.

"New Rules, New Tools." 2001. *Smart Business*, April.

"New Zealand: Singapore Trade Deal." 2000. *Oxford Analytica*, November 14.

Nickell, Stephen J. 1996. "Competition and Corporate Performance." *Journal of Political Economy* 105(4):724–46.

Noll, Roger. 1999. "Telecommunications Reform in Developing Countries." Working Paper 99-10. American Economics Institute and Brookings Joint Center on Regulatory Studies, Washington, D.C.

Noorbakhsh, Farhad, Alberto Paloni, and Ali Youssef. 2001. "Human Capital and FDI Inflows to Developing Countries: New Empirical Evidence." *World Development* 29(9):1593–1610.

Nordhaus, William D. 2001. "Productivity Growth and the New Economy." Working Paper 8096. National Bureau of Economic Research, Cambridge, Mass.

OECD (Organisation for Economic Co-operation and Development). 1999. *The Role of Telecommunications and Information: Infrastructures in Advancing Electronic Commerce.* Paris.

———. 2000. "A New Economy? The Changing Role of Innovation and Information Technology in Growth." Paris.

———. 2001a. "Innovative Networks: Cooperation in National Innovation Systems." Paris.

———. 2001b. "Insolvency Systems in Asia." Paris.

Ohmae, Kenichi. 1990. *The Borderless World.* New York: HarperCollins.

Okamoto, Yumiko, and Fredrik Sjöholm. 1999. "Protection and the Dynamics of Productivity Growth: The Case of Automotive Industries in Indonesia." *Economics and Finance* 324.

O'Keefe, Brian. 2001. "Closing in on Cancer." *Fortune*, September 17.

Oliner, Steve, and Daniel J. Sichel. 2000. "The Resurgence of Growth in the Late 1990s: Is Information Technology the Story?" Finance and Economics Discussion Series 2000-20. Federal Reserve Board, Washington, D.C.

"One to Watch." 2001. *Red Herring*, April 1.

"Online Finance: The Virtual Threat." 2000. *Economist*, May 20.

Overholt, William H. 1999. "Thailand's Financial and Political Systems: Crisis and Rejuvenation." *Asian Survey* 39(November–December):1009–35.

Ozawa, Terutomo. 2001. "The 'Hidden' Side of the 'Flying-Geese' Catch-Up Model: Japan's Dirigiste Institutional Setup and a Deepening Financial Morass." *Journal of Asian Economics* 12(4):471–91.

Pacific Economic Cooperation Council. 1999. "Assessing APEC Individual Action Plans and Their Contribution to APEC's Goals." Trade Policy Forum, Manila.

Pack, Howard. 2001."Technological Change and Growth in East Asia: Macro Versus Micro Perspectives." In Joseph E. Stiglitz and Shahid Yusuf, eds., *Rethinking the East Asian Miracle.* New York: Oxford University Press.

Palim, Mark R. A. 1998. "The Worldwide Growth of Competition Law: An Empirical Analysis." *Antitrust Bulletin* 34(1):105–45.

Panagariya, Arvind. 1999. "Preferential Trade Liberalization: The Traditional Theory and New Developments." University of Maryland, Department of Economics, College Park, Md. Processed.

———. 2001. "The Indian Diaspora in the United States." *Economic Times*, May 23.

"A Panda Breaks the Formation." 2001. *Economist*, August 25.

Parente, Stephen L., and Edward C. Prescott. 2000. *Barriers to Riches.* Cambridge, Mass.: MIT Press.

Park, Yung Chul, and Jong-Wha Lee. 2001. "Recovery and Sustainability in East Asia." Working Paper 8373. National Bureau of Economic Research, Cambridge, Mass.

Parker, Stephen, and Sungho Lee. 2001. "Did East-Asian Developing Economies Lose Export Competitiveness in the Pre-Crisis 1990s? Assessing East Asian Export Performance from 1980 to 1996." Asian Development Bank Institute, Tokyo. Processed.

Pederson, P. O. 2001. "Freight Transport under Globalization and Its Impact on Africa." *Journal of Transport Geography* 9(2):85–100.

Peking University, Tsinghua University, and University of South Carolina. 2000. *The Economic Impact of the Coca-Cola System on China.*

Perkins, Dwight H. 2001. "Industrial and Financial Policy in China and Vietnam: A New Model or a Replay of the East Asian Experience?" In Joseph E. Stiglitz and Shahid Yusuf, eds., *Rethinking the East Asian Miracle.* New York: Oxford University Press.

Persaud, Avinash. 2001. "The Knowledge Gap." *Foreign Affairs* 80(2):107–17.

Pohjola, Matti. 2000. "Information Technology and Economic Growth: Introduction and Conclusions." In Matti Pohjola, ed., *Information Technology, Productivity, and Economic Growth: International Evidence and Implications for Economic Development.* Helsinki: World Institute for Development Economics Institute.

Porter, Michael E. 1998. "Clusters and the New Economics of Competition." *Harvard Business Review* 76(6).

———. 2001. "Strategy and the Internet." *Harvard Business Review* (March).

Porter, Michael E., Hirotaka Takeuchi, and Mariko Sakakibara. 2000. *Can Japan Compete?* London: Macmillan.

Posen, Adam S. 2001. "Japan 2001—Decisive Action or Financial Panic." International Economics Policy Briefs PB01-4. Institute for International Economics, Washington, D.C.

"Praying for Rule of Law." 2002. *Far Eastern Economic Review*, June 27.

Pritchett, Lant. 2001. "Where Has All the Education Gone?" *World Bank Economic Review* 15(3):367–92.

"Problematic Newcomers." 2001. *Oxford Analytica*, September 20.

"Pulling Away." 2000. *Far Eastern Economic Review*, February 10.

"Quantum Leap." 2002. *Far Eastern Economic Review*, July 14.

Quintyn, Marc, and Michael W. Taylor. 2002. "Regulatory and Supervisory Independence and Financial Stability." Working Paper WP/02/46. International Monetary Fund, Washington, D.C.

Rauch, James E. 1999a. "Business and Social Networks in International Trade." University of California, Department of Economics, San Diego. Processed.

———. 1999b. "Introduction to Symposium on 'Business and Social Networks in International Trade.'" *Journal of International Economics* 48(1):3–6.

Rauch, James E., and Vitor Trindade. 2002. "Ethnic Chinese Networks in International Trade." *Review of Economics and Statistics* 84(1):116–30.

Rauch, Jonathan. 2001. "The New Old Economy: Oil, Computers, and the Reinvention of the Earth." *Atlantic Monthly*, January.

"The Real Trouble." 2001. *Economist*, July 28.

Reynolds, Stephen E., Somchai Ratanakomut, and James Gander. 2000. "Bank Financial Structure in Pre-Crisis East and Southeast Asia." *Journal of Asian Economics* 11(3):319–31.

Robertson, Peter E. 2000. "Diminished Returns? Growth and Investment in East Asia." *Economic Record* 76(235):343–53.

Rodrigo, Chris G. 2001. *Technology, Economic Growth and Crises in East Asia.* Aldershot, Hants, U.K.: Edward Elgar.

Rodriguez, Francisco, and Dani Rodrik. 1999. "Trade Policy and Economic Growth: A Skeptic's Guide to Cross-National Evidence." Working Paper 7081. National Bureau of Economic Research, Cambridge, Mass.

Rodriguez-Pose, Andres. 1999. "Innovation Prone and Innovation Averse Societies: Economic Performance in Europe." *Growth and Change* 30(1):75–105.

Rodrik, Dani. 1998. "Why Do More Open Economies Have Larger Governments?" *Journal of Political Economy* 106(5):997–1032.

———. 1999. "The New Global Economy and Developing Countries: Making Openness Work." Policy Essay 24. Overseas Development Council, Washington, D.C.

———. 2000. "Institutions for High-Quality Growth: What They Are and How to Acquire Them." Working Paper 7540. National Bureau of Economic Research, Cambridge, Mass.

Romer, Paul M. 2000. "Should the Government Subsidize Supply or Demand in the Market for Scientists and Engineers?" Working Paper 7723. National Bureau of Economic Research, Cambridge, Mass.

Rozman, Gilbert. 2002. "Can Confucianism Survive?" *Pacific Affairs* 75(1):11–37.

Sakakibara, Eisuke, and Sharon Yamakawa. 2002. "Regional Integration in East Asia: Challenges and Opportunities." Background paper for *World Bank East Asia Study*. World Bank, Washington, D.C.

Saxenian, Annalee, and Jinn-Yuh Hsu. 2000. "The Silicon Valley-Hsinchu Connection: Technical Communities and Industrial Upgrading." University of California, Department of City and Regional Planning, Berkeley.

Scherer, F. M. 1999. "Retail Distribution Channel Barriers to International Trade." *Antitrust Law Journal* 67(1):77–112.

"Scientists with Business Flair in Demand." 1998. *Science*, August 6.

Scollay, Robert, and John Gilbert. 2000. *New Sub-Regional Trading Arrangements in the Asia Pacific*. Institute for International Economics, Washington, D.C. Processed.

———. 2001. "New Regional Trading Arrangements in the Asia Pacific?" Policy Analyses in International Economics 63. Institute for International Economics, Washington, D.C.

Scott, Allen J., ed. 2001. *Global City Regions: Trends, Theory, Policy*. New York: Oxford University Press.

Shapiro, Carl, and Hal Varian. 1999. *Information Rules: A Strategic Guide to the Network Economy*. Boston: Harvard Business School Press.

Shaw, Stephen M., and Feng Wang. 2002. "Moving Goods in China." *The McKinsey Quarterly* (2). Available on www.mckinseyquarterly.com.

Shin, Dong-Ho. 2001. "An Alternative Approach to Developing Science Parks: A Case Study from Korea." *Papers in Regional Science* 80(1):103–11.

Sicular, Terry. 1998. "Capital Flight and Foreign Investment: Two Tales from China and Russia." *World Economy* 21:589–602.

"Singapore: Internet Control." 2001. *Oxford Analytica*, September 5.

Sleuwaegen, Leo. 1998. *Cross-Border Mergers and EC Competition Policy*. Oxford: Blackwell.

"South Korea Upwardly Mobile in Telecoms." 2002. *Financial Times*, August 5.

"Southeast Asia: Cyber Threats." 2001. *Oxford Analytica*, April 3.

"Southeast Asia Steps up Removal of Trade Barriers." 2002. *Financial Times*, July 8.

"Southeast Asia: Sullied Central Banks." 2002. *Oxford Analytica*, April 30.

Spear, Steven, and H. Kent Brown. 1999. "Decoding the DNA of the Toyota Production System." *Harvard Business Review* 77(5):96–106.

"Spending Spree." 2002. *Far Eastern Economic Review*, June 13.

Spiegel, Mark M. 2001. "Financial Development and Growth: Are the APEC Nations Unique?" Working Paper PB01-04. Pacific Basin Working Paper Series. Federal Reserve Bank of San Francisco, San Francisco.

"Storage Titans Would Rather Fight than Connect." 2001. *Red Herring*, September 15.

"Survey of Cambridge." 2001. *Financial Times*, September 11.

Symeonidis, George. 2000. "Price Competition and Market Structure: The Impact of Cartel Policy on Concentration in the UK." *Journal of Industrial Economics* 48 (1):1–26.

"Taiwan: Banking Burdens." 2000. *Oxford Analytica*, November 28.

Tanzi, Vito. 2001. "Globalization and the Work of Fiscal Termites." *Finance and Development* 38(1):34–37.

Taylor, Timothy. 2001. "Thinking about a New Economy." *The Public Interest*: 3–29.

Teixeira, Diogo B. 2000. "E-Commerce: What Role Will Banks Play in the Future?" *Payment Systems Worldwide* (Winter).

"The Telecos Work Part II." 2001. *Financial Times*, September 6.

Temple, Jonathan. 1999. "The New Growth Evidence." *Journal of Economic Literature* 37(1):112–56.

———. 2001. "Growth Effects of Education and Social Capital in the OECD Countries." Discussion Paper 2875. Center for Economic Policy Research, Washington, D.C.

"Thailand, Bank Consolidation." 2002. *Oxford Analytica*, April 25.

"3G by Any Other Name." 2002. *Economist*, January 12.

Thun, Eric. 2000. "Growing Up and Moving Out: Globalization in the Taiwanese Textile/Apparel and Automotive Sectors." Industrial Performance Center Working Paper 00-007. Massachusetts Institute of Technology, Cambridge, Mass.

Thurbon, Elizabeth. 2001. "Two Paths to Financial Liberalization: South Korea and Taiwan." *Pacific Review* 14(2):241–67.

Trajtenberg, Manuel. 1999. "Innovation in Israel 1968–97: A Comparative Analysis Using Patent Data." Working Paper 7022. National Bureau of Economic Research, Cambridge, Mass.

"The Truth about Internet Fraud." 2001. *Smart Business*, April.

UNCTAD (United Nations Conference on Trade and Development). 2000. *World Investment Report 2000.* Geneva.

———. 2001. *World Investment Report 2001.* Geneva.

UNESCO (United Nations Educational, Cultural, and Scientific Organization). 1999. *UNESCO Statistical Yearbook, 1999.* Paris.

———. 2000. *World Education Report 2000: The Right to Education.* Paris.

"United States: Productivity Performance." 2001. *Oxford Analytica*, May 18.

"University Industry Cooperation in High Technology." 2000. *Japan Inc.*, July.

Urata, Shujiro. 2001. "Emergence of an FDI-Trade Nexus and Economic Growth in East Asia." In Joseph E. Stiglitz and Shahid Yusuf, eds., *Rethinking the East Asian Miracle*. New York: Oxford University Press.

Urata, Shujiro, and Hiroki Kawai. 2000. "The Determinants of the Location of Foreign Direct Investment by Japanese Small and Medium-Sized Enterprises." *Small Business Economics* 15(2):79–103.

———. 2001. "Technological Progress by Small and Medium Firms in Japan." In Farrukh Iqbal and Shujiro Urata, eds., *Small Firm Dynamism in East Asia: Evolution and Determinants*. Washington, D.C.: World Bank Institute.

Urata, Shujiro, and Kozo Kiyota. 2000. "Service Trade in East Asia." In Ito Takatoshi and Anne Krueger, eds., *Services Trade in the Asia-Pacific Region*. Chicago: University of Chicago Press.

"Valley of the Deals." 1998. *Far Eastern Economic Review*, November.

van Ark, Bart. 2002. "Measuring the New Economy: An International Comparative Perspective." *The Review of Income and Wealth* 48(1):1–14.

van den Berg, Leo, Erik Braun, and Willem van Winden. 2001. "Growth Clusters in European Cities: An Integral Approach." *Urban Studies* 38(1):185–205.

Vatter, Harold G., and John F. Walker. 2001. "Did the 1990's Inaugurate a New Economy?" *Challenge* 44(1):90–116.

Viscusi, W. Kip, John Mitcham Vernon, and Joseph Emmet Harrington. 2000. *Economics of Regulation and Antitrust*, 3rd ed. Cambridge, Mass.: MIT Press.

Wallsten, Scott J. 1999. "Competition, Privatization, and Regulation in Telecommunications Markets in Developing Countries: An Econometric Analysis of Reforms in Africa and Latin America." World Bank, Washington, D.C. Processed.

"Wal-Mart Develops a Taste for Japan." 2002. *Financial Times*, May 3.

Warren, T. 2001. "The Application of the Frequency Approach to Trade in Telecommunication Services." In C. Findlay and T. Warren, eds., *Impediments to Trade in Services: Measurements and Policy Implications*. Sydney: Routledge.

Wei, Shang-Jin. 2000. "National Openness and Good Government." Working Paper 7765. National Bureau of Economic Research, Cambridge, Mass.

Wells, Louis T., Jr. 1993. "Mobile Exporters: New Foreign Investors in East Asia." In Kenneth A. Froot, ed., *Foreign Direct Investment*. National Bureau of Economic Research Project Report. Chicago: University of Chicago Press.

Wheeler, James O., Yoko Aoyama, and Barney Wolf, eds. 2000. *Cities in the Telecommunications Age: The Fracturing of Geographies*. New York: Routledge.

Whelan, Karl. 2000. "Computers, Obsolescence, and Productivity." Finance and Economics Discussion Series 2000-6. Federal Reserve Board, Washington, D.C.

White, Lawrence J. 2001. "Financial Regulation and Economic Development: An International Perspective." In Shahid Yusuf, Simon Evenett, and Weiping Wu, eds., *Facets of Globalization: International and Local Dimensions of Development*. Washington, D.C.: World Bank.

Willcocks, Leslie P., and Robert Plants. 2001. "Pathways to E-Business Leadership: Getting from Bricks to Clicks" *MIT Sloan Management Review* 42(3):50–59.

Wilson, John Sullivan. 1998. "Telecommunications Liberalization: The Goods and Services Connection." World Bank, Washington, D.C. Processed.

Winters, Alan. 1997. "What Can European Experience Teach Developing Countries about Integration?" *World Economy* 20(7):889–912.

———. 1999. "Regionalism versus Multilateralism." In Richard Baldwin, Daniel Cohen, Andre Sapir, and Anthony Venables, eds., *Market Integration, Regionalism, and the Global Economy*, Cambridge, U.K.: Center for Economic Policy Research.

Wirtz, Jochen. 2000. "Growth of the Service Sector in Asia." *Singapore Management Review* 22(2):1–16.

Wiseman, Alan E. 2000. *The Internet Economy: Access, Taxes, and Market Structure.* Washington, D.C.: Brookings Institution Press.

Woo-Cumings, Meredith. 2001. "Miracle as Prologue: The State and the Reform of the Corporate Sector in Korea." In Joseph E. Stiglitz and Shahid Yusuf, eds., *Rethinking the East Asian Miracle.* New York: Oxford University Press.

World Bank. 1999. *World Development Report 1999/2000: Entering the Twenty-First Century.* New York: Oxford University Press.

———. 2000. *Trade Blocs: A World Bank Policy Research Report.* New York: Oxford University Press.

———. 2001a. "Special Focus: Financial and Corporate Restructuring—an Update." *East Asia Update* (March). East Asia and Pacific Region.

———. 2001b. *World Development Indicators.* Washington, D.C.

———. 2002. "Asia Rebounds, but for How Long?" *East Asia Update.* East Asia and Pacific Region.

———. Forthcoming. *Cultivating Creativity: The Foundations of Economic Growth in East Asia.* New York: Oxford University Press.

World Economic Forum. 2000. *The Global Competitiveness Report 2000.* New York: Oxford University Press.

———. 2001. *The Global Competitiveness Report 2001.* New York: Oxford University Press.

Wyplosz, Charles. 2001. "How Risky Is Financial Liberalization in the Developing Countries?" Discussion Paper 2724. Center for Economic Policy Research, London.

Yang, Shinku, and Erik Brynjolfsson. 2000. "Intangible Assets and Growth Accounting: Evidence from Computer Investments." New York and Cambridge, Mass.: New York University and Massachusetts Institute of Technology. Processed.

Yen, David C., and David C. Chou. 2001. "Wireless Communication: The Next Wave of Internet Technology." *Technology in Society* 23(2):217–26.

Yusuf, Shahid. 2001. "The East Asian Miracle from the Perspective of the Turn of the Millennium." In Joseph E. Stiglitz and Shahid Yusuf, eds., *Rethinking the East Asian Miracle.* New York: Oxford University Press.

Yusuf, Shahid, and Weiping Wu. 1997. *The Dynamics of Urban Growth in Three Cities.* New York: Oxford University Press.

Yusuf, Shahid, Ho-Chul Lee, and Akifumi Kuchiki. 2002. "Reviving Japan's Economy: A Suggestion for a Consumer-Oriented Policy." DRG Working Paper. World Bank, Washington, D.C.

Zanfei, Antonello. 2000. "Transnational Firms and the Changing Organisation of Innovative Activities." *Cambridge Journal of Economics* 24(5):515–42.

INDEX

ABOUT THE AUTHORS

Shahid Yusuf is Research Manager in the Development Economics Research Group at the World Bank.

Simon J. Evenett is Director of Economic Research at the World Trade Institute in Berne, Switzerland. He completed the research and drafting of this study while an economist in the Development Economics Research Group at the World Bank.